A FEVER OF MUHAMMAD

A Movie of the World
Francis Ford Coppola, Francis Lang,
John Travolta, Peter Falk,
and Rickie Lee Jones are
and survive to tell the Tale!

By Tom Canford

Edited by Jonathan May

HOLLOW SQUARE PRESS

Not a soul
But felt a fever of the mad and play'd
Some tricks of desperation. All but mariners
Plunged in the foaming brine and quit the vessel,
Then all afire with me: the king's son Ferdinand,
With hair up-staring, – then like reeds, not hair –
Was the first man that leap'd, cried, 'Hell is empty,
And all the devils are here.'

The Tempest,
by William Shakespeare
Act I. Sc ii, l. 208-215

"Tom, you're steppin' in high cotton!"

Annie Lee May,
upon hearing tales told by the
author about his experiences
working on movies

TABLE OF CONTENTS

INTRODUCTION TO A MOVIE PUBLICIST
(The Editor Greets His Readers)

Meet Tom Canford. Actually, you can't, because Tom Canford never really existed except as a name on his published works. All you directors, stars, supporting actors, extras, and production staff who worked with him on movies knew him as Tom Miller. Later on, after Tom has his say-so, I'll elaborate on the choice of pseudonym.

Tom had been working as a staff publicist for movie companies for several years before he took his first job as unit publicist (and if you don't know what that is, I'll let Tom explain it in good time. And yes, the job *has* changed a lot since then). His unit publicity career lasted from 1970 until 1987 and involved the following films:

Alex in Wonderland (1970). Donald Sutherland, Ellen Burstein, Jeanne Moreau. Directed by Paul Mazursky.

Shaft (1971). Richard Roundtree, Moses Gunn. Directed by Gordon Parks.

The Gang that Couldn't Shoot Straight (1971). Robert De Niro, Jerry Orbach, Lionel Stander, Jo Van Fleet, Leigh Taylor-Young. Directed by James Goldstone.

The Wrath of God (1972). Robert Mitchum, Rita Hayworth, Frank Langella, Victor Buono, Ken Hutchison. Directed by Ralph Nelson.

The Effect of Gamma Rays on Man-in-the-Moon Marigolds (1972). Joanne Woodward, Nell Potts. Directed by Paul Newman.

The Last American Hero (1973). Jeff Bridges, Valerie Perrine, Gary Busey, Art Lund, Geraldine Fitzgerald, Ned Beatty. Directed by Lamont Johnson.

Three Tough Guys (1974). Fred Williamson, Isaac Hayes, Lino Ventura, Paula Kelly. Directed by Duccio Tessari.

The Happy Hooker (1975). Lynn Redgrave, Jean-Pierre Aumont. Directed by Nicholas Sgarro.

Mikey and Nicky (1976). John Cassavetes, Peter Falk, Ned Beatty. Directed by Elaine May.

Matilda (1978). Elliot Gould, Robert Mitchum, Lionel Stander, and an actor in a fake kangaroo suit. Directed by Daniel Mann.

Boardwalk (1979). Ruth Gordon, Lee Strasberg, Janet Leigh, Lillian Roth. Directed by Stephen Verona.

Blow Out (1981). John Travolta, Nancy Allen, John Lithgow, Dennis Franz. Directed by Brian De Palma.

The Chosen (1981). Robby Benson, Barry Miller, Rod Steiger, Maximilian Schell. Directed by Jeremy Paul Kagan.

So Fine (1981). Ryan O'Neal, Jack Warden, Mariangela Melato. Directed by Andrew Bergman.

Tattoo (1981). Bruce Dern, Maude Adams, Leonard Fry, John Getz. Directed by Bob Brooks.

Easy Money (1983). Rodney Dangerfield, Joe Pesci, Jennifer Jason Leigh, Geraldine Fitzgerald, Tom Ewell. Directed by James Signorelli.

Harry & Son (1984). Paul Newman, Robby Benson, Ellen Barkin, Morgan Freeman, Joanne Woodward. Directed by Paul Newman.

The Cotton Club (1984). Richard Gere, Diane Lane, Gregory Hines, Lonette McKee, James Remar, Nicolas Cage, Bob Hoskins, Fred Gwynne, Gwen Verdon. Directed by Francis Coppola.

Berry Gordy's The Last Dragon (1985). Taimak, Vanity, Faith Prince. Directed by Michael A. Schultz.

A Gathering of Old Men (TV) (1987). Louis Gossett, Jr., Richard Widmark, Holly Hunter, Will Patton, Woody Strode. Directed by Volker Schlöndorff.

Without further ado, let me turn you over to my friend Tom. I think you'll enjoy making his acquaintance or renewing his acquaintance, as the case may be.

Jonathan May

A FEVER OF

THE MAD

ENDLESS ARE THE ORGIES
(A Dedication)

You always wanted a memoir from me, Ruth. Well, you got one. Of warts and weasels and occasionally the winsome. My career in movies.

Let's begin with Ruth Pologe. It doesn't necessarily begin there, but Ruth is as good a place to begin as any.

Ruth Pologe was a character.

I say that affectionately.

She had balls enough for two longshoremen and a hairdresser.

Ruth Pologe was head of publicity at American International Pictures in New York City, and she prided herself on being a ballbuster. Her official title was Eastern Director of Publicity. She was adorable in that role, full of bluster and bark, her blond hair flying and falling in flagrant disregard of fashion.

Every morning a mound of pills was colorfully laid out on her desk. She seemingly and separately agonized over each pill before swallowing it, and with each swallow savored the bile of whatever else her position required that she swallow that day. By noon the pills were gone.

She was technically, as marriage vows had it, Ruth Pologe Levinson. But she had small professional use for that appendage and neither did we, however deferentially we treated Irwin Levinson when he came to call.

Levinson? In New York City, wasn't the name on every corner? Up and down West Forty-seventh Street, for instance. Whereas, *Pologe.* Ah. The name struck terror in the hearts of men. If not titters.

Pologe. Think apology and you have the pronunciation.

You almost had to apologize when you said you worked for her.

"How do you stand it?"

I loved the woman.

We all did. In varying degrees on variable days. Think adorable when you think Ruth Pologe.

She took movies seriously, especially American International movies, movies that were hers to shepherd unscathed and unsheared through the minefield of second and third string New York film critics.

She took *De Sade* seriously, even though it was an incredible turkey of a film that starred Keir Dullea in his first screen appearance since *2001: A Space Odyssey.*

De Sade was AIP's big budget hopeful for the year of its release.

I walked into her office the morning after its premiere. (The premiere was as disastrous as the film.) She had her head in her hands and her pills pushed to one side of her desk. She had been perusing the reviews. In those days New York had several morning newspapers, as well as what hit the stands in the afternoon.

"No quotes," she moaned. "No quotes."

I was what they called AIP's newspaper contact as well as its trade contact, meaning it was my job to deal with screenings for newspaper and trade critics and take them to two- and -three martini lunches at Sardi's.

As if, in the case of *De Sade*, it would do much good.

I had seen the reviews. I pointed out something in the *Daily News*. Might this be a possibility?

She circled it boldly and triumphantly. "This is it!"

She had her quote and ads were immediately prepared featuring it. The quote even appeared on the marquee of the Times Square theater playing the film.

Kathleen Carroll called. "How could you do this to me?" she asked. Somehow word had gotten back to her that I had been responsible for taking her unceremoniously out of context, using what she had meant pejoratively as a box-office enticement. Not that it enticed many.

Her review had included an exasperated ". . . and endless are the orgies."

Endless are the orgies.

With Kathleen Carroll's name attached, we had our quote.

"WHAT'S A NICE PERSON LIKE YOU DOING IN A JOB LIKE THIS?"
(The Craft of the Unit Publicist)

Robert Mitchum and Rita Hayworth!

Together again.

"I met her first when she was thirteen," says Mitchum. You wonder at such a statement.

Rita joins us on the porch of the ages-old Catholic Church in La Luz, Mexico, where the stars are putting the finishing touches to <u>Ralph Nelson's action</u> adventure <u>The Wrath of God</u>, in which Mitchum plays a renegade-priest-with-machine-gun and Hayworth plays Frank Langella's God-fearing but recently-ravished-by-bandits mother.

"It's the first time I've ever been ravished by bandits," says Rita. "But I was ravished by Jose Ferrer. In a movie. Does that count?"

Mitchum and Hayworth appeared in Fire Down Below *in 1957, and it was Mitchum who persuaded Miss Hayworth to accept the present role. "She's very withdrawn," says Mitchum. "Very shy."*

"I'm not that shy," said Miss Hayworth, playfully kicking at his shins. "I'm shy because I was working in Tijuana when I was, like, thirteen."

"That should make you aggressive. I've known girls working Tijuana when they were thirteen. All of them aggressive, stopping you on the street."

"I wasn't working Tijuana, Bob! I was working in Tijuana. I was dancing with my father when I was

_ᴜɪ_ shows a day. And I had to go to Chula _ᴜᴜ_ across the border between shows for school lessons. I always resented it. I hated being different. I wanted to go to school regular hours like the rest of the kids."

"You told me you made Blood and Sand when you were thirteen," said Mitchum, slyly twittering. "You mean you went to school in Chula Vista, danced in Tijuana, and made Blood and Sand all when you were thirteen years old? You were a swinging teenager."

"I made Blood and Sand when I was, like, nineteen."

"The same year I made Desire Me. Like, when I was twelve and a half."

"Who was in that movie?"

"Me."

"Idiot. Who else?"

"I think Doris Duke."

Miss Hayworth laughs. "Whatever happened to Doris Duke?"

"She got rich. She made a killing in the stock market."

"Wasn't there something about a husband? Crushed in a gate or something? Some kind of mess."

Mitchum nodded. "A mess.—I saw her in Paris recently. She looked well."

"I wish I were in Paris now. Or the south of France. Isn't there a picture I can do in the south of France?"

"I tried to get them to do this one there. So it's 1920 and a Latin American country. We could have faked it. Here we are 7,700 feet in the Sierra Madres, and if we'd played our cards right we could have been in Nice."

"I don't like Nice," said Rita. "It's too fattening."

"Nice is?"

"France is. Especially when you love frog legs Provençale."

"They've got frog legs in Guanajuato, for Christ sake. Guanajuato – what do you think it means? Jumping frog. You're in frog country."

"And you'd better jump," said producer-director Ralph Nelson, gently nudging Miss Hayworth to tell her she was wanted for the next scene.

"I love to jump," said Miss Hayworth, rising. "I used to play leap frog — "

"Maybe in Tijuana, when you were thirteen?" said Mitchum with a smile.

Rita smiled back after pantomiming a slap to Bob's cheek.

The Wrath of God, *based on a novel by James Graham, co-stars Victor Buono, John Colicos, Ken Hutchison, and Paula Pritchett. Director of photography of the MGM release is Alex Phillips, Jr.*

You have just read what is known as unit copy, a feature, rarely used anymore and rarely used then (in 1972), written by the unit publicist, myself, as part of a voluminous amount of copy prepared for the film that turned out to be the last in which Rita Hayworth appeared, all on the slim chance that the film would be a major hit and major background on it would be needed.

The film was a major bomb (although *I* liked it!), but I think there were political (intra-studio) reasons for its being virtually thrown away by MGM (but that is another story).

I'm here to talk about the job of the unit publicist.

If you have only a vague idea what a unit publicist is, join the vast club out there. Many a neophyte producer doesn't know either. Not to mention some of the more seasoned ones. It is a profession only dimly understood and appreciated even less.

On the first day of production of *The Chosen*, I introduced myself as the film's unit publicist to one of the young co-stars, Barry Miller. He said, with more chastisement than sympathy, "Don't you know how little respect people have for you?"

Robert Mitchum told me in his laconic way of one film where the production manager told him they were going to have to get rid of the publicist. "Why?" Mitchum asked. "I like him." "Because," said the production manager, "he's a cocksucker." "In that case," said Mitchum, "you better get rid of the director as well."

Mitchum smirked. "Besides, isn't that the first requirement for being a publicist?"

When I didn't respond, he said, "I hope you know I'm kidding."

As laconic as he, I replied, "I hope you know I hoped so."

You would think that a seasoned producer like Joseph E. Levine of Embassy Pictures would have a clearer idea than most of what a unit publicist does. Nevertheless, two days after the completion of principal photography on *Tattoo*, he sent me word that I was dismissed, my job done. I sent word right back: my job wasn't done by half. If I left then, he would sacrifice all writing materials that would be needed at the time of the film's release: final production notes, biographies of all the principals, synopsis, features on the art and history of tattooing, etc., copy that would normally be incorporated into press kits for distribution to the media at the time of the film's release) His associates passed the word along to him (I tried to deal with him as indirectly as possible at all times). I could imagine him going into one of his famed tirades, screaming that I was cheating him, demanding to know why I hadn't written the stuff earlier (quick answer: no time, too busy with all the other stuff that a unit publicist is involved with during shooting). He passed the word along to me, "You got one more week."

I pulled the material together in less time than that, actually, and got it to Levine. I'd been told that he wanted to read every word. He did, that night. Next day I ran into him in the lobby of his office building, and he beamed at me. "I read what you wrote. I like it. I didn't know you guys did that."

(Translated: "I didn't know unit publicists wrote the kind of polished copy that appears in press kits." The mind boggles.) At the time of *Tattoo*, Levine was a veteran producer and distributor with more than twenty solid and successful years behind him. I had worked on his staff in 1967 at the time both *The Graduate* and *The Producers* were being released and had written and supervised hundreds of weekly mailings to exhibitors and press about both films. I wondered if Levine thought I'd made it all up out of my head without a bedrock of unit copy to guide me. Did he think the unit publicists acted merely as a guide or deterrent to visits from the press?

His reputation for firing unit publicists was notorious, and hilarious stories (well, hilarious to those who heard them later) were told in the industry about at least two such firings. I had been determined to make it through *Tattoo* and had concluded that staying out of his way was as good a way as any of assuring job longevity. It almost backfired on me. After I had successfully eluded Levine for two weeks, he paid a rare surprise visit accompanied by his chauffeur to the *Tattoo* production office. Eyeing me, he raised his walking stick like a wand and advanced on me like something wicked come this way from Oz, shouting, "I've caught you at last!" He struck me as funny, a demented Frank Morgan, but he seemed determined to strike me otherwise. "I've never struck anybody in twenty years," he said, plainly demonstrating his intention of remedying that. I tried to laugh it off as the joke it clearly was not and got out of the office fast while everybody including the chauffeur looked on dumbstruck.

On *Tattoo* I had not only Levine to deal with toward the tail end of his producing career but Bruce Dern as well. Dern had a wicked sense of humor that I often enjoyed, particularly when I wasn't its target. In the film Dern played a characteristically psycho role with a degree of personality carry-over from character to actor but insisted from day one that the character was not a psycho: he kidnapped and tattooed girls not because he was crazy but because it was his way of expressing love. Five years after the film's release, Dern admitted in print that the role was as over the edge as any he'd ever played, and God and every movie-goer knows that Dern has played some lulus. But during production, Dern was like Rodney Dangerfield demanding respect; he wanted respect for his character, and this attitude didn't make life any easier for me or for the unit photographer, whom I supervised. Dern insisted that no photographs be taken of him when he was engaged in a "menacing gesture." After I argued with him about the need for stills of a scene in which his character sticks a hypodermic needle into the arm of co-star Maude Adams, he started giving me a new (fortunately temporary) salutation when I appeared on set: scumbag. Imagine a nice person like me in a screaming match with Bruce Dern as you've seen him on screen at his most characteristically psycho! Indeed, what *was* I doing in a job like that? Later on I shouted him down after he had blown up at me because I had shown some photos of Bruce to his wife and to Maude Adams before he saw them. It's not the way a unit publicist likes to work, nor should he have to. Still, playing the heavy opposite Bruce Dern was sort of fun as long as such scenes were minimal. Most films are fun. At least in retrospect. While you're working on them, the stress is such that you hardly have time to notice.

On the set of Paul Newman's *The Effect of Gamma Rays on Man-in-the-Moon Marigolds*, once I'd gotten to know Newman well I asked a favor of him. "A favor? Sure. What?"

I asked him if he'd mind signing a book I had bought, *The Films of Paul Newman*.

He blushed and said he was on his way to direct a scene, but he'd be back.

No sooner had he left the room than Joanne Woodward's stand-in and two extras came running over to me. "What did you tell him? He turned beet red!"

I explained. The stand-in looked shocked, then amused. "But didn't you know? He never signs autographs!"

The funny thing was, I *never* asked stars to sign autographs (well, rarely). And here I'd asked the one star who made it a point and a policy never to give them. I felt extremely foolish. I could have kicked myself. Newman was one of the nicest people with whom I had ever worked, and now I felt I'd endangered my relationship with him.

About fifteen minutes later, Newman was back. He nudged me as I sat working at one of the tables. "Where's your book?"

I gave it to him. He scribbled something, then pushed the book back to me, and waited until I read the inscription. It was my turn to blush. He laughed and went back to the set. The stand-in and her friends came running back to me, astonished that they had witnessed Paul actually autographing something. I was pleased to show them what he had written: "To Tom—a ray of intelligence in a vocation not noted for it—Paul."

A plus for me, and grateful was I for it; but what a rap for my vocation. I think that one of my qualities that Paul responded to was my restraint, the low-keyed way in which I worked. Also I had done my homework. I had seen the play on which the film was based and I knew its history and critical reception. I knew everything there was to know professionally about Newman and Joanne Woodward, his wife and the film's star. *Restraint* and *preparation*: two good words for all budding unit publicists to know.

Speak of a Hollywood publicist and the image is still likely to be something like the character Lee Tracy played some sixty years ago in the Jean Harlow film *Bombshell*: quintessentially hot-shot, high-powered, fast-talking. Not unlike that other well-known characterization of the Hollywood publicist in *A Star Is Born*, played in various versions by Lionel Stander and Jack Carson. A few of these types may still be around, but their numbers are few and more likely to be found with an independent or "outside" public relations agency than with a studio. Such outside agencies have moved into the void left by the closing or truncating of the studio publicity offices.

So what is it that a unit publicist *does*? And why a *unit*? And if an outside agency is on the film as well as a unit publicist, what does *it* do?

In the heyday of the Hollywood studios, each production was called a unit and given a unit number. A studio staff publicist would be assigned to the unit to be responsible for all copy written about a film during its production (biographies, news releases, photo identifications and captions, etc.). Hence unit publicist. Normally assignment to a unit had depended on availability, and a producer or director for the most part had no input or much interest in who was assigned as publicist. It was assumed, irrespective of truth, that whoever it was would probably be a spy for the studio, and the impression of unit publicist as antagonist remains in residual form today. The term persists as something of an anachronism, being used as a shorthand for function rather than denoting a line between the production and the parent body's publicity department.

Some unit publicists call themselves by other titles and may be billed as such: publicity coordinator, production publicist, public relations, publicist. The search for other nomenclature is understandable. The term "unit publicist" sounds to some who practice the profession not only arcane but archaic and denotes too much the functionary. A name to define the present function has not been found. (I like "information coordinator.")

The person who filled this job was not widely credited on screen until the early 1970s. I received my first screen credit in 1974 with *The Happy Hooker* for Cannon Films, having already worked without film credit on four films for MGM (*Alex in Wonderland, Shaft, The Gang That Couldn't Shoot Straight,* and *The Wrath of God*), two for Twentieth Century-Fox (*The Effect of Gamma Rays on Man-in-the-Moon Marigolds* and *The Last American Hero*), and one for Paramount (*Mikey and Nicky,* filmed in 1973 but not released until 1976). The Publicists Guild made no issue over screen credit, and the individual publicist had to use such leverage as he or she could.

I had asked for this credit on *The Last American Hero,* and executive producer Joe Wizan told me that I would get it but couldn't deliver on his promise. Studio brass vetoed it, saying that it was not studio policy, the job being seen traditionally as (and in fact was) an extension of the studio's publicity department.

So what does a unit publicist do?

First and foremost, you deal with attitudes. More often than not, you are working in a maelstrom of conflict, tension, personality, and politics. You must mobilize the good will and support of just about everyone in every department, but particularly the department heads, all of whom you need favors from at one time or another. The publicist must declare allegiances but not too loudly. You must keep distances but be able to close a distance swiftly when necessary. Axes fall on the most exalted heads, and you must not be standing so near to the beheaded that you trip over the head as it rolls.

If there is a star (that is, *star! **Superstar!***) on a film, the publicist often works through the star's personal public relations agency. All interviews that the star does are either set up by or cleared through the agency, with the publicist arranging for the time and location of the interview. (But beware of the bugs: if an interview is to be done on location, bet on it that the shooting location or time will change without notice. The publicist will arrive with the interviewer to find the crew wrapping up to move to a new location and the star dismissed for the day.)

To write production notes that will be used in the press kit, the publicist must gather, from a wide variety of sources and people, the necessary material, a process that is on-going throughout the shoot. (But Publicist, beware of not doing your homework ahead of time. "What have you done in the past, Mr. Mitchum?" is not a question you want to ask.) The publicist writes these notes sketchily at the start of or even prior to principal photography, revising and enlarging them into as complete a set of information about the production as can be mustered by the time the film wraps or as soon thereafter as possible. The facts ideally include a film's start and stop dates, locations, anecdotal material about the shooting, biographical information on the principals, sources for the screenplay, and a thematic description of the project that may touch upon but does not necessarily reveal narrative materials.

In addition to biographies of the principals, a publicist would sometimes be asked to write feature stories. This type of story could at one time be assured of publication in small-town newspapers, usually picked up from the elaborate press books featuring copy along with advertising mats for the film in question. Press books are rarely prepared anymore, although they were still being done on the first few films I worked on at MGM. They are collector's items now.

The unit publicist would write column items, either for immediate placement with a local or syndicated columnist or for use at the time of the film's release. Of course, by time of release the items might no longer be current, but the column planter (Mike Hall in New York was my favorite) would still be able to use them. Columns did have to be filled, and it was important to get the titles of new releases into print in whatever context. Examples:

Filming a "safe" scene for The Last American Hero, *Jeff Bridges, driving his own racing car, became interlocked with a stunt driver's vehicle, spinning both cars into a spectacular crash. Director Lamont Johnson called it the best "stunt" in the picture, and luckily nobody was hurt.*

Joanne Woodward dreamed she got up, put makeup and costume on, and did a scene for The Effect of Gamma Rays on Man-in-the-Moon Marigolds *just before her alarm went off and she had to get up and do exactly what she had dreamed.*

Okay, sometimes it is a stretch!

Filler copy is anecdotal material that is usually indistinguishable from a column item except that preferably the column item is shorter, pithier. Filler is suitable for special pages and columns such as "Page Six" (*New York Post*) and "People Page" (*New York Daily News*). Editors and copy writers frequently embellish them with additional material obtained from other sources or perhaps from a follow-up call to the publicist.

A bit of filler as written:

They laughed when he sat down to play dept. But not at Richard Gere who in The Cotton Club *plays his own cornet. Gere played the horn as a teenager but took it up in earnest to portray a jazz musician who likes musically to prowl with the black cats of Harlem. He studied with famed horn men Warren Vaché and Jim Maxwell, and one of the key turns he plays is Louis Armstrong's "The Butter & Egg Man."*

As it appeared on the "People Page" of the *New York Daily News*, December 12, 1983:

Richard Gere loves to blow his own horn, and that's just what he'll be doing in the upcoming movie, Cotton Club. *But before you go getting the wrong impression about Mr. G, we're speaking about trumpets - not self praise.*

Gere had to play the horn in the flick, so jazz great Warren Vaché was brought in to give the star pointers on how to fake playing the instrument.

But it turned out that Gere played *the trumpet when he was in high school. So Vaché gave him some real lessons. When director Francis Coppola wandered into one of the sessions he was so impressed with the mellow sounds Gere was producing that he decided to use him on the soundtrack.*

Look out, Al Hirt.

Since the publicist can't always be present on set, he must rely on friends to provide him with the latest amusing tidbits. His being tied in with the gossip crowd is functional as well as fun.

The unit publicist provides the distributing company with a cast and crew list as soon into production as possible. He writes identification captions for all photos taken by the stills photographer, mostly black and white, which come to him on contact sheets, approximately thirty-five shots to the page. These ID captions do just what the name implies: identify the actors, not necessarily frame-by-frame, but by sheet or roll if a roll is devoted to one scene and one set of actors. Also the action of the scene is cursorily described. Here's an example from the first two sheets for *The Cotton Club*:

SHEET 1
1 Speakeasy. Sol Weinstein (JULIAN BECK), in hat, described as "death Yiddish style," is the bodyguard of Dutch Schultz as well as his personal hit man; here he is keeping an eye on Dixie Dwyer, played by RICHARD GERE.

28-33 In beard and glasses, director FRANCIS COPPOLA.

34-35 Sol Weinstein (JULIAN BECK).

SHEET 2
1-4A See above.

5-22 Speakeasy. Musicians.

23A Asst. director ROBERT GIROLAMI, actress NOVELLA NELSON and other actresses.

24 GREGORY HINES & FRANCIS COPPOLA.

25-39A L to R: MAURICE HINES, SR. and son GREGORY HINES. Production shot.

31-35 GREGORY HINES & COPPOLA (in white hat) watch videotape playback of a scene just recorded.

When *The Cotton Club* wrapped on December 13, 1983 (not taking into account the two weeks of additional shooting in the spring of 1984), still photographer Adger Cowans had shot 410 rolls of black and white film that had to be so captioned.

The unit publicist is the custodian of the photographer's color slides (or transparencies), selecting from them something that may be suitable for immediate deployment, say to *Time* or *Newsweek* for their "People" and "Newsmakers" pages. He shows both contact sheets and transparencies to those principal players whose contract specifies that he or she has "kill rights," meaning that the actor has the right to prohibit the use of a contractually specified percentage (it could be as much as 50 percent, sometimes 100 percent) of all photographs in which the actor appears, whether taken by unit or special photographers. "Showing" the contact sheets sounds easier than it is. A set of all contact sheets in which the actor's photograph appears must be relinquished to the actor, who may take two days or two weeks to slash, with a red china marker, through each frame determined to be unflattering. The publicist then has to prepare a list of all "kills," which is sent to all pertinent parties: distributing company, outside PR agency, and anyone else who has been authorized to receive a set of contact sheets. The unit publicist must ascertain at the start of production who has kill rights and begin the process of kills immediately with any actor having that right because of the limited time involved.

Given the expense (up to a dollar per page), the number of contact sets authorized to be printed is limited. Ordinarily the distributing company gets a set, and a set is retained in the production office for ready referral during the making of the film. The outside publicity agency, if there is one, gets a set. The unit publicist, who works most actively with the contact sheets during production, of course has his own copy. In some instances the stills photographer is allowed a set.

Especially when established stars and directors are involved, many productions maintain a "closed set" policy: press access is prohibited or limited to special and favored cases. The policy is guaranteed to engender hostility in the local press when a big star arrives in town to film and tells the publicist that he or she will have neither the time nor the energy to do production interviews. The publicist must relay this information to a lot of angry and disappointed people. A closed set doesn't make a publicist's life any easier. He would much rather look at the shooting schedule and the schedule of press visits and say, "Sure, come along, how's Tuesday? Maybe you can eat with Francis during his lunch break."

Every publicist should have this slogan on a framed sampler facing his desk: Watch Your Words Carefully! A slip before the press or even the star's personal public relations people can lead to misunderstanding, a strained relationship with the star, or outright disaster. A case in point:

In Florida on *Harry and Son*, I got a call authorized by Paul Newman's PR people in California from a reporter for *USA Today*. Wally Beene, a Rogers and Cowan account executive, had sent the reporter a photograph taken by stills photographer Ron Phillips showing Newman as a construction worker walking an exposed beam twenty stories high. The reporter asked how the shot was taken. I told him a platform just big enough for the camera, cameramen, sound people, and equipment had been built about three feet below the beams and a camera was trained upward at Newman on the beam. The reporter had another question: "I hear Paul is scared of heights?"

Jesus, Tommy, when will you learn to keep your mouth shut? I had mentioned to Wally that when Paul came down from the beam, he joked, "Put me in a racing car any day at any speed, it's better than being up there standing still!" Wally had been amused, and I could understand why he wanted to pass it along to the reporter. Instead of saying something smart and noncommittal like "Not that I know of," I proceeded to give the reporter an off-the-cuff version of what I was later to write in the production notes: "He (Newman) finds it ironic that he should be playing a construction worker in *Harry and Son* because of a mild apprehension he harbors about heights. He enjoys being at the helm of a speeding car on a racetrack because, as he says, there on terra firma and himself driving, he feels in control. So he found it funny that his stomach should threaten flip-flops at the thought of heights. His own apprehension did not extend to his character's (Harry), however, and he put his qualms on hold for the scene in which Harry walks the bare beam of a skeletal building to ask a foreman about a job, then grows dizzy and sinks to a sitting position on the beam (for it is Harry's health and not any apprehension about heights that causes the dangerous dizzy spell). Newman found it exhilarating walking an exposed beam twenty stories high. Still, he was just as glad to get back with both feet on the ground."

The day the picture and nine-paragraph story appeared in *USA Today*, I arrived on set totally unaware of its publication. Paul and Robby Benson were doing a scene in a bowling alley coffee shop. Paul was playing from a seat at the counter. I slipped into a booth that I hoped was out of the actors' line of vision. After the scene was finished, Paul came over to where I was sitting and said casually, "Tom," as though in greeting. I replied, "Paul."

"How did that happen?" he asked.

I was confused and showed it.

"*USA Today*," he said. "It's right there in print, in this morning's paper—'Tom Miller says Paul Newman is deathly afraid of heights.'"

My body temperature must have shot up five degrees. Joanne Woodward joined us, asking Paul, "What's the problem?"

"The *USA Today* story," he said.

Joanne looked at me sympathetically. "That was unfortunate."

Paul sat in the booth opposite me, his eyes as piercingly judgmental as they were blue. "You're here to protect me," he said. "This is all make-believe. The movie, me—all image. When you destroy any portion of the image, you destroy it all. You've got to be extremely careful what you say to these people."

When I found a copy of *USA Today*, I became, if anything, angrier than Paul. I told him so at the dailies that night. "I've been grossly misquoted!"

"Don't worry about it," said Paul, sipping a Budweiser, "but join the club."

Joanne said, "Now you know what we've been going through for years."

Some would say the *USA Today* story is innocuous, merely anecdotal, *publicity*, after all. Perhaps, but it was nevertheless wounding, in a sensitive moment, to Paul Newman and doubly wounding to me because of the distortion of information that I had given the story's writer. Imagine then how wounded a director or actor can be by a *truly* malicious item and story, which the Jack Matthews piece in *USA Today* was not. During the making of *The Cotton Club*, malicious items appeared repeatedly about both Francis Coppola and Richard Gere. On separate occasions each of them expressed to me their paranoia and frustration with the same words: "They all hate me." One of the few things on which actor and director totally agreed.

The unit publicist is a trouble-shooter on locations, especially when the company is filming street scenes to which the public has access or scenes in a private or commercial establishment which the company has rented but over which it lacks total control of access. (A real horror story occurred during the first week of location shooting on *The Cotton Club* when the proprietor of the building where we were filming decided to ride our publicity coattails by personally inviting local New York City television crews to visit our location in his building, but that's a story that deserves fuller treatment elsewhere.) The publicist, often with the help of production assistants, tries to dissuade free-lance photographers or, failing that, to block their view. But the company may not forbid the taking of photographs on public streets, and photographers know it.

It is considered important, especially during the early weeks of production, that the unit publicist as representative of the company control the distribution and release of photographs. The work of unauthorized photographers is usually inferior to that of unit or special photographers for obvious reasons, and frequently the unauthorized pictures end up in sleazy publications. When a film has a star like Newman, Gere, or John

Travolta, it is virtually impossible to keep the unwanted photographers away; and there are times when, from a public relations standpoint, it is to the film's advantage to let them get their shots. Freelancers can be tenacious, worrisome, and obnoxious, especially when too relentlessly denied. Most of the earlier photographs published during the making of *The Cotton Club* were unauthorized.

When a special photographer is authorized to work in addition to the unit photographer, a host of in-house clearances must be obtained and a platoon of people notified, especially if a special photo session (i.e., away from the set) is planned. The director, assistant directors, makeup, wardrobe, hair, production manager, director of photography, stills photographer, gaffers, electricians, props, set dressers—in some cases all must be notified either by the publicist or by the production office staff. The publicist may need the help of some or all of these departments in setting up a photo session for the special photographer. The photographer arrives for special session work with an assistant, sophisticated strobe lights, umbrellas, light stands, and other equipment. Either the cinematographer or the production manager will notify the camera local (in New York, Local 644). If the special photographer is not a member of this local, the company must pay a stand-by union photographer one day's wages for each day the special works. The stills photographer will not be happy about the special's presence because of what he or she perceives to be royal and preferential treatment given the special and believes that he or she could do as good a job as the special if only given equal opportunity and cooperation. The stills photographer is also irked because magazines give a special's work preference and photo credit, which the unit photographer rarely receives. (It is an injustice that I've tried to correct on my later films, most successfully with Adger Cowans on *The Cotton Club*, his work being regularly credited by magazines. But *The Cotton Club* was a special case: I had control of all photographs taken by the stills photographer throughout production and for several weeks following completion of principal photography, when finally I was allowed to turn them over to the distributing company, Orion Pictures.)

When a special photographer is hired, the actors to be photographed must be notified and their schedules cleared. In some cases a star has approval and veto power over a special photographer, if not overtly then covertly. It isn't easy to clear schedules. The photographers often must be locked into specific days because of their own busy schedules. The unit publicist works with other production people in ascertaining what days would be best. The photographer will want the star to be working in a scene crucial to the movie, preferably one offering great visuals. Events may knock the shooting schedule askew so that neither the star nor the crucial scene is before the camera on the day the special arrives to work. The publicist hastily tries to arrange for the star to be brought in for the day for a special photo session (usually this possibility has to be foreseen and the star's cooperation obtained in advance).

Photographs authorized, unauthorized, special, and unit take up an inordinate amount of a unit publicist's time. Even with a plethora of magnifying glasses and loupes and light boxes, I sometimes felt I was going blind looking at all the tiny frames and color transparencies, trying to be properly judgmental about them.

Should an outside public relations firm be assigned to the film, some of the duties of the unit publicist, especially those pertaining to initial and preparatory press contacts, may be performed by this agency. The agency's term of employment is usually from pre-production through release of the film, most likely a period of a year or more. The agency may plant column items sent to them by the unit publicist or items that they themselves originate. At the same time, of course, the agency will be working with and for other clients: other films, stars, rock groups, circus acts, restaurants, night clubs, whatever. The agency will work closely with the distributing company in the long-range planning of stories about the film, especially with regard to placement in magazines whose content must be planned and prepared some months in advance.

For a film that didn't want production publicity (well, Coppola didn't), *The Cotton Club* broke records for press mentions: we were always on the tip of an anonymous tongue. Yet while the picture did okay at the box office, it did not do spectacularly well. It received rave reviews and pans, and it was the subject of extensive magazine and newspaper coverage with major photographic layouts. Still, despite its cause célèbre status in New York and Los Angeles and the feeling of those who worked on the film that it had been publicized to death, it did not draw in compelling numbers the moviegoers that its producers and distributing company had anticipated. And perhaps being over-publicized was part of the reason.

As for my next movie, *The Last Dragon*, as the film was known during production before acquiring Berry Gordy's name as part of its title, it too had a closed-set policy during production, and, unlike *The Cotton Club*, was able to maintain it. There were few mentions of it in the press, certainly none in the gossip columns, because that was the way Berry Gordy wanted it. He wished to avoid the overexposure to title and entity that perhaps had caused other films to be less than honestly evaluated in the inevitable arena of contagious critical comment. It was easy to keep *The Last Dragon* quiet. It had no money problems (comparatively speaking). Berry Gordy, its executive producer and the founder of Motown, kept the lowest of profiles. When the picture opened, hardly anyone had heard of it—so much so that hardly anyone outside the obligatory daily newspapers reviewed it. The lack of production publicity did not hurt *The Last Dragon* at the box office. It became one of the year's sleeper hits, without to my knowledge a single magazine review to its credit. It did get nice words from Roger Ebert of the *Chicago Sun-Times* and David Hinckley of the *New York Daily News* and a belated four-weeks-into-its-run rave review by Joel Siegel on *Good Morning, America.*

A publicist beginning work on a film never knows, nor does anyone else connected with it, if it is going to be a hit and/or an "important" film. In retrospect, if it bombs, you might recollect that you said to yourself when you first read the script, "But how can they shoot this garbage?" Or, "How can they go with that has-been director?" Or, "Don't they know this actor is going to sink it?"

But hope springs eternal. Or at least a semblance of it should for the unit publicist who must prepare intelligent, usable background material and copy for each of his films. Just in case.

"ON THE WHOLE I'D RATHER BE IN PHILADELPHIA"
(Elaine May's *Mikey and Nicky*)

In retrospect you look back and wonder how you could have allowed yourself to be so demeaned. Not that I felt demeaned at the time. I felt richly rewarded, even privileged, to be in the vortex of such horseshit. Now as I look back, I find myself plunged into the immediacy of the moment. It is as fresh now as it is then. And the whole thing is a hoot.

I'm the unit publicist on *Mikey and Nicky* and its director, Elaine May, is not supposed to know I exist. I'm not to go near the set. She is not to lay eyes on me. If she did, I'm told, she would freak out. Sounds remarkably like the basis for a Nichols and May comedy sketch.

What kind of job is this, to go to Philadelphia on a movie location and be told you are to stay in your hotel room? Hey, it's okay, right? Cushy job. Paid vacation. I have the new Ross MacDonald novel, *Sleeping Beauty*, and when I'm through with that I've got E. M. Forster's *Howard's End*, which I've always wanted to read. I've got a TV and the Watergate hearings are on. More than enough to entertain me.

But it is not. The more I think about it, the more pissed I get. The real entertainment is out there, where I'm supposed to be working. I'm being paid to watch Elaine May, Peter Falk, and John Cassavetes make a movie. Somehow I've got to get in there and watch it.

Now this is the summer of 1973. If you know your Watergate you've probably already figured out that date. Paramount's big publicity guns are trained on *The Great Gatsby* shooting in Newport. Socialite extras, twenties fashions, Stutz Bearcats, and all that. And Robert Redford in the title role of Jay Gatsby. Glamour! Lights! Media! Elaine May, on the other hand, doesn't want so much as a cap pistol pointed at *Mikey and Nicky*.

One week before principal photography is to begin, before the cast and crew assemble at their Philadelphia location and the cameras start rolling, Elaine's novice producer Michael Hausman remains adamant about not wanting a unit publicist on the picture.

For one thing, he's trying to palm it off as an independent production, trying to hide the fact that it is bankrolled by Paramount and is already on Paramount's release schedule. He'll get union concessions this way, or possibly he can bypass the union entirely. By union, I mean Teamsters. Even though the rest of the crew is union, he doesn't want Teamsters. He doesn't envision any need for them. To use Teamsters would inflate the budget considerably. My presence would bring on the Teamsters, he's afraid. I'd be plastering the name "Paramount" all over the trades. In every press release and column item.

I am anathema. Cries of "Leper!" will be heard all over the city when I arrive to claim my position as the film's unit publicist.

Gordon Weaver is Paramount's director of publicity, and, bless him, he's determined that I shall go to Philadelphia. Talking soft and silky and rationally, he convinces Mike Hausman that it is essential to have a PR guy around, at least for the first three or four weeks, if for no other reason than to gather production and program notes for use as a press kit when the picture is released. And the presence of a movie company and bona fide movie stars in Philadelphia is obviously going to excite a hell of a lot of hoopla. Somebody will have to handle the hoops. Is Hausman prepared to? Of course not. Nobody seems to know what a unit publicist does until he or she needs someone to do what a unit publicist does. We get no respect. Low man on a very tall totem pole. (Although we're looked on sometimes with envy too, don't you think, seeming to do nothing and hobnobbing off-camera with stars and sitting in director chairs and being allowed other tokens of privilege.)

Entertainment editors. Reporters. Columnists. Journalistic would-be starfuckers. (If that isn't one word, it ought to be.) Hey, Hausman, won't they all wish to take note of the fact that Columbo, the incredibly popular TV detective of the baggy trench coat, Peter Falk himself, will be working in their city for the entire summer, along with his actor/director buddy and frequent collaborator, John Cassavetes?

Have you any concept, Michael Hausman, any idea, of the barrage of phone calls the production office will be getting? Who will take these calls? Who will meet with those clamoring for access to Falk and Cassavetes, be the intermediary in granting or denying access as well as scheduling and presiding over interviews? You, Mike? Elaine May will be directing her third picture in the city of her birth. A story there. The film will be shot exclusively in Philadelphia and exclusively at night. A story. The unit publicist must gather all this information for future if not present use. Not to mention the Philadelphia press who will want to know and deserve to know details about the film's production. The company will have a public relations problem if these concerns are not addressed promptly and politely. Will Hausman have the time and inclination to deal with them?

Mike got the point. "Send me somebody," he said. I was the one Gordon would send. Gordon called me to his office overlooking Central Park from the Gulf and Western Building on Columbus Circle, and we spoke to Mike by telephone. Mike had caveats and conditions, and almost the first thing he said to me was, "Elaine mustn't know."

"Mustn't know what?" I wanted to know.

"That you're in town. Who you are," Mike said.

"You must be kidding."

"I'm serious."

"But she'll *see* me."

"Where?"

"On the set."

"You won't be on the set."

"If I'm not on set, where will I be?"

"In your room, writing."

"What am I going to write?"

"Make it up."

Gordon laughed. Mike laughed. All three of us, long distance laughing. All of us recognizing that it was loony bin time.

Make it up. It was a refrain I was to hear often during the next three weeks, especially from Peter Falk. If his director was mad, he harbored an even wilder madness of his own.

"Believe me, Tom, trust me. I know Elaine," said Mike. He'd been her production manager on *The Heartbreak Kid.*

"With Elaine you have to insinuate yourself. She likes familiar faces. What she doesn't like are strange faces that turn out to be publicity faces. Maybe we'll let her see your face gradually, maybe the second week, maybe she'll accept it. But please God she never finds out you're a publicist sent by Paramount. She'll think you're here to spy on her."

I sneaked into the City of Brotherly Love on the rainy Sunday night of May 20 before the picture was to start shooting the evening of the following day. To add to the welcome, or lack of it, I arrived in the middle of both a thunderstorm and a taxi strike. Five of us and our wet umbrellas were crowded into a private automobile, one of many pressed into service for the emergency. Like an airport van, it made all the hotel stops. Mine was the Warwick. "It's where the stars stay," someone said. The movie company was staying there, and the production office was on the top floor in the penthouse suite.

My room was nice enough, but I was disappointed that it contained two double beds which took up most of the space. Also there was no refrigerator, no hotplate, no kitchen nook. The refrigerator I would most acutely miss. I had forgotten to specify it when I made my deal. I would never forget it again. The bathroom was a charmer, old squared little white tile on the floor and a massive porcelain bathtub and sink. It was nine-thirty in the evening. I called the production office. Surely somebody would be there the night before principal photography was to begin.

Somebody was. The voice sounded like Elaine May's. I had come a cropper. I had to report to somebody that I was here, didn't I? But what if this was Elaine? What would I do then?

Her name was Nola, she said, "Assistant to the Director." Nola Safro, and that is indeed how she was listed on the crew sheet I would later receive. A name like that deserves an actress behind it. Especially with that voice.

"And who did you say you are?"

I told her, but I didn't say I was the unit publicist. I still wasn't sure but what I had Elaine on the line. Traps, I feared, were everywhere.

Her voice lowered an octave. She whispered into the phone, "Oh yes, Mike told me about you. Come up tomorrow morning."

I asked her if there was a bar in the hotel where I could get a drink and a snack.

"It's closed on Sunday," she said. She mentioned a bar about a block away. Even though it was still pouring, I went there. Not much in the way of food, but everything else was choice. A gay bar. Interesting that Nola Safro should have sent me there. I didn't even know the lady, and here she was, my Good Samaritan.

I met Nola Safro the next day and still wasn't certain that she wasn't Elaine May. I'd met Elaine some years before at a Bring Your Own Bottle party at Ben Bagley's. She was with lyricist Sheldon Harnick to whom she was later, if briefly, married. I'd seen her in performance with Mike Nichols both in cabaret and on Broadway. I felt sure I would know her if I saw her. I eyed Nora Safro very carefully.

She was rubbing lotion into her skin and complaining about dishwater hands. She had just come from Elaine May's suite where Elaine, on this first day of shooting of her new film, was hard at work scouring her dressing room table with a very soapy and wet steel wool scouring pad. So much, in Elaine's opinion, for the Warwick staff.

Nola introduced me to three other women working in the office: Shelly, Jackie, and Pat. Jackie turned out to be Elaine's cousin and became a major source of information. Pat, the office manager, was involved romantically with (or was she married to?) Mike Hausman. The office manager designation was her own idea. In another company she would likely have been called the production secretary.

I was delighted when familiar and friendly faces began to turn up, crew members I'd worked with on other films. Bob Visciglia, the prop man, I had worked with on *Alex in Wonderland*, and Randy Munkacsi, the stills photographer, on *Shaft*.

Bob Visciglia was trying not to worry. He had just reviewed the extended shooting schedule of Elaine's two previous films. Such a schedule overrun for *Mikey and Nicky* might mean the loss of another job he had lined up.

He tried to look at it optimistically. "They've got Falk only for the summer, right? So how can they not finish on time?"

Had I been endowed with prescience, I might have replied, "Let me count the ways!"

I was handed a cast and crew list that gave their room numbers at the Warwick. It surprised me to see that I was on it, room 937, and that it succinctly and without equivocation gave my crew position as that of publicist.

Now who was kidding whom? Elaine May wouldn't see this list? Why the subterfuge?

Elaine was in 1108, Cassavetes in 808, Falk in 1008. The 08 series seemed to be choice. And I ended up in the 37 line with no refrigerator.

Shelley offered me a granola cookie. She gave me a list of nearby health food stores that I might like to try if I were "into that kind of thing."

Shelley's two cats were in residence in the office, one of them embarrassingly in heat. I patted it and tried to focus its attention elsewhere.

Putting down one phone and in the process of picking up another, Mike Hausman greeted me and said he would drive me that afternoon to the night's location and give me a tour. I scrounged from him a list of locations (guarded zealously by Pat) despite his misgivings about allowing me to see it. Did he think the list would be published the next day in a bordered box on the front page of the *Inquirer*? I assured him I would not deal in location specifics when speaking with the press.

The production office staff was housed in the larger of two living rooms in the penthouse suite, which you had to pass through to get to Mike's office in the smaller room. One of the bedrooms was the company's editing room where film editor John Carter (not on Mars but sometimes I pictured him as wishing he were) would work with two assistants on state-of-the-art editing machines and Movieolas. The room would be used for a brief while for storage of exposed film, but the cans of film would quickly proliferate in seemingly autonomous self-duplication like the bass fiddle in a W. C. Fields two-reel comedy. More space would have to be found. Another bedroom, the office of the location auditor, would become a much-frequented and much-argued-in room.

Until a typewriter could be arranged for me, Pat let me borrow one of the office machines.

Mike Hausman became greatly concerned when he learned what I immediately would be up to: composing and transmitting to both the *Hollywood Reporter* and *Daily Variety* in Los Angeles a key cast and crew list for publication in the current Production Chart listings of each of the periodicals. The listings are by studio, and if a film has no studio affiliation it is listed as an independent. Mike did not want *Mikey and Nicky* listed as a Paramount Picture but instead placed with the independents with "Mikey and Nicky Productions, Inc." as the identified producing organization. Toward the end of production he would allow it to be announced that the film was a Paramount pick-up, one that Paramount had bought in on after the fact rather than before.

But it was not to be.

Before I was brought in, the Paramount publicity department had already distributed press releases announcing its participation in the project, and the film's title had appeared in the press as a Paramount release. I had to follow Paramount's lead in this decision and not Hausman's.

Mike was not happy. More than ever he feared that stressing Paramount's proprietary interest would up the ante with the various unions with whom he had to deal. He was still trying to keep the lid on that somewhat agitated Pandora's Box.

It took three days to resolve this situation, three days during which I was to refrain from direct communication with the *Reporter* and *Variety*. While it wasn't an easy time, I became grateful for the respite; for during that period the original director of photography was replaced or had resigned, and the first assistant cameraman (the focus cameraman) departed shortly thereafter. Some claimed for the latter an incipient nervous breakdown.

Production Chart listings in 1973 usually cited eight members of a film's personnel: producer, director, author of the screenplay, director of photography, film editor, art director, sound man, possibly the production manager (Mike Hausman was serving in this capacity as well as producer), often the first assistant director, and, at least in the *Hollywood Reporter*, the unit publicist. Directly under the film's title, in smaller print, came the names of actors thus far cast.

Our credits were few, and two of them were Elaine May's as director and scenarist. She also had penciled herself in to play a featured role but didn't want that fact revealed. The other listings were the two for Hausman, Vic Kemper as director of photography, editor John Carter, assistant director Pete Scoppa, and me. Hausman told me to keep it trim. Ordinarily Anthea Sylbert as art director would have been listed, but she was by union affiliation a costume designer and had not yet ironed out several union wrinkles that would allow her to surface safely in her new designation.

Other films listed under Paramount's banner that first week of June 1973 were *The Little Prince*, *Ash Wednesday*, *The Parallax View*, *The White Dawn*, and Zeffirelli's *Camille*, a film shortly to be aborted. *The Great Gatsby*, not due to begin shooting until June 11, was not yet listed.

Mike elaborated a bit more on why he wished to keep the company free of Teamster drivers. The rap on Teamster drivers is that they drive and nothing more. Often they drive to a location chauffeuring an actor or delivering material and then remain there on call, perhaps until the end of the day's shoot, free until then to play cards, shoot the breeze, snooze, or whatever. Their inert presence and high visibility being so can be demoralizing to a highly active, harried, high-voltage crew.

The company would be working in a close radius from the Warwick. The small amount of driving to be done could be handled by Hausman's unit manager John Starke or a couple of production assistants or even Hausman himself. The fewer the better.

Ultimately Hausman's concern was budgetary. It was very important to him that he hold costs down. Paramount's then president Frank Yablans had already been contacted by the Teamsters union with a complaint about the lack of union drivers. Yablans had instructed Hausman to put two Teamster drivers on salary with the promise that the salaries would not be charged against Hausman's budget.

I was typing advance production notes in my room that first morning when the phone rang. Nola. Could I please hurry back to the production office? A reporter from the *Philadelphia Bulletin* had turned up with his editor's instruction not to come back until he had a story on the film.

Luckily, I had on my own time and without recompense researched the director and stars the previous week in New York (this, my usual habit and preference, tended to save a lot of time and heartache later on). I had read Elaine's script and had seen the film's location schedule. I felt prepared to talk about the film in general terms.

When I walked into the office, Joe Adcock, the reporter, was asking questions and taking notes about the office cats. Shelly was amused that Adcock's demanded story should have reduced him to such a task. There was also a flurry of concern among the staff, passed on to me later, as to how Adcock might use the cats metaphorically.

The paranoid mind boggles.

To escape the confusion and distraction of the cats, I suggested to Adcock that we go to the Warwick lobby for a chat.

He asked, "Is the title *Mikey and Nicky* perhaps a play on Mike Nichols?" I loved the connection and wished I had thought of it. I told him that I didn't know, but by all means use it. (In the story published the following day in the *Bulletin* he did use it, and I was quoted profusely and authoritatively.)

"What is the film about?" Adcock asked.

"Next train out, guy," I could hear Hausman's voice whispering in my inner ear by way of warning.

With some trepidation I summarized Elaine's story and theme. In ideal circumstances I would have been allowed to confer with the director or producer before becoming a spokesman. I was in dangerous territory, winging it like this.

"It's about a man in the organization . . ." I began. I was treading barefoot on shards of glass. Through experience, I knew enough to eschew the inflammatory word *Mafia*, either specifically or generically. On two films, *Shaft* and *The Gang That Couldn't Shoot Straight*, protestations in the form of threats had caused me to mitigate terminology. "A man in an organization who thinks there's a contract on him but he's not sure and he can't figure out who. . ."

I resented not having been prepped. I had no idea the tone Elaine intended to take in filming her screenplay. I thought it was a comedy.

Jackie had said, "Oh, no, she's going to be deadly serious with this. Don't ever dare say it's a comedy."

"But I laughed out loud when I read it."

"I did too, but don't let anybody else hear you say it."

After Adcock left with something resembling a story, I realized that I had to do repair work with Philadelphia's other two newspapers. I couldn't have it appear that we were favoring the *Bulletin*. I called the entertainment editor/movie critic of the *Inquirer* and gave her a variant of the rundown that Adcock had received. I stopped just short of telling her about the office cats. Adcock mentioned the cats but used them circumspectly as office color. The staff was relieved.

The *Inquirer* story was accompanied by a morgue photo of Elaine that made her look like an ingénue. The *Bulletin* ran an uncharacteristic photo of our director, widely grinning, looking as hair-sprayed and bouffant as any 1950s West Texas debutante. "Where did they get *that* picture," Shelly gasped. The *News* merely carried column items. It was agreed on penalty of death that no one would show Elaine any clippings. She wasn't likely to come across the stories on her own. "She never looks at a paper," Jackie said.

Both the *Inquirer* and the *Bulletin* gave the name of what would be our location for the first three weeks of shooting, but no harm done. It was all interior and all at night. It was the abandoned Essex Hotel at Thirteenth and Filbert Streets, about a block and a half from Philadelphia's instantly recognizable landmark city hall. In *Mikey and Nicky* it would be called the Royale Hotel. The Essex had been closed for seven years, since October 1966.

Hausman drove me to the Essex early the first night of shooting, about five o'clock. Elaine wouldn't be there for a couple of hours yet. Peter Falk was already there. Mike introduced me to him on the run. I sat with Falk in a red cracked-leather booth in what had been the hotel restaurant while Mike went to see about things on the second floor where crew were setting up for the shooting of John Cassavetes's opening scene, the first scene of the film.

Peter Falk would not be needed for hours. He was early because he would rather be where the action was than hanging about his hotel room waiting for his call. He was playing aimlessly with a deck of cards. He looked at me as if I were lying when I told him I was the publicist. It made sense to him when I told him that Elaine didn't know I was there and as far as Mike Hausman was concerned would never know.

Falk grinned. "I won't say anything."

He wanted to show me something. We walked around what was left of the restaurant and its kitchen.

"It looks like it was walked out of like on the last day of the world, right? Look at it—menus. Two of them here open where somebody left them, like they just ordered, or maybe not even ordered yet. Look at the water glasses. The inner rings. Lower and lower on the glass as the water evaporated. And look over here. Crumpled napkins on the tables . . ." There were three tables still with used napkins on them. "There were even dirty dishes, they tell me. They cleared out some of this crap before we moved in. The prop guys. But go in there in the kitchen and look around."

He followed me in.

"Pots and pans. All this heavy artillery hanging from the ceiling. Like bats. Did you ever see so many cobwebs? Is that bat or rat shit on the floor? Is that like dirt you've ever seen before? And have you looked in any of the rooms upstairs?"

"I'm not allowed in any of the rooms upstairs."

Falk chuckled. "Elaine's not here yet. Come take a look. I'll be with you. Nobody's going to eat you."

We left the kitchen and returned to the restaurant and walked past what had been the cashier's desk where an old dusty cash register was still stationed, its empty money drawer hanging open.

"Funny how they can do that. Just walk out and leave a place. Even Cokes in the Coke machine. Just walk out and leave everything and put a padlock on the door."

Like Columbo, he tried to puzzle it out.

"What did they do, suddenly go bankrupt? Were they evicted? Some terrible plague?"

I hoped one day to uncover the mystery of the Essex Hotel. I fancy that Columbo and I working as a team might have been able to. We never got the chance.

Falk took me to the upstairs shooting area. With all the two-by-fours being slung about and hazardous objects and workers' tools at every turn, with every inch of space crowded with a crew unhappy with your usurping any more of their space, we didn't stay long. I appreciated the tour but didn't find it particularly rewarding. The walls were solid. The rooms were small. How much better it would have been, I thought, to have removable walls, expandable space. I wondered what could be achieved shooting in this dump that couldn't have been achieved so much easier in the comfort of a studio.

Joe Adcock's story in the *Bulletin* the next day would feature the Essex prominently. He managed to interview carpenters and other members of the crew. He found David Moon, the scenic artist, smearing Vaseline on a wall before covering it with plaster. "That way the plaster will chip off easily and give us that seedy hotel look." Giving the Essex a seedy hotel look was like adding fuzz to a caterpillar. Anthea Sylbert had spent her day exchanging a bathroom with a closet and moving the door of Nicky's (Cassavetes) room a few inches so that a clean line of corridor would be visible when the door opened.

It was inevitable that Mike Hausman would see me. I was braced for it. Seeing that I was with Falk, he didn't say anything. His grin said it all. When it was nearing time for Elaine to arrive, he instructed a production assistant to drive me back to the hotel.

There were plans for Mayor Frank Rizzo to visit the Essex Hotel on Wednesday evening about five o'clock, just before shooting started. Elaine May, Falk, and Cassavetes would act as guides showing the mayor and his aides through the rubble that was our location. Newsprint and broadcast media were invited.

If the media were invited, surely it followed that I, the company's resident public relations person, would also be there, perhaps—dare I hope?—even participate in the event. No longer the leper on the ninth floor.

"I don't follow your reasoning," Mike said when I broached the subject.

"Hey, Mike, I'm the publicist, remember? I deal with the media."

"Uh uh, not on this occasion. Betty Croll will deal with the media."

Betty Croll of the city representative Henry Bollinger's office had found the hotel and other locations for the company. The mayor's visit would be a hug-fest of a photo opportunity for Mayor Rizzo and Peter Falk and payback to Croll.

"And what am I going to be doing?" I asked.

"Oh, you can be there, I guess. We'll pretend you're a reporter. I've got it all figured. We like you, Tom, we're glad you're here."

I felt the sentiment was sincere and the sarcasm only a tart twist of lemon for flavor. I said, "As long as I'm posing as a reporter, I think I'll pose a few questions for Elaine." Mike's look told me I was kidding.

The visitation scheduled for Wednesday did not take place but was rescheduled for the following Tuesday, this time at the mayor's office. Instead of Mayor Rizzo coming to us, we had to go to him. It was labeled a courtesy call on the mayor by May, Falk, and Cassavetes.

The morning after the first night of shooting, I was in the hotel lobby at eight on my way to breakfast. I met the crew coming in from the night's work. I ducked behind a pillar and a potted palm in hopes of getting a glimpse of Elaine. Not to be. I wouldn't get to see her until the press conference in the mayor's office.

But at least I tried.

I pulled the unpardonable on the third night of shooting and showed up on my own at the Essex. Elaine and other key personnel were on the second floor shooting. I could see no harm or threat so long as I stayed on the ground floor. I sat in one of the restaurant booths and had coffee with Jackie in the middle of all the rubble. Mike spotted me. Despite his beard that could have been swiped blithely from a Smith Brothers cough drop box, I'm convinced I saw him blanch.

"What are you doing here?"

"Well, I . . ."

"Come on."

He led me outside to the car, politely but pointedly held the door open for me, and drove me personally back to the hotel. He let me out. "Go to bed." He said it gently, apologetically, and humorously. Then he drove off.

I didn't go to bed. I went to a bar.

Let me pause a moment for Jackie Peters, the production assistant and crew feeder. It didn't take long for me to realize that she and the ubiquitous Nola were the real line of communication, tenuous and surreptitious as it might be, to Elaine May. Each of them could pop into May's eleventh floor suite at will. Jackie was definitely someone to cultivate. And besides, she was nice.

After Joe Adcock had come up with the idea of the film's title being a play on the name Mike Nichols and since he had already used it in the *Bulletin*, I had the bright idea of recycling it as a news item for the trades or perhaps the *New York Daily News*, either as conjecture or as something commented on by Elaine.

I asked Jackie to query Elaine about it. Jackie left the office, went down to Elaine's suite, soon returned, frowning. "Elaine wants to know, has that been used?"

"No," I said.

Jackie was relieved. "Elaine says not to use it."

"But it's already *been* used."

Jackie said severely, "You just said it hadn't."

"I mean, not by me. It's not mine. It's Joe Adcock's. It's in his story today in the *Bulletin*." Didn't anybody take a look at the story, I wondered.

Jackie was horrified. "Oh, my God!"

"I just wanted to give it to somebody else. I thought Elaine might get a kick out of it or something, maybe comment on it."

Jackie shook her head. "Forget it. Let's just hope she doesn't see the story. I don't think she will."

"Did you tell her who I was?" I asked.

"What do you mean?"

"Elaine. When you asked her about the item. Who did you say wanted to know?"

"Oh, just some guy in the office," said Jackie.

"You didn't say the publicist?"

She looked at me pityingly. "Are you kidding?"

Jackie resembled a ripe and unpolished Rita Hayworth. She had been a cabaret singer and had appeared in one or two movies. She was now in charge of feeding a crew on location. On that first day of production she didn't have a clue where to start. She was blithely winging it. She hadn't yet firmed up the night's menu, the mode of delivery, or even the supplier. She wasn't particularly worried. She was making phone calls, stating her problem, taking bids. She stuck her hand over the receiver to ask, "Do you think they'd like ham sandwiches?"

My startled expression was her answer. She wrinkled her nose, considered a moment, then told the man on the phone she'd get back to him.

"If worse comes to worse, we can always call McDonald's," she said.

"At midnight?" I didn't think so.

If I were Jackie I would be worried. The crew, to be fed at two in the morning, would expect hot food, ample in quantity, and exemplary in quality. There would be a lot of bitching if it wasn't.

It was when I was having coffee with her in the booth at the Essex that I had learned that she was Elaine's cousin, their mothers being sisters. She and Elaine were the same age. From about the time they were nine, they grew up together after their fathers, independent of one another, were killed in automobile accidents. Their mothers converged on Chicago with their daughters to live with a brother, Elaine's and

Jackie's uncle, who managed a nightclub. The germ of *Mikey and Nicky* originated in this uncle's story, Jackie hinted, something that had happened in the early stages of the Second World War or just previous to it. After three years in Chicago, the whole family including the uncle moved to Los Angeles where the girls attended junior high school and Fairfax High. Elaine Berlin, as she was then, didn't stay at Fairfax long. While a student there, she met and married upperclassman Marvin May. Elaine was sixteen at the time. Jackie, Elaine, and their menfolk would double-date in a coupe with a rumble seat, and they would flip to see which couple got the choice rumble seat. Elaine and Marvin usually won. The birth of a daughter (Jeannie Berlin) put an end to Elaine's rumble seat days as well as to her formal education, although she had a long history of being a notorious truant. Elaine parked her child with her mother and enrolled for acting lessons with Stanislavsky-trained actress Maria Ouspenskaya, a Hollywood character actress mainstay from the mid-thirties until her death in 1949. When Elaine's marriage to Marvin broke up after two years, she left Jeannie in her mother's care and returned to Chicago, where she sat in on whatever classes appealed to her and attended whatever extracurricular events she chose at the university (although she never officially enrolled). It was a course that eventually and happily led to Mike Nichols.

And fame.

Which brings us back to Mayor Michael Rizzo.

Mike Hausman told me to be in the lobby of the Warwick at three forty-five and he'd have a ride for me. When I got to the lobby, Peter Falk, John Cassavetes, and Gena Rolands, Cassavetes's wife and frequent leading lady in films he directed, were already there.

Falk introduced me. Cassavetes was surprised to learn that a publicist was on the picture. "How come I haven't seen you around?"

Between us, Falk and I told him how come. Cassavetes snickered. Gena Rolands smiled at me sympathetically and shook her head to convey understanding. She was visiting from Los Angeles, she said, and would be in Philadelphia only a few days.

Mike Hausman and his unit manager John Starke joined us in the lobby. Mike hustled me out of the hotel and had Starke take me on to City Hall. Mike said he would bring the others.

John Starke circled City Hall before we found a parking place. We waited for the party in the other car to arrive. When they didn't show up after about five minutes, we wondered if perhaps they had managed to get there before we did. We went on up to the floor where the mayor's office was located. A City Hall aide came running and asked frantically, "Where are they? It's four-fourteen!"

Neither John nor I was surprised. He had waited in enough automobiles and beside enough elevators to know that you do not get Elaine May anywhere on time. He told me that once he had waited for her in his car for thirty minutes in front of the Warwick to take her to location. She finally emerged breathlessly to admonish him, "You must learn to be on time, John. We're on a budget, you know, and time is money."

The corridor outside the mayor's office was jammed with reporters and camera crews and with what looked like half of the city's civil servants, at least those who worked at City Hall, all of them Columbo fans.

I mumbled excuses for the tardy arrival of our stars. As hostility built, directed at us, of course, since the stars were nowhere in sight, John suggested urgently to me that we get the hell out of there.

Just as we were beating our hasty retreat, the elevator doors opened and out stepped, voila!—*The Stars!* There was pandemonium, everybody jockeying for position or for whatever they could get of Peter Falk: a touch, a feel, a look, a picture. Maybe even a piece. He was pushed, the rest of us pushed along with him, by the sheer momentum of the crowd, toward the mayor's office. A buxom blonde of uncertain years threw her arms around him. Ordinarily the publicist would have been running interference for him, but I wasn't supposed to let the mask drop in front of Elaine. Still, at Falk's elbow, I tried to help as best I could to extricate him from the woman's grasp. She pleaded with Falk to have dinner at her house with her, her husband, and their sons, all of whom loved him like she did. Falk, nearly smothered by her, tried to be gracious. "What a shame," he said, as he unwound the woman from his body. "I've got to work tonight, but thanks anyway."

"Hi, Columbo."

"Hey, Columbo."

Flashbulbs were in full frenzy. Guards, still trying vainly to admit only the invited or the privileged and to control the mob, were shunted aside. Even the guards wanted to look at Columbo and speak to him.

John Cassavetes, looking heavy at the waist due to a too-tight shirt complete with colors and stripes befitting the hood character he plays in the film, was not the object of adulation that Peter Falk was. Falk was dressed in a soft suede sports jacket. Many in the crowd seemed upset that he wasn't wearing Columbo's trademark trench coat.

As John Starke and I pushed into the mayor's office directly behind our stars and Miss Rolands, Elaine May was pushing out.

John looked at me and said unbelievingly, "Now where's *she* going?"

"To pee?"

"She's bolting!" said John.

She was looking for a telephone, it so happened. A weird time to make a call. She looked like a hoyden, a confused child in this noisy crowd, tall for her age, a tomboy picked up off some softball diamond wearing faded jeans and a jacket. Once the guests and the mob of reporters got herded inside, the doors to the mayor's inner office were closed behind us, and here we all were without the director.

Nobody knew who she was. I wondered if she'd be let back in.

Peter Falk and John Cassavetes posed dutifully standing, with Mayor Rizzo sitting in his chair at his desk. Photographers positioned and repositioned themselves to get the best shots. Frank Rizzo had the dazed look of a heavyweight prizefighter after too many blows to the head but still a winner, arms raised, grinning. He had never seen this many reporters and photographers. Rizzo, a big Nixon supporter, had a face as straight as Vice President Agnew's, which probably didn't help him much since the Watergate containment was coming apart daily at the seams. He may not have been the size of the great Italian boxer Primo Carnera, but alongside Peter Falk and John Cassavetes he gave that impression. Rizzo invited Falk to sit in his impressive swivel chair. Falk did. A reporter asked Falk why a film company would want to film a crime drama in Philadelphia, an obvious political needle since Rizzo was having internal

(City Hall) as well as external (the streets) criminal problems. Recognizing the question for what it was, Falk had an adroit reply.

"Not because of the crime," he said. "There's no crime in Philadelphia."

It got a big laugh.

Falk and Cassavetes concurred that they found Philadelphia more to their liking than they could have possibly imagined. They did lay it on a bit thick. "You can even walk the streets without fear," said Falk. Rizzo smiled slightly and looked pleased for the cameras.

"I don't understand Philadelphia's bad rap," said Falk. "Mention Philadelphia anywhere in the country and they laugh. It's a joke. Why is it a joke? Because of W. C. Fields. What was it he said—you know, the inscription he wanted on his tombstone?"

John Cassavetes was pleased to supply it. "'On the whole, I'd rather be in Philadelphia.' It's his epitaph."

It was all going a little fast for Rizzo. He wanted somebody to explain it.

"On the whole, he thinks he might prefer Philadelphia to being in a grave, or perhaps in the hereafter," explained Falk.

He should have left it ambiguous. Rizzo was indignant. "Who said that?" he demanded. He looked angrily at Cassavetes as if it had originated with him.

"W. C. Fields, I think," said Falk, bemused by Rizzo's peevishness. The whole scene was showing signs of turning into a public relations disaster. "W. C. Fields was born in Philadelphia, you know."

Rizzo glowered at the snickering reporters. He was an ex-cop. He plainly wanted to arrest someone. Anyone.

"Elaine May was born in Philadelphia too," contributed John Cassavetes, trying to skateboard off a touchy subject and careening into the rock wall of Rizzo's lack of knowledge about Hollywood. The mayor didn't know who Elaine was. I wondered if he knew who W. C. Fields was. Elaine had slipped back into the room and was seated on a couch against the rear wall.

Again the still-glowering mayor asked, "Who?"

"*Elaine May*!" exclaimed Falk. To him it was an explanation in itself. The whole conversation was preposterous. Falk was about to break up.

I'd been aware that Elaine was sitting a few feet from where I stood and that she was trying to be polite to a woman who had surmised that Elaine had something to do with the movie. She was pitching Elaine about a Fourth of July program she was planning for Independence Hall in hopes that Elaine might use her influence as the director's assistant, or whatever she was, to get the stars there.

"Come on up here, Elaine," coaxed both Peter and John.

The press swiveled to look. Elaine reluctantly rose to push her way through the crowd to be introduced to Mayor Rizzo. One or two photographers took pictures. The others couldn't be bothered.

Cassavetes introduced her to the mayor. "I was just telling His Honor that you were born in Philadelphia."

"Oh?" said the mayor vaguely, still confused as to who she was. "When was that?"

With her many years in show business, Elaine recognized this as a throwaway line. She responded with a throwaway smile. John Cassavetes laughed at nothing in particular, directing his laughter to his shoes.

After giving Elaine May the quick once-over, Mayor Rizzo looked across the heads of the crowd in search of someone. "But where is your director?" he asked, mystified. "Let's get your director up here."

He meant Mike Hausman. I think.

Peter Falk, embarrassed, said with a small flourish to Ms. May, "But this *is* our director." Rizzo stared at Elaine in disbelief. Falk added, trying to cover the faux pas of Rizzo's expression with what he hoped was a pleasantry, "It's the age of Women's Lib, you know. Now it's come to Hollywood."

After Rizzo presented each of them with autographed coffee-table picture books of Philadelphia, Elaine May returned quietly to the back of the room while the clusters of reporters gathered around Falk, Cassavetes, and Rizzo. During much of the exchange I had stood off to the side whispering with Gena Rolands. While Elaine was distracted with Rizzo, I circulated, surreptitiously distributing press handouts I'd prepared giving information about the film.

With the mayor's part in the press conference officially over, Cassavetes tried to explain the film's premise and story line to reporters. He beckoned me to help him out. "You have something on it, don't you?" I handed him some of the fact sheets, which he passed along to reporters. Elaine saw it all. So did Mike Hausman, who caught my eye and winked.

Elaine beckoned to Gena and whispered into her ear, shielding her mouth with her hand. Who was I? she wanted to know. Gena said she didn't have a clue. "But I saw you talking with him," said Elaine.

"Do you think he might be with the mayor?" said Gena, enjoying the conspiracy of silence about me.

Mike Hausman said we had to leave. Peter Falk said, to no one in particular, "Get me out of here!" Newly emboldened by the excitement and by my own tentative steps toward assertion of professional identity, I took hold of his arm and forward-pushed and stiff-armed him out the door and into the corridor, where we were immediately surrounded by Columbo lovers, importuning. Pencils and scraps of paper were pushed forward. Falk stopped and signed several.

Somebody whispered to me that the other members of our party were waiting in the lobby. Rather than wait for the elevator, we opted for the circular stairway, taking it at a fast clip before other Columbo fans gained on us. In the lobby at the foot of the staircase Elaine May was waiting for us. Her bent arm rested on a stanchion. She watched our descent with curiosity. I felt her eyes on me every step of the way. I was aware that my face was being memorized. Peter Falk and I reached the main floor with no words spoken between us, and I got the feeling that neither he nor John Cassavetes wanted to compromise my shaky position with Elaine any more than it already was.

I said nothing.

She said nothing.

I parted with Falk, made eye contact with no one but John Starke, walked briskly to the exit with him, and was out of there.

At the hotel I made notes, showered, and turned on the local evening news coverage of the event. There was a lot of Peter Falk and Mayor Rizzo but little of Elaine May and John Cassavetes except for an almost subliminal glimpse of Cassavetes, in high spirits and humor, laughing and nudging Elaine to step forward and assert herself, and Elaine, highly amused, nudging

Cassavetes back with her shoulder, daring him to do likewise.

Then I treated myself to a cocktail and a wonderful dinner at a restaurant recommended by Nola. Already I had learned to place great trust in Nola's recommendations.

One day I had encountered her in a local health food store. I was picking up a cup of Dannon plain yogurt. Nola said with a slight discouraging shake of the head, "Elaine eats Erwin."

I had never heard of Erwin yogurt. My hand hesitated over a container. "Oh, try it," said Nola, "you'll love it. Put the Dannon back. Erwin has a thin crust of cream. Don't look at the price. It costs more but quality always does."

There was a distinct difference in price: Erwin, fifty-one cents for seven ounces, thirty-three cents for Dannon. Nola pronounced it a pittance. She handed me the Erwin. It would be a discovery and an adventure, she said. "Splurge."

I found out that Elaine also had an enthusiasm for a beverage supplement "from a combination of protein sources" called Tiger's Milk. Later when I mentioned that to Peter Falk, he said, mocking Elaine's enthusiasm while remarking her energy, "Seriously, I think she milks her own tigers."

The *Philadelphia Daily News* feature on the meeting at the mayor's office carried a photo of Falk, Cassavetes, and the mayor.

Columbo, the idol of every cop in America looked a little beat, like maybe he had been out all night working on a very important case and needed a little sleep to get moving again . . .

Columbo really had been out all night—shooting scenes for the movie Mikey and Nicky, *an underworld flick being filmed on Locust Street. Columbo is not Columbo in the movie, though. He is Mikey, a Greek gangster. John Cassavetes is Nicky, another Greek gangster.*

The filming starts in early evening and goes on until dawn, which means Columbo doesn't get to bed until 8 in the morning. But yesterday he got to visit an old cop who made it big in politics. It must have been a hurried trip because he forgot his trench coat, the Columbo trademark.

This ruined Frank Rizzo's opening line.

"My daughter told me to tell you to get a new trench coat," the Mayor said.

"She'll put me out of business," Columbo said.

John Cassavetes received a mention, but there was none for Elaine May.

That evening I got off the elevator in the Warwick lobby to find Nola, Mike, and Elaine immediately in front of me. They were conferring and didn't see me. Nola stood removed from them by a pace, waiting to be admitted into the conference. Mike was laughing and recalling anecdotes to Elaine about the press conference. He mentioned the story and pictures in that day's *News*. He picked one off the hotel newsstand rack. Elaine glanced at the photo and smiled. At that point Mike spotted me. Thinking that my moment surely had come, I stepped forward to be introduced.

Nola Safro's hand reached out to restrain me, and Mike did his familiar blanch. Executing some nimble choreography, he stepped between Elaine and me. While facing her and throwing nervous banter, he motioned me away. The gesture was redundant. I had already gotten the point: I was still persona non grata. I back-stepped to the nearest elevator.

I had finished reading *Sleeping Beauty* and *Howard's End* and was almost through with *The Digger's Game*, a new George V. Higgins novel. I knew every interesting bar in Philadelphia. I spent Memorial Day weekend in New York. My friend Jonathan would come down to visit me the following weekend. I wasn't sulking.

I wrote notes to Peter Falk and John Cassavetes which I slipped under the doors of their suites. There would be no opportunity for interviews, but I passed along the more important requests just the same. The *Mike Douglas Show*, originating in Philadelphia, was especially eager to have them. Schedules wouldn't allow.

And there was the cop who had been calling me for two weeks about Peter Falk. The man was in charge of getting celebrities to visit sick and dying ex-policemen in hospitals. His eagerness to land Falk for this purpose bordered on the abusive. He could not comprehend the meaning of a tight schedule. Dutifully I kept feeding the request to Falk. There was one dying retired cop in particular who was "going fast," and it was his last wish that he get to see Columbo in the flesh.

Falk called me in my room Saturday just after noon. I was on the way out to lunch with my friend from New York. After lunch we had planned to see the Liberty Bell.

"I guess we ought to do this one, right?" said Falk.

I said I thought we should. I would arrange it. The police would send a car for us, I had been told, and it would take about ten minutes each way. They had promised to have Falk out of there in less than fifteen minutes. Falk sighed. He had heard it all before. He would be gone at least an hour and a half. "Well, okay," he said.

I called the cop to tell him that Falk was prepared to go. The cop said in mournful reproach, "Too late, the man just died."

When I got the chance, I told Peter Falk that I'd like to sit with him and get his answers to questions Paramount wanted to pose for use in a press kit feature called "Roundtable Discussion."

"Where did you get the questions?" Falk asked.

"I made them up."

"Then make up the answers to go with them."

I laughed. He laughed. "I'm not kidding," he said. "It's all a bunch of you know what anyway. So you make up the answers. You can do it better than I can."

I told him okay but that I would show him the answers so he could correct them.

"I don't want anything to do with them," he said.

Cassavetes, on the other hand, invited me to his suite where he answered each of my questions, some at length, then listened to those I'd written for Falk. He thought it hilarious that I should have to make up the answers. He helped me with some of them and got a kick out of doing so.

Of course, Falk's "answers" were predicated on what I knew about him. Cassavetes wondered if it was in good taste to refer to Peter Falk's false eye.

My question: How do you remember your childhood? (Like the false eye, what problems did it create for you in your relationships with friends, at school, in your aspirations? And later, re your interest in art?)

I justified the question as legitimate. I'd seen the matter discussed in stories and biographies of Falk. The answer I gave, taken from source materials, was: "My eye was taken out when I was three years old. A malignant tumor. I was self-conscious about it, the glass eye, until about the time I started playing ball and going to the gym. Then it became a joke. From then on I could live with it."

Cassavetes still had a copy of the production notes I had distributed at the press conference. He took me to task on a couple of points. I had referred to Elaine as a woman director. "Ah, but she isn't," said Cassavetes with a point-making smile. "She is a director who happens to be a woman. That fact out of the way, she is the finest actor's director I've ever worked with."

"Really?"

"Yes, really. Why do you say 'really'? Are you surprised?"

"Kind of, I guess."

"Why?"

"Well, it's a terrifically complimentary statement to make about a director, particularly this one."

"Why particularly this one?" he asked.

"The way I hear she works. Some interpret it as the method of a director . . ." (I searched for words that wouldn't offend. I couldn't find them) ". . . who hasn't got a clue as to what they're ultimately up to."

Cassavetes smiled, shaking his head. "She knows. Believe me, she knows."

I had heard the story of the fake stairs at the Essex, for instance. For the film, the Essex's lobby had been redesigned and made smaller. The original stairway from the lobby to the second floor was unusable. When Elaine prepared to shoot the lobby scene, she became disenchanted with the location of the stairs. Where they were negated some specific action and business that had just occurred to her. The scene had to be postponed while the set was redesigned and the stairs located elsewhere, a delay of at least a day. I suggested to Cassavetes that another director—indeed most directors given such a situation—would simply have re-thought, re-staged, re-choreographed the scene and worked with what was there.

"And with another director you could conceivably get a piece of hackwork," said Cassavetes. He hastened to add, no doubt sensing that I was going to, "And conceivably not."

"Why do you say she's the finest actor's director you ever worked with?" I asked.

"She gives, or suggests, or makes available so much for an actor to work with. Aside from in this instance providing the script which she wrote herself, and let me tell you it's one of the tightest I've ever read. She provides the props, the set—having worked it all out in advance with the prop guy and the art directors—and so forth. And she has a concept of character and direction that allows for flexibility in the actor's development of his characterization."

I asked Cassavetes, who was known as one of the industry's top improvisational directors, if he expected to contribute any directorial input in the making of this movie.

"Oh, come on!" he said. "This is Elaine's. I'm merely acting in it. She's a joy to work with. I can hardly wait to see the movie.

"As for improvisation," he continued, "I think singling me out as an improvisational director, or singling Elaine out, is to impose a category that I question even exists. I mean as something apart. What director directing films doesn't improvise?"

He mentioned Frank Capra as a case in point and as a surprising influence on his own work. He had recently read Capra's autobiography. "Like Capra says, no two directors work alike. In the thirties, Gregory La Cava and Ernst Lubitsch, for instance. Lubitsch approached his films like an architect. His scripts were as highly detailed as blueprints. La Cava couldn't be shackled to the chart systems of a script.

"But no director can be. I don't think even Lubitsch was. Actually making the movie is like doing the final draft of the script, especially for the director like Elaine who has written the script. No, I take it back. I guess editing is the final draft, but the director has a hand it that too, or should have.

"I've had a script for every film I ever did except *Shadows*. I had a script for *Husbands*. I had a script for *Faces*. I had a script for the new one." (*A Woman under the Influence*, on which principal photography had been completed, the editing of which Cassavetes interrupted in order to appear in *Mikey and Nicky*). "Wrote them myself. But a director has to let the scenes and the script breathe, expand, amplify.

"That's what Elaine's doing with this picture. Only with this difference: after she has allowed you, the actor, to open up, expand, really explore the character and situation in a certain scene, she'll guide you back, funnel you back, into the script.

"In the first scene, Peter and I played it every possible way, we're all over the room. Sometimes we said the lines Elaine's written, sometimes we didn't."

"Doesn't she complain?" I asked. "You said it's the tightest script you ever read. Why can't you respect its tightness?"

"It's because we respect its tightness that we can play with it," he said. "She would never ask that it always be done just the way she wrote it. Because something better might come out of it. A line, a quality, a mood. Like I say, filming the scene is like doing another draft. Oh, believe me, she goes back to the script, believe me she does. I got a note from Nola last night." He showed it to me.

Elaine says learn the lines.

"I've learned the lines. She knows I have. I'm just not married to them. I've never expected any of my actors to marry themselves to my lines. What this note says is, 'Now let's get back to the script.' Tonight, then, thanks to this note, I will speak the written lines. Sequentially."

One evening I planned to have dinner with our editor, John Carter. Before we finalized out plans, I was invited by our old friend from City Hall, Betty Croll, to have dinner with her and her husband at an Italian restaurant of some repute. I asked if Carter might join us. They were delighted.

I picked Carter up at the editing room. We were going out the door when a phone call came from the set. Elaine. Could Carter please hurry over to the Essex to confer with her? I called Betty Croll and told her we might be late.

At the hotel, Carter disappeared upstairs while I sat with Peter Falk in a booth on the main floor. He had a chessboard and pieces on the table in front of him, a game frozen in progress. Unlike acting, chess is something Falk refuses to improvise. He takes as long as twenty minutes to make a move. He was glum, preoccupied, in no mood for conversation. I slid silently from the booth and busied myself elsewhere until Carter returned.

On our way to the restaurant, Carter told me what the meeting with Elaine was all about. She needed advice on how to move her actors from one playing area to another to accommodate snippets of the scene that, wildly improvised, had already been shot. She wanted to match those sequences with what she hoped would now be a close adherence by the actors to the structured script. It wasn't going to be easy.

I had my spies on set. The crew. Especially those I'd worked with before. I was fed anecdotes, items, observations.

Randy Munkacsi's problems as stills photographer were almost a match for my own. Elaine excluded him from many set-ups, sometimes arbitrarily, sometimes excusing it to lack of space. At times she would allow him to stay but tell him, "Don't shoot this." Ordinarily a stills photographer is allowed to shoot during camera rehearsals. Elaine didn't believe in camera rehearsals. She filmed her rehearsals, fearful that she would lose an inspired bit of spontaneity if she did not, some great piece of business, or some expression that might not be recaptured on succeeding takes. The sound of the stills photographer clicking away could be a distraction and might also be recorded by the sound equipment. As a result, Munkacsi was severely limited in what he could shoot and resorted to being as surreptitious as I. When I left Philadelphia at the end of my three weeks, I hadn't seen a single contact sheet of Randy's work. Usually by the third week of a film I have seen and usually captioned at least thirty contact sheets with approximately thirty-five exposures per page. Randy was even restricted from taking production shots: photographs of technicians at work in conjunction with actors or in setting up scenes, shots of the director off-camera doing her job. Elaine simply did not want to be photographed, didn't want to see a camera pointed even vaguely in her direction.

"You didn't take a picture of *me*, did you?" she would scold.

Randy learned to fudge. "It was a shot of Cassavetes," he would say, neglecting to mention that Elaine was also in it. Once he admitted, "There might be just a portion of you in it." She replied, "I hope it's not the portion I think."

Randy complained to me during the second week of production, "It's getting so that every time I raise my camera, she gives me a dirty look."

A gaffer from California said, "I've never seen anything like the way she directs. We'll have the setup one way, then she'll get a wild hair and decide to do it another way, and we have to change it. I'd tear my hair out if I had any."

I suspect that Elaine's style of directing was more difficult for the cameramen than for anyone else, especially the focus cameraman. The actors had no set marks to which they had to adhere during scenes. "The trouble is," a cameraman told me, "they can move wherever they want whenever they want, and we're supposed to keep them in frame and in composition and in focus." Small wonder the original director of photography and his focus cameraman left after a few days' shooting.

There were complaints that she couldn't do "pick-up" scenes: scenes in which the actors pick up dialogue at a specific line or bit of business and reenact for the camera only the required portion of the scene rather than the entire scene. "Invariably, she'll reshoot the entire scene rather than do a pick-up," said an assistant director. "She doesn't edit in her head." Needless to say, reshooting the entire scene is costly in money, temper, and time. Although the method had paid off for Elaine in her previous two films, *A New Leaf* and *The Heartbreak Kid*, very few (if any) other directors would have been allowed the leisure and license she enjoyed on *Mikey and Nicky*.

On Thursday, June 7, the exhausted company finally finished at the Essex Hotel; and so glad was everyone to get out of there, it seemed almost like a wrap. It must have been because of the prevailing mood that I dared slip a note under Elaine May's door. "Don't shoot, but I'm the publicist," it began. I went on to tell her that Guy Flatley wanted to come to the location to do a Sunday "Arts and Leisure" piece for the *New York Times*, focusing either on her as director or on the film. "If it's impossible to speak with you, he'll be happy just to do a production story." I pointed up the advantages.

The note was intercepted by Nola Safro.

"I found your note," she said, with an enigmatic smile on her face.

Oh God! I thought. Is there no way to pierce this barrier?

"Did you show it to Elaine?"

She shook her head slowly. "It's best she doesn't see it."

I tried not to let my frustration give rise to anger. Nola was not unsympathetic. She knew a *Times* story was important. However, Elaine had already promised another *Times* movie writer, Mel Gussow, a story. "When the time comes, she'll give Gussow a story, but not till the picture's finished."

Gussow wrote for the daily paper, Flatley for the Sunday edition. Why couldn't each of them have a story, I argued. "She doesn't even have to talk to Flatley. Just let him come visit for a day or two."

Nola looked at me with pity. I still didn't get it, did I? I still didn't realize just what we were dealing with. Her look gave me a small shiver.

One morning I was sitting at someone's vacant desk in the production office when Elaine came in and sat down at a desk in front of me. If she noticed me, she gave no indication. She wrote something on a notepad, tore out the note, and went to the editing room. It was the first and last time I saw her in the office. It was like working with Garbo.

When Elaine returned from the location at eight in the morning, she sometimes went directly to the editing room for two or three hours before finally retiring to her suite. The doors to the editing room were always tightly closed. John Carter had been given two assistants and additional equipment to help deal with the voluminous amount of film being shot.

On the next to the last day of shooting at the Essex, John Cassavetes accidentally struck a female extra with a bottle thrown from a second story hotel room window supposedly to land at the feet of Mikey (Peter Falk), who was standing in the street below. His aim was off and the bottle hit the woman in the head. She was rushed to the hospital.

Thursday's papers carried the story along with the additional information that the woman was filing suit for $10,000. Cassavetes visited her in the hospital. Falk himself wrote her a letter describing her as ". . . a terrific person . . . really nice."

The bottle is crucial to the action. Nicky is holed up in the downtown hotel room. It's night. He's desperate, certain they're out to get him. He needs help, medicine, food. He's got an ulcer. Who can he turn to? Who but Mikey, his childhood buddy with whom he had joined the syndicate or gang (anything but mob or Mafia) on a buddy basis like some guys join the Navy. But what if it's Mikey who has the contract on him? Trusting no one but with no one else to trust, Nicky calls Mikey and tells him to come to a certain street corner and come alone. Nicky has to make sure that Mikey *is* alone. Once certain, he'll let Mikey know how to find him.

Now comes the bottle and the towel.

When Nicky sees that Mikey is alone, he wraps a towel around a bottle and throws it into the street to land at Mikey's feet. A clue to his whereabouts. The name of the hotel is on the towel. Mikey gets the room number from a recalcitrant clerk, rushes up to Nicky's floor, and raps on the door. Nicky, still apprehensive, won't open the door.

"Come on," cries Mikey, "it's me, Mikey. I came as soon as I got your towel."

A funny line. Quintessence of Elaine May.

Then I heard they weren't using it in some of the takes. I told Jackie I thought it a crime if they didn't use it. It was too good a line to waste.

"I don't think it was there originally," Jackie said.

"What do you mean, 'originally'?" I asked.

"It wasn't in either the play or the script," she said. The work had started life as a one-act play.

"You mean she just recently added it?"

"No," said Jackie, "I think *they* might have."

They could only mean *them*. "You mean Falk and Cassavetes came up with it?"

"Hey, that's how they work. It's how they all work. Of course I don't know. I admit it *sounds* like Elaine.

So much so that I said, "It *has* to be Elaine."

"Maybe that line," Jackie said, "but they put *some* things in. They got together and rehearsed long before any of us ever saw a shooting script."

I began to think that it must have been in rehearsals that the script turned into a comedy. In the process of filming it, Elaine was trying valiantly to reposition it on its dramatic foundation.

"It's what worries Elaine so much," said Jackie. "Everybody thinks it's going to be a comedy. It's what they expect of her. It *is* kind of funny though, isn't it?"

She said that Elaine complained about being unable to resist laugh lines and situations that occurred naturally to her comic imagination but that had no relevance to the tone and mood of the scene. Sometimes she didn't resist but realized it would be something else she would have to worry about later in the editing room.

It was editor John Carter who brought me the big news about myself: Elaine was considering me for the third male lead in the movie.

"What!" (Actually I think I had at least three exclamation points in my voice.)

"Yes," said Carter. "She's seen you around. She thinks you'd be great as the killer in the car."

I couldn't interpret the smile playing about his lips. Was he putting me on, or was *she* doing so using him as her conduit? Carter was not one to play practical jokes or speak frivolously.

"You say she's seen me. Where?"

Carter shrugged. "City Hall, for one thing. You've been on the set a couple of times. She's seen you with me. Yours is a familiar face to her now. She wants a familiar face in that role."

The killer/contract man had little dialogue. His role consisted primarily of driving an automobile though the dark late night streets of Philadelphia or sitting in the parked car waiting for his mark to appear.

I was never approached officially about the role. Elaine decided that Paramount president Frank Yablans should play it. He refused. She then offered the role to Bob Fosse. When he turned it down, Ned Beatty was cast. Carter assured me (or teased me) that Elaine did have me marked as camera potential and would use me yet.

On the night of Friday June 8, the company was filming at Dewey's Coffee Shop at Fifteenth and Locust Streets, not far from the Warwick. In the scene, Mikey comes into the coffee shop at a gallop to purchase either cream or milk for Nicky, whose ulcer is acting up. Nicky has a stopwatch, and if Mikey is not back at the hotel with the milk in ten minutes, Nicky will know that he has taken the extra time to tip off the mob as to his whereabouts and that it is he who has the contract on Nicky. The scene involves a confrontation between Falk and a slow, obstinate counterman who refuses to sell Mikey any cream unless Mikey also buys the coffee that the cream would ordinarily be sold with. Argues the counterman, otherwise how would I know what to charge for the cream? (It had struck me as sort of a riff on the famous restaurant scene with Jack Nicholson in *Five Easy Pieces.*) A brief scene, really, just a page and a half out of some 129 script pages.

The counter was a kidney-shaped affair with a wide, gleaming, Formica-slick surface. On the far side of the counter, out of camera range, sat a multitude of extras, only a few of whom would be used. Standing in front of the counter, Elaine whispered to her assistant director, Pete Scoppa, while looking circumspectly at me. Scoppa was already in costume and makeup to play the counterman. He tried to follow her discrete indication. His range was afield. She focused him on me. He shook as head. As did crew people. She argued with them, all of them looking in my direction while pretending to look beyond me.

I was starting to feel that maybe there was virtue in staying in my hotel room.

Elaine wanted to use me in the scene. Scoppa told her she couldn't. I wasn't an extra. She had contracted for extras. She was paying for extras. "Use an extra," he told her.

Later he told me the real reason they wanted me instead of an extra. "We expected violence."

I don't know who they told Elaine I was. We were still maintaining the fiction that there was no publicist with the company. None of the extras had the look she wanted, she told Scoppa. The look that I had. I wonder what that look was. She capitulated sullenly and picked a male from the pool and placed him on a stool at the counter. She looked at him through the camera lens and immediately had him returned to the pool. Another was selected who also didn't meet with her approval anymore than the first. He was dismissed. She looked longingly at me. Pete Scoppa shook his head in grave discouragement. She looked vaguely around for another idea.

Someone or something for Peter Falk to play off. And there they were. They had just been brought in.

Doughnuts.

Sitting almost directly opposite me on a table behind the counter, the doughnuts were to be used for decoration and props. They were in a fresh, grease-stained, highly fragrant cardboard bakery box, gorgeously glazed, tempting even to someone like me who avoided pastry as the harbinger of hypoglycemic plague.

Elaine fixed on the doughnuts. She began fondling them. Carefully. Appraisingly. One by one. Testing them for—whatever. Firmness? Weight? Who knows. Bob Visciglia, whose province as prop man the doughnuts were, joined her in the exercise. He fondled the doughnuts too. I doubt seriously whether he had any more idea what he was feeling for than I did. Perhaps I do him discredit. I did admire his bravura in faking it, if that is what it was. Doughnuts were separated. This one rejected, that one chosen. That one returned to the box to be shoved under the counter, this one proudly to go to onto a counter display plate. Some doughnuts rejected by Visciglia were reclaimed by Elaine. She had second thoughts about some of her own choices, but not like she did about Visciglia's. Evidently he never learned the trick. She returned most of his selections to the greasy box and replaced them with doughnuts chosen by herself. There was a fair amount of anguish and soul-searching over a couple of the doughnuts before their proper niche was decided. She felt, selected, rejected, and transferred doughnuts for a period of fifteen minutes. Why some were rejected as unfit for camera and others chosen to make their wild cinematic debut was never revealed to those of us who were watching.

Once her selections had been made and placed on the display plate, she then began to arrange them to suit her artistic or esthetic sense. Some doughnuts on the bottom she pulled from the pile and put on top. Some on top she tucked in among those at the bottom or arranged somewhere in the middle. When her back was turned, a little boy, son of one of the camera operators, grabbed one and began to eat it. He was hustled outside. No one mentioned it to Elaine, but when she turned back to the plate, she immediately knew something was wrong. She was momentarily puzzled but cast no blame. She merely rearranged.

When she finally thought it was perfect, she paced the plate of doughnuts on the counter where it would be in the forefront of the shot and put a plastic orange cover over the plate. She looked at the plate through the camera. What she saw did not please her. She removed the cover and looked again. Still she was dissatisfied.

Most of the company, except for a precious few of us who were hypnotized by her obsessiveness, were oblivious to her, perhaps consciously so, immersed in business, problems, and conversations of their own.

She put the carefully organized display plate and its orange cover out of camera range. She then set the box of rejected doughnuts on the counter. She looked through the camera again, smiled. It was what she wanted. She was ready to shoot.

I asked Pete Scoppa what had been the point. His expression said, "Huh?"

"The doughnuts," I explained.

"For Falk to work with, if he wants."

"How?"

"However he wants. If he wants. They're there to use if he wants to, like you'd be if I'd let her use you. She'll never tell him how to use them. They may suggest something to him. Like you might have, if you were in the scene. Then again he may ignore them. We'll just have to wait and see."

Which still didn't really explain the fifteen minutes of feely-touchy with the fried and sugary dough.

The camera operator seemed to read my mind. Like many of the crew, he had worked with Elaine before. He told me that he had never seen her quite so compulsive. I wondered if possibly what looked like compulsiveness might not be her way of psyching herself up for the scene. Or down, as the case might be. Perhaps she was blocking out action, testing camera angles in her head as she fiddled about. In any case, I marveled at what I'd been watching. I realized that I'd been witness to an improvised sketch containing in its own inadvertent way as much satiric wit as a Nichols and May parody, just nonverbally. But who dared laugh? It was enough, in my precarious position, just to look.

Certainly Peter Falk had been given something to work with. He had his choice of an individual doughnut, the collective doughnuts, the doughnuts and the box together in a cataclysmic orgasm of business, or portioning this wealth of material, first the doughnuts and then the box. Also provided for him were a crumpled napkin, a coffee cup with dregs of coffee remaining, and silverware lying about. Somehow it all came together in my head as confirmation of what John Cassavetes and Peter Falk had both told me about Elaine May: that she is the best actor's director in the business, always giving the actor something to work with, beginning as author of a tightly constructed plot, characters realized in depth and relating to one another in interesting complexity, dialogue that skips off the page like bullets to explode with a zing of wit upon delivery, on down to the coffee dregs and doughnut details of the night's lunch-counter accoutrement.

Lights.

The scene was ready for filming. Since Elaine did not stage camera rehearsals, the camera would turn on every bit of action. She was after spontaneity, which she believed might come at the very beginning. She didn't want to miss a thing.

Camera.

Action!

In his contretemps and frustration with the counterman, Peter Falk attacked the doughnuts in every conceivable way, all on the first take.

He slung them, spit on them, threw them, kicked them, and stomped them. How easily it could have been me!

Scoppa was slaughtered along with the doughnuts.

Falk's hands were as busy as his feet. He was a madman.

The little boy who had appropriated a doughnut gasped at a particularly bit of brutal nastiness visited upon Scoppa. His mother clasped her hand over his mouth.

Watching the take, you felt for Scoppa. You wondered if he wasn't going to come out of this more dead than alive. You sensed his astonishment and anger as well as his regret at having taken the role. Now you realized why they had one of the crew take it: an actor would sue.

The level of anger and violence exhibited by Falk was totally unexpected (except for Scoppa, surely, who having forewarned me of violence must have expected it, if not to this extent and virulence). Everyone was watching spellbound, Elaine visibly ecstatic. Falk's performance was totally mesmerizing. One had to resist the impulse to run out in front of the camera to save Pete Scoppa.

Falk jumped onto and over the counter to clutch his hands about Scoppa's neck and start strangling him, jerking him backwards, forwards, sideways, banging him against the counter repeatedly in the struggle. (Scoppa showed me his back the next day. It was a ribbon of welts, black and blue and purple.)

When the take was over, it took at least five minutes before Falk's anger subsided and his breathing became normal. He strode back and forth behind the stool where I was sitting, trying to come down from his adrenaline high. He glanced at me. More like a glare. Still partially in character, I realized. Mikey still lived within him. The glare contained a plaintive quality, however, that was not Mikey's but Peter Falk's: the look already contained an apology. As he caught his breath, his look became gentle and Columbo-ish. I still chose to avoid his eyes. The man might have been acting but he was not kidding.

The scene was shot fourteen times that night. And that was the master shot alone. Then came the same scene with close-ups. The doughnuts disintegrated. In some takes, Falk merely threw and broke plates and stayed on his side of the counter. In others he used doughnuts like grenades. When the doughnut supply ran out, the prop man was reduced to Scotch-taping doughnut pieces together for subsequent takes. Aesthetics be damned.

Falk apologized to Scoppa after the first take, but his anger and how he acted on it, how he acted it out, was no less restrained during all of the following takes.

The most horrendous take for Scoppa, if one can be singled out, was one prior to which Elaine had taken Scoppa aside to tell him, "This time, be evasive."

What does she mean? Scoppa wanted to know.

"Don't give him the right answers. Don't give him his cue. Let's rattle him a little."

Scoppa was apprehensive, but he couldn't very well tell Elaine he didn't think it was a good idea. He merely voiced the opinion that he thought Falk might be rattled enough as it was.

With trepidation Scoppa begins the scene. Falk enters and speaks his first line. Scoppa replies with something totally out of left field but still in character. Confusion and anger flood Falk's face as he tries to continue the scene as written while Scoppa continues playing it as thought the script were foreign to him, stepping on some cues, oblivious to others.

Again Falk jumps the counter, this time with a fork raised in his hand. It is raised to stab Scoppa, who knows he's in heavy-duty danger. He runs from behind the counter and swings around two female extras having coffee and pastry and disappears behind a stanchion, yelling as he went, "This guy's out of his head!" All the while Falk is pursuing him brandishing the fork, Elaine yelling, "You're getting out of camera range!" and Scoppa replying, "And that's where I intend to stay!"

And then he ran out the door onto the street, Falk snarling and snapping behind him like the Hound of the Baskervilles. At this point the action moved out of my field of vision, and I can't vouch for precisely what happened next. I do know that Falk was somehow stopped and subdued and that Scoppa was persuaded to do yet another take. The more fool he.

John Cassavetes was a recipient of Elaine's directorial tricks as well. In one scene, Nicky has to back through the open door of his hotel room with a gun in his hand. In one take, Elaine told an assistant to close the door without letting Cassavetes know about it. The cameras turned. The scene played. Cassavetes went to the door and banged into it. He was furious, certain that some luckless crew member had screwed up. He threw his gun at the door and kicked it, then banged his head against the door. Elaine May, a shy grin on her face, said quietly and sweetly, "Cut."

One night while the crew was setting up to film a sequence on the sidewalk in front of the Essex, Elaine watched as an inebriated derelict wandered among the crew. She approached the man and asked if he would do her a favor: would he please stop the two gentlemen who were presently to come around the corner and ask them for a cigarette? The request confused the man, but he was game to oblige. When Falk and Cassavetes turned the corner and came into camera range, the bum did exactly as instructed. The two actors so convincingly improvised a scene on the spot with the man that wardrobe man Dick Bruno, thinking them to be shooting the breeze with the bum between takes, walked into the shot and adjusted Cassavetes's coat collar. Elaine screeched to Bruno, "Leave that collar alone! You are never to touch that collar again!"

Bruno was humiliated. He said to me, "It's my first goof in twenty years in the business. I didn't even see the camera."

Which was exactly how Elaine liked it. For the camera to be invisible.

When she set up the scene again, Cassavetes yelled to Bruno, "You're on, Dick!"

To make up for lost time (we had already fallen a week behind schedule in the first three weeks of filming), the company began working on Saturdays. On Saturday June 9, I had an early dinner with John Cassavetes and his son Nick at Bookbinder's, a seafood restaurant just half a block from Dewey's Coffee Shop of doughnut fame. Cassavetes was scheduled to report for work right after the meal.

Recognizing Cassavetes, the hostess at Bookbinder's wondered why he hadn't been working the night before. She had seen Peter Falk beating up on some poor man in the coffee shop. He was still beating up on him when she went to bed. Since her apartment was in the next block overlooking Dewey's, she had had a good view. Cassavetes explained that he had not been in that particular scene. The conversation switched to the Kentucky Derby that had been run that afternoon with Secretariat the Winner.

"Mr. Falk is no slouch at racing either, is he?" said our hostess. "My neighbor heard a bunch of racket about five this morning and looked out and saw the man Mr. Falk had been beating up on come running out of the coffee shop and around the block with Mr. Falk following him with a fork. But the funny thing was, she said she couldn't see a camera anywhere."

John Cassavetes agreed that it was a funny thing. A perplexing thing. But making movies often was a funny thing.

A message I carried with me when I left the movie after my three weeks on location.

By the end of August of 1973, well over the optimistically envisioned eight weeks shooting schedule, it was clear that the movie could not be finished that year. Peter Falk had to return to California and to his baggy trench coat. The new season's episodes of *Columbo* were ready to roll. The company shut down, not to resume again until well into 1974 when Falk would again be available. Early in 1975 I began to hear rumors that principal photography had at long last been completed.

On the average film of that time, approximately 400,000 feet of film were exposed.

On Elaine May's *The Heartbreak Kid* between 600,000 and 700,000 feet were shot. Nicolas Sgarro was Elaine's script supervisor on both *A New Leaf* and *The Heartbreak Kid*. I became acquainted with Sgarro in 1975 when I worked as publicist on *The Happy Hooker*, which he directed. He told me that having seen how Elaine worked on *A New Leaf*, he had suggested to her that to facilitate matters two cameras be used simultaneously on *Heartbreak*. Big mistake. Like treating a diabetic with Godiva Chocolates. The raw stock bills were enormous. Even so, not as enormous as on *Mikey and Nicky*.

Over one million—*one million*—feet of film were shot on *Mikey and Nicky*. About 200 miles' worth. It was to be something of a record. By comparison, about 250,000 feet were shot on *The Happy Hooker*.

Not all of the long post-production period of *Mikey and Nicky* was spent in trying to untangle and match film. Sound too was a problem. The sound man had experienced as much difficulty as the focus cameraman in adjusting to the working methods of the director and the two stars. Asked to specify just what the difficulties with the sound were, Elaine May said, "I'm just trying to fix it so you can hear it."

Mikey and Nicky was released in December 1976. It received almost unanimously bad reviews. Two exceptions are worth noting. Gene Shalit, reviewing for *The Today Show* on NBC, picked the film as one of the ten best of the year. Stanley Kaufmann of *The New Republic* named it as *one of the ten best of the decade*.

Time may be proving Shalit and Kaufmann right. When the restored print was released in 2004 prior to the DVD release, *Mikey and Nicky* was viewed as a major work of art.

"STEPPIN' IN HIGH COTTON"
(Francis Coppola's *The Cotton Club*)

The Cotton Club was politics and confetti, at the time of its production in 1983 one of the largest and most expensive Tinkertoys in the history of motion pictures. Film-making as circus and circus as metaphor, a three-ring psychodrama in the minds and psyches of the film's key players and crew, principally enacted on the sound stages and dressing rooms and other production seats of power of New York's old historic Astoria Studios (in ignominy, rechristened Kaufman-Astoria after a present owner).

As the film's unit publicist, unable to be everywhere at once—eyes, ears, head straining, alert, craning, turning from ring to ring, always aware of having just missed something by a beat, coming in on the whispered residue of an incident—I turned more and more to messengers of information, runners of rumor, acolytes of anecdote, bearers of the magic password "Have you heard the latest?" who enlisted themselves in my service: the wardrobe people, the sound men, grips, smoke blowers (oh yes, lots of those), senior production personnel, secretaries, the janitorial crew, production assistants, director confidants, stars.

Some, their identities unknown to me to this day, skipped me entirely. With hotlines of their own to gossip columnists and others, they reported the latest set outrage or the newest behind-the-camera skirmish, incidents printed day after day under the by-lines and aegis of Liz Smith (*New York Daily News*), Suzy and

"Page Six" (both in the *New York Post*), and others. Most of these tales out of school involved top-billed Richard Gere, director Francis Coppola, and producer Robert Evans (with whom Coppola wasn't speaking and who was also barred from the set, part of Coppola's agreement to direct the film).

Before I became associated with the picture, *The Cotton Club* was already becoming something of a legend, blazing through the media sky like a long-heralded comet that was fully and flagrantly to live up to expectations, never to disappoint those who daily gathered to shake heads and marvel in voyeuristic glee at the sparked tracery of its passing.

For a film that didn't want production publicity, *The Cotton Club* broke records for press mentions. Never out of the news, the title and production were always on the tip of an anonymous tongue. Yet most messengers of information came to me not because they expected their latest fun item to see immediate print but because they quickly and correctly perceived in me one highly appreciative of a good story. The messengers came not only to deliver goodies but to receive them. They whispered to me; I whispered to them. The good old barter system at work. We were living through a phantasmagorical soap opera only a few scenes of which any one of us was privileged to experience personally. Each of us was getting only snatches of the drama, sometimes the buildup but not the payoff of the comedy. We traded the connective tissue of our respective narratives, mine for yours, yours for mine. Together perhaps we would have a joined piece of the larger unknowable puzzle. Now we find us another piece: where does it fit? The messengers and I bonded in a spirit of mirth that helped dispel the ditziness and puzzlement of it all, the prevailing feeling of uncertainty and surrealism encountered everywhere, in every department. Our laughter grew therapeutically brazen.

One of the things that made it fun was the paranoia. Paranoia rode trick ponies throughout the circus tent. I had to walk a political tightrope and still keep an eye on the ponies and twirling bodies in all the rings.

Take Coppola, for instance. Ringmaster in a pas de deux with his own paranoid pony. Now on it, now off, dragging his practiced feet on the ground or holding them together, extended, aloft, now to this side, now to that, maintaining balance yet sometimes dangerously off-balance, poised to topple any minute: stay out of his way.

It became my mantra.

* * *

In the spring and summer of 1983, gossip columnists reported that black technicians were being sought for crew positions on *The Cotton Club*. Good luck, I thought, finding an experienced black unit publicist. I knew of none. Not on the East Coast. A black stills photographer was rumored to have been hired, Adger Cowans, said to be good but difficult. A black stills photographer meant that it would be easier for the company to justify a white publicist. I went after the job. I had qualifications, and I had precedent. I was publicist on the first big black action film produced by a major studio, MGM's *Shaft* in 1971. I had worked successfully not only with Gordon Parks, Richard Roundtree, and Moses Gunn on that film but also with

Ben Vereen, Ossie Davis, Ruby Dee, Isaac Hayes, and Fred Williamson on later projects.

By the time of *The Cotton Club*, the outside public relations agency had increasingly usurped the studio publicity department's importance and function, even in the hiring of a unit publicist. It was not good news to find out that the PR agency on *The Cotton Club* was Zarem, Inc. Bobby Zarem was under contract to producer Robert Evans. I hadn't a prayer of a chance. I wouldn't be Bobby's fifth let alone first choice for unit publicist. Bobby and I had worked together (if you can call it that) on the Ryan O'Neal comedy *So Fine*, a title that did not at all reflect my relationship with Bobby.

To my surprise I received a call on July 12 from Mark Kane of the Zarem office asking about my availability for *The Cotton Club*. Oh shit. Did I want to work with Zarem again? What was I to do? I needed the job. It promised to be a long one. I took a deep breath and said "Yes."

An appointment was set for me to meet with Fred Roos at the Kaufman-Astoria Studio.

Astoria Studios had opened in Queens on September 20, 1920, as Famous Players/Lasky Studio, also known as Eastern Service Studio, across the East River from Manhattan. It became identified with Paramount Pictures through a series of financial maneuvers on the part of Adolph Zukor, who had co-founded it with Jesse Lasky. The Marx Brothers movie *The Cocoanuts* was made there while they were appearing on Broadway in *Animal Crackers*. In later years *Wolfen, Hair, Arthur,* and others had been made at the studio, but no production had spent as much time there as *The Cotton Club* would. It was a labyrinth where I was often to explore and just as often to get lost. There were uninhabited areas that smelled of clay and decay, a shambles of dirt and rotted wood. It was rumored that the ghost of the recently deceased Gloria Swanson walked there, and Coppola himself would later claim to have seen her during one of her nocturnal visits during pre-production when he was sleeping over at the studio in the star suite first occupied by Swanson. Swanson had made a number of pictures at the studio, including two directed by Allan Dwan, for whom the studio was built. Dwan had not liked working in Hollywood.

Fred Roos had co-produced a number of Coppola's movies including *Apocalypse Now*. On *The Cotton Club* his title was casting consultant. Obviously he would have greater responsibilities on the film than was currently being acknowledged.

I arrived for the interview. Roos was out of the office, but Bobby Zarem and Mark Kane were there. Zarem wore a short-sleeved cotton shirt, unbuttoned to his navel, no undershirt, the shirt stained with circles of moisture. Kane, himself narrow, had a buttoned-down look, jacket with narrow lapels, narrow tie. He looked remarkably cool for such a hot day. No air conditioning. The room's one window was wide open to admit what, if a breeze, was certainly sporadic and just as certainly tropical. Zarem positioned himself flat on the floor, clasped his hands behind his head, and commenced sit-ups. A bulky guy. While he wore his weight well, you could appreciate his wanting to wear some of it off. His hair was wispy, balding on top, the side hair worn long like Benjamin Franklin. It was always in disarray, I remember, sort of endearing. He had a habit of sculpturally worrying strands of it with a finger.

Roos came in, stepped across Zarem, and settled down behind his desk. His face was oval and pasty, owlishly pulled in on itself. He reminded me of a character out of Mark Twain, a riverboat captain without his cap. His eyes were active and searching, seemingly several beats ahead of his thought processes, and those swift enough. His arms rested on his desk. He held my résumé before him in both hands like a helmsman at the wheel of his boat, trying to sight in the clear horizon of my professional past the readings of a possible and future rock or sandbar that might interfere with the proper passage of the good ship *Cotton Club* should I be aboard it.

Zarem began pitching me, ticking off the titles of my films despite the fact that Roos had my credits right in front of him.

Roos asked about films on which I'd worked with Robert De Niro and John Travolta. I caught the drift. There were rumors that Richard Gere was out and that either of these two might be in.

Likely a closed set, Roos said, no press allowed. Special photographers, maybe, depending on Coppola and Gere, both of whom he thought at present to be opposed to the idea. The key lay with Coppola. If he approved, Gere must be persuaded to cooperate. I took that comment to mean that the securing of such cooperation would lie with me.

Zarem took umbrage, claiming a proprietary interest in Gere. He would deal with Richard himself, he said. For my own protection. "After all, he slugged his last publicist, and she was a woman."

Not a unit publicist, I learned, but a publicist with the PR agency representing him at the time he was starring in *Bent* on Broadway. The alleged slugging had taken place in front of the theater.

Roos asked me to wait in the production office. Cramped space, four desks, a clutter of boxes and paperwork. The production office coordinator was a friendly face, Grace Blake. I knew her from *Shaft*. In the only chair designated for visitors was another friendly face, Gregory Hines. I knew him only from his work. He sat like an errant child in the principal's office. An earring dangled from the lobe of one ear. Perhaps he was to be chastised for the earring. Precipitously, in introducing myself to him, I told him I was to be the film's unit publicist. Bite your tongue, Tommy. Grace Blake clapped her hands. Big grin. "Wonderful!" Gregory beamed (and he did have one of the best beams in the business). If it made Grace happy, it made him happy. I felt like a jerk. Roos and Zarem were probably in there already on the phone offering the job to another publicist.

Grace was a black woman who had been born in Venezuela but raised in Trinidad. She brought a nice touch of earth mother and Whoopi Goldberg to the office. The production office was no place for a pretender. I told her and Gregory I was going to take a look around.

The Cotton Club set, already fabled in press mentions, was dark, the area lit by minimal work light. I was within hailing distance of the production office should anyone call for me, separated from it only by black cycloramic drapes and hanging flats on which were painted Harlem brownstones circa the twenties. A young man in a green Lacoste shirt appeared from behind the drapes with the suddenness of a thrown stone to catch me singing to myself. He saw something elementary in me that amused him. An acceptable Richard Gere substitute, I thought. An adroitness in his walk, something insinuating. A moustache, which I could have done without and so could he. A haircut on the square side. A winning dollop of hair falling gracefully over his forehead. His body not on a par with Gere's. Gere's stand-in, maybe? Something lacking. Gere's savoir faire. Probably an electrician or gaffer. Bookkeeper? Someone who had been told he looked like Gere and was doing his admirable best to emphasize various small points of resemblance. He looked like a nice guy, though, and I thought it would be pleasant to get to know him.

Before we had a chance to talk, Roos and Zarem called me back into the office. "Don't call us, we'll call you," they said in essence. They did manage to say it a little bit nicer. But when I left them that day, I really didn't expect to hear anything from them again.

But they did call.

And called again.

The hiring dragged on for days. My asking price? I named a figure. Nobody fainted. The same money I had received a few months earlier working on the Paul Newman movie *Harry and Son* in Florida.

Days passed. No word. Rumors. Coppola preferred a female publicist. Everybody's choice, Ann Guerin, was committed to Robert Redford and *The Natural*. Scott McDonough, a former Woody Allen unit publicist, had been offered the job.

I had an informant friendly not only with Guerin and McDonough but with key crew people. "You're not to repeat this to a living soul," she said, "but I got it from a virtually unimpeachable source. Richard Sylbert is out. Even though the principal set's his and already built. Coppola's deal is, he can hire and fire as he chooses once they start shooting. Gere is probably out, too. They've got somebody standing by. Travolta, maybe. They may use the pissing in the street thing against him."

Poor Richard. He had been arrested in Greenwich Village for relieving himself at the corner of Tenth Street and Greenwich Avenue, presumably into a church bush. (Living in the Village myself, I figured that if they arrested everybody who was doing that, the jails would be filled and they'd have to borrow from New Jersey and Connecticut.) A woman unsympathetic to public urination, no matter how urgent the need, had flagged a police car. The leaky perpetuator was hauled off to the nearest precinct. "He claims he's Richard Gere." He was fined. The *New York Post* had fun with it.

(Immediately Coppola had incorporated the incident into the script, and it was still in the first draft I read. Gere's character is spotted by two talent scouts while making wee-wee. Immediately recognizing his potential, they arrange for a screen test that lands him a contract. I teased Richard, telling him how gleefully I was looking forward to the filming of that scene. Could we expect a close-up?

"I'm not filming it, Tom. Francis put it in as a joke. Lower your expectations, sir! Or as the case may be raise them.")

But back to matters at hand. Zarem and company told me they were talking to no one else but me.

Bullshit.

"It will be resolved today."

More of the same.

Three days later: "It's pretty certain that you have the job. You still want the picture, don't you?"

And the next week, stringing me along until they could see which way Scott McDonough was going to jump: "You still want the picture, don't you?"

Later: "You're the one we want to do the movie, as long as you want to do it."

Scott flipped out. At least he dropped out. He told my informant, "They can have Tom. He'll be good for the movie. They're playing too many games. Now they want me to come in for yet another interview, this time with Dyson Lovell. I'm not going."

I wasn't surprised when I got a call to go to a meeting with Dyson Lovell.

He was the Evans hurdle. I had, I thought, already cleared the Coppola hurdle. This was phase two in a psychological tug of war for a compromise publicist, one who, on the basis of past credits and associations, was unlikely to favor either faction, not to mention favor Richard Gere. It became clear to me that if I had ever known or worked with Richard Gere, I wouldn't get the job. No wonder Scott dropped out.

Lovell was in his forties, I imagine. Nice looking. He was dressed casually in pale blue-jeans with a red belt and a white short-sleeved shirt with a few top buttons open to expose his bare chest. His ample but trim body looked like it would not disgrace itself on a squash court.

"I'm not at ease with interviews of this nature," he said. "I never know what to ask or how to proceed."

I gathered he was leaving it to me to begin. His attitude and attire suggested casualness and indirectness as the best approach. There was a massive calendar covering two walls of his office like a mural. On it were penciled names of characters and indications of scenes. Mrs. Flegenheimer? I didn't know her. "Is she the Madame in whose house Dutch Schultz hangs out?"

"No," said Lovell, "she's the mother in whose house he hangs out."

Too late I remembered. Dutch Schultz's real name was Arthur Flegenheimer. It would have been a plus had I remembered sooner.

He asked what I had worked on. I told him, emphasizing Paul Newman (always a safe bet). We traded stories, remembrances. I felt easy with him and he with me. He said, "Just let me tell you. It's a minefield here. You will have to keep your wits about you. Be very careful as you pick your way through."

There was foreboding in those words. Also prophecy.

I had the job, I thought. Or did I? Three days later, still no word. Thursday. The picture started Monday. I called Lovell's office. His assistant, Jim Kelly, apologized. "Our fault. I'm sorry. We only just now spoke with Mark and told him to proceed with negotiations for you."

The following afternoon I saw David Golden, the production manager. I had with me a list of particulars and specifications I wanted worked into my deal memo (this is one of the most important lists a publicist can make). Salary, expense account, private office, refrigerator and other niceties, everything I could think of that I might require. He looked at my list askance. He expelled his breath. A heaven-help-me sigh. He would have to refer it to higher authority, he said. Wait outside.

He spoke with associate producer Milt Forman. I heard Forman say, "Scale." I said from the doorway, "I won't work for scale." They said they'd have to talk to Fred Roos. Wait outside.

The Cotton Club main set was fully lit and unoccupied. I began to investigate. Production designer Richard Sylbert joined me. He surprised me by knowing who I was. "I hear you're joining us," he said. I brought him up to date. He smiled wryly. He had been there. "Get your money. Don't settle for less," he said. Easy enough done if you're a Richard Sylbert.

He wore a safari jacket, his costume. I never saw him without it. He wore it like a talisman, as I suspect also was the pipe he always carried in his breast pocket, hand, or mouth. Sylbert had designed several films directed by Mike Nichols, among them *The Graduate*, *Carnal Knowledge*, and *Who's Afraid of Virginia Woolf* for which he had won the Academy Award. He had also designed *Reds* and *Shampoo* for Warren Beatty and *Chinatown* for Roman Polanski. At one time he was vice-president in charge of production at Paramount Pictures, replacing Robert Evans who had moved on to being an active producer. "That was fun for a while. I didn't have to worry about such weighty matters as 'Where's that doorknob?' But then I began to miss this end of it. The position of vice-president in charge of whatever was, I discovered, not such the kick I thought it might be. I got back into production design."

He was pleased to have the chance to talk about his present work.

"The Cotton Club changed its décor every six months. The film will reflect that. The club represents the gangster's idea of the South. Magnolias, cotton fields, steamboats, banjos, mammies in bandanas, all the stereotypes."

They were all represented on the walls of Sylbert's set. Initially there were supposed to be three big Cotton Club shows as well as the three décor changes, but during production the number was dropped to two.

He had been hired by Robert Evans long before it was known who the film's director would be and had worked pretty much on his own from various Mario Puzo scripts. "Which quickly supplanted each other," he said. After three years of pre-production—yes, Virginia, *three*—Coppola was signed to write and direct, bringing with him Albany novelist William Kennedy as co-writer. Sylbert didn't have to change any of his designs or concepts for the club after Coppola signed on. "Although," he said ruefully, "obviously I'm not used to working like this."

Nor was Coppola, who usually worked with production designer Dean Tavoularis. The hard fact that Tavoularis was in New York and was seen frequently in Coppola's company did not help dispel rumors of Sylbert's imminent dismissal. (Actually, Coppola and Tavoularis were planning another film, not to be realized.)

"I had to proceed like a detective researching the club. Not only is it gone but the entire block it stood on has since been trashed, turned into an apartment development. A shame. I also felt that memory played tricks on many who worked at the club. They remember it as larger. We established that it was ninety-eight feet by seventy-two feet. My researchers found a picture taken in 1930 when RKO sent someone to photograph the room and chart its dimensions. The Schomburg was a great help to me." He was referring to the Schomberg Center for Research into Black Culture, a branch of the New York Public Library in Harlem. "Then I found some marvelous archival film shot inside the club."

(When later I was able to see this archival footage myself, I was astonished to see how closely Sylbert's set matched the interior of the real Cotton

Club. After *The Cotton Club* wrapped, the Smithsonian Institution got in touch with me about the set. They wanted to acquire it. They were a day late. Half of it had already been dismantled, one of its wall murals donated to the Museum of the Moving Image at the Astoria Studio. When I told Sylbert about the request, he said with regret, "Too bad they didn't ask sooner. It would have been like having the original club in mint condition.")

I was paged.

Fred Roos had said no to my major requests, I was told. He lowered my asking price to what I had received a couple of years before on *Blow Out*. Clearly unacceptable.

What I found very interesting was what he *did* approve: a proviso whereby my salary would go up should Zarem quit or be fired. He called Zarem and read it to him. Zarem had a shit fit, which somehow pleased me. However, in that event Roos would allow my salary to rise only to my current asking price. If Zarem were kicked out, as the rumor mill had it he would be, my responsibilities would double, a staggering prospect on a production of this size.

I called Zarem and told him I was out. They could find someone else. Zarem screamed at me not to do anything foolish. He wanted to talk to Milt Forman. Maybe something could be worked out. He added, "We're all very upset with you. It wasn't the money so much as the other requests you brought in!" Like I was asking for caviar on my desk every afternoon, roses every morning. (I was eventually to get the roses. An unexpected admirer.) "And you *are* asking two hundred dollars above what anybody else is."

I loved that. After their telling me they were talking to no one else!

"Bobby," I said, "I told you two weeks ago what my asking price was. The picture starts Monday and here I am haggling details late Friday afternoon. The whole thing stinks."

"The picture starts Monday?" said Zarem. He sounded like it was news to him. Maybe it was. "But there's no script yet."

He told me to please hold tight until he could talk to Forman.

Forman's secretary could see that I was seriously upset. She told me her boss was on the phone with Zarem. "But it's about you," she said, adding conspiratorially, "go on in."

Forman looked like Groucho Marx on a straight day after the jokes have dried up. He motioned me to sit. He cupped his hands over the mouthpiece to conclude his conference with Bobby.

"Let's talk realistically," he said, waving my list of particulars. "What is it that bothers you? Is it the money?"

Of course it was the money!

But by now it was many other things. Scott McDonough, where art thou now!

He tried and failed to locate Fred Roos. "I'd prefer that he talk to you since he was the first to okay you, but okay then," he sighed, reluctantly taking responsibility. He named a figure one hundred dollars less than my initial asking price. With an alacrity that surprised both of us, I accepted. He seemed relieved. We went to Golden with the news.

Forman again raised the Zarem clause. It had clearly had its effect. Zarem was an Evans man. Coppola didn't want him. He would likely go. Simple as that. I wanted more money for the extra responsibility.

"But it's demoralizing to Bobby," said Forman. "I urge you to drop it. I've never seen anything like this and I've been in the business a long time."

By this time the poor man looked like he had been in the business a long time, the men's ready-to-wear business. Furthermore one on the verge of bankruptcy. His wilted pants and shirt looked like something from a fire sale. The job was taking a toll on him.

"Zarem's got a contract," he stressed. "He won't be let go. We'd have to pay him off, and we're not going to do that."

(I smile sadly in retrospect at the irony of that statement. Too many with contracts would eventually be paid off and let go, including Milt Forman, Dyson Lovell, and David Golden. Zarem miraculously managed to hold on. But just barely.)

I let the Zarem proviso go, which surprised Golden. He said he would have my deal memo typed and ready for my signature Monday morning on location.

It was over.

I had the job. I felt a little sick. I also felt exhilarated.

Which one of the reputed monsters would attack first? Coppola? Evans? Gere? Some jealous underling? As it turned out, I have never known a first week of shooting on any film that was a bigger horror show than *The Cotton Club*, and the horror and turmoil came from a totally unexpected source.

* * *

We were filming in a charming Victorian-styled building, newly renovated, that housed a restaurant, a bar, and various rooms available for special events. Its proprietor, inspired by the Prohibition Era nature of the film, envisioned converting one of his rooms into a Speakeasy. My conflict with the man stemmed from his determination that our presence in his premises should result in a windfall of publicity for himself and his establishment. My orders were that reporters and television crews were not to be allowed on or near any of our sets at any of our locations, a policy that was to prevail throughout the production, rarely modified. We were scheduled to shoot interiors in the building for three days. The three days stretched unmercifully into a full work week. I had welcomed having our kickoff shooting in a private establishment leased to us. Control of access by press and others (particularly freelance photographers attracted by the bait of Richard Gere and Francis Coppola and the air of notoriety already surrounding the film) would be greatly simplified. Or so we thought.

On the morning of the second day, I was transcribing notes from the day before in my apartment. Grace Blake called: I was urgently needed on the set. An ABC News team was there. *Inside* the building. Invited by the proprietor. Of all the gall! I was furious. The action was unprecedented in my experience. I got to Brooklyn as quickly as I could. Three ABC News people were in the proprietor's anteroom, the proprietor in his office with the door closed. I explained to the news team why they couldn't be allowed to shoot. The proprietor snapped open his door and told me briskly to step inside.

"When I'm through here," I said.

"Now."

Fu Manchu had spoken. I couldn't believe this guy.

Politely but firmly, I refused. He ordered me off the premises. I told him that as part of the company leasing his building I was as privileged to use it as anyone else. As long as the company was here, I would be here. (We were paying $75,000 for the use of the building for three days, a sum that was to escalate greatly when we were forced to stay two extra days.)

I went on about my business, leaving the ABC News team where they were. They said they had to stay until they got orders from their assignments chief. The proprietor had told them to sit tight and it would all be resolved. I passed word to production assistants, assistant directors, whomever: under no circumstances was the ABC team to be allowed anywhere near the sets, nor were they to have access to holding areas where costumed extras were on call and waiting.

An hour later, the location manager, Chris Cronyn, introduced himself to me. It was an indication of the atypical circumstances that we hadn't even met yet. He suggested that we meet with the proprietor. What the hell for? I didn't see the point. I'd made my case clear. No press allowed, period. Cronyn, the son of actors Jessica Tandy and Hume Cronyn, had a persuasiveness about him, a sense of proportion and reason. I finally acquiesced to the meeting.

The proprietor wanted to make a deal: let ABC News return the following morning to interview Richard Sylbert and to photograph sets on which we wouldn't be working.

Simply stated, no. I wouldn't even approach Sylbert about it. I spun a little web of lies. Publicity about the production design was incorporated in the larger plan worked out by the Zarem Office and Orion Pictures for the movie's release campaign, I said, and anything now would be exceedingly premature. (Plan, I thought to myself, what a joke. The Zarem office didn't have a clue, let alone a plan. Nor did Orion. Nor did any of us. Here I was talking about a plan for publicity when there was barely a plan for making the movie. We were two days into shooting and Richard Gere hadn't shown up for work and it was unclear whether he would. In the meantime, scenes were being improvised and actors being thrown before the camera in situations unfamiliar to them on sets not yet ready. It was pure chaos. And I was talking about a plan!)

But it was why he had decided to rent his building to us, the proprietor said; it was self-aggrandizement (not that he used that term, mind you, nor did he mention the $75,000 plus that he was being paid). He had been overjoyed, he said, that The Cotton Club was to film here because then the press would come and see his "lovely rooms." His lovely rooms would be featured in picture and prose in newspapers, magazines, television, and any media currently known. It would be the making of him. It was pitiful. Why wouldn't we allow photographers into his lovely rooms? That was all he asked.

The man simply had no understanding of the concept of a closed set. I was making myself hoarse trying to explain it. How I wanted to slug this bastard. His lovely fucking rooms. There would be no interest in his building, I told him, no matter how lovely the rooms, were we not working here. If photographers were allowed in, it will be us they would be taking pictures of, not his lovely, empty rooms. But the man knew all this. He smiled the smile painters of biblical scenes inevitably ascribe to martyrs. What I *would* do for him, I said, offering a compromise, would be to write about his building in my productions notes which would be distributed to the press at the time of the film's release. I would write about the building's magnificent grand ballroom, its fantastically high ceilings, the stately elegance and aplomb of the four or five mahogany bars. The beautiful old mirrors, the plush turn-of-the-century furniture in the lobby, Cronyn interjected, caught up in the music. The palms and greenery, the grand staircase, I continued. The stained glass, the murals said to be of museum quality, brass fixtures from the gaslight era, original frescoes. We were on a jazz riff, Cronyn and I, rattling off what I would write about, me on tenor sax, Chris on trumpet. We had the proprietor's rapt attention, his body almost moving to the beat.

As if we had a deal, he asked a favor in return: a picture of himself with Coppola, Gere, and Gregory Hines. Sure thing. Even though to my knowledge I hadn't meet Gere yet, I said I would try to arrange it.

The ABC team was still in the anteroom when Chris and I emerged from the fray, the smiling proprietor trailing us. He told the ABC people that he thought it would be all right with me if they shot the entrance to the building, our crew at work unloading trucks and doing stuff, maybe a few costumed extras. Incredible! We hadn't got through to him at all. I said okay to everything but the extras. The ABC team went to work. The footage appeared on national television, in what context I don't know. I never saw it. My sister in New Mexico called to say she had seen me on TV, even though it was only the back of my head. She described the pink shirt I had been wearing. Had I known I might have turned around.

But it wasn't over yet.

The man's maneuvers, his reversals, his flip-flopping positions, his conciliations swiftly followed by confrontations over the next three days were positively vertiginous. It was strictly Looney Tunes time; but although I recognized it for the cartoon it was, I couldn't laugh at it. I never did feel that the man had anything less than respect for me as an opponent, despite his practiced melodramatic way of studying me when I was otherwise occupied, his chin pulled low, his eyes not so much tracking me as keeping periodic tabs on me. Even when he was being affable, I wondered what he was up to. Within minutes I usually found out. He could spin his moods like a top. I'd like to say he didn't faze me, but don't tell my stomach that.

Wednesday was relatively quiet, even though I did have to head off at the pass another TV crew that the proprietor forewarned me he had invited. I called the Zarem office and let them act as intermediary on that one; but when the crew didn't arrive, the proprietor knew I was still waltzing around the room with him. There was no way he was going to keep me off the floor.

Enter Barrie Osborne. I'd seen him on the set conferring with top echelon people, including Coppola. No idea who he was, nor his position. No one able to tell me. Not on the crew list. Moderately tall, relatively slim, in his middle to early thirties, maybe older. He wore contact lenses, which accented his eyes because of his discomfort with them. His eyes often smarted. He exercised his eyelids in an attempt to relieve the irritation. Affable, considerate.

"I'll be working with Francis as a kind of line producer," he told me.

There were a lot of chefs on *The Cotton Club* who were not allowed to cook. Barrie Osborne was to be the head cook, invested with more and more authority as key Robert Evans people were removed from the decision-making process. He had been production manager on *Apocalypse Now*, Grace Blake told me. "He bailed Francis out of a lot of problems. He's married to an Oriental woman. Maybe because of that he knows how to deal with foreign-type people. He was on that movie for a year and a half." He had also worked as Coppola's assistant director on *The Godfather, Part II*. All told, a most impressive career. In later years he served as executive producer of *The Matrix* and as producer of *The Lord of the Rings* trilogy, on which he also directed several scenes.

Line producer. One of those ambiguous titles that can mean almost anything. So many ambiguous titles in the movie business: producer, executive producer, associate producer, executive in charge of production. They will mean different things on different films. An honorary title, a putter-together of the package, a supervisor of the production, a money-raiser, a needy relative of some High and Mighty. Whatever Barrie Osborne's written job description was, he certainly managed to be a powerful and important force on *The Cotton Club*.

On Thursday morning, after we thought the situation contained, the proprietor informed me that he would "pull the plug" on us at twelve noon that day and the company would be evicted from the premises. We would no longer be allowed to film in his building unless a TV crew was allowed in to roam at will and film us at work. He was shutting us down. It was no longer just a publicity problem.

Key company people were finally made aware of the stomach-churner I had been having all week. Barrie Osborne joined me in trying to reason with the man. The proprietor told Barrie, nodding in my direction, "He's worn me out." From that moment my stock began to rise. I have to hand it to the man. He had worn me out too.

Barrie, Fred Roos, assistant director Henry Bronchtein, Chris, unit manager Meg Hunnewell, Robert Spiotta (president of Coppola's beleaguered studio, Zoetrope, which would receive the nebulous screen credit "From Zoetrope Studios"), all got into the act. We met in clusters, removed from but in full view of the proprietor who glanced at us from time to time trying to assess the import of his ultimatum and what our countermove might be.

Someone suggested that Robert Evans be brought in by limousine to talk with the TV people about how long it had taken him to get this project underway. Meg said, "That's all it would take to shut us down permanently, to show Robert Evans on TV." I didn't quite understand the import of that, but there seemed to be general agreement to let that particular sleeping dog lie.

Okay, how about if we let ABC come the following morning? A bit of craftiness here, since if all went well we'd be out of the building by noon today. Of course this was the height of absurdity. Nothing ever went well on *The Cotton Club* production and wouldn't in this case. I objected: if we let ABC come, the other two networks, CBS and NBC, would know about it as they always did; and down the line we would be obligated to them. Spiotta agreed with me.

There was talk of restraining orders, and calls were made to lawyers ever though we all thought it was too late for that kind of thing. In the meantime it was decided that we should use the ABC invitation as a stalling device. The proprietor was told that he could call ABC and say they could come Friday about noon. We thought that would end our problems with him for the rest of the day. Oh, sure.

During lunch break, an NBC team showed up believing that there was an understanding that they could shoot the sets while cast and crew were at lunch. Barrie and I explained to NBC anchorwoman Anna Bond that the company had nothing to do with the invitation to the premises and why we couldn't permit television coverage at this time. In order to placate, we did escort her and her crew of two to our hot set where we'd be filming after lunch: a numbers racket bank in Harlem in the late 1920s, an impressive, beautifully researched and decorated set that unfortunately had to be given short shrift in the movie. Gregory Hines and Larry (not yet Laurence) Fishburne would be in the scene.

The proprietor, feeling betrayed again (wouldn't he ever), uncaring about our equal sense of betrayal, then had the front doors of the building locked so that no one could enter or exit. People who needed to go to the trucks were forced to go through side doors and walk around the building.

The NBC people were also made captive, detained in a bar off the main lobby and treated to a drink on the house and a summary of the building's history. The proprietor unlocked the doors when Anna Bond and her work party were ready to leave. On the way out, Bond said to me: "I know ABC is coming tomorrow. If they get something and we don't, don't say I didn't warn you."

Somehow the proprietor got wind of our hopes for an early wrap on Friday morning. He counteracted by telling the ABC people to come not at noon but at nine o'clock. He also told the ABC assignments editor that the crew would be allowed access to principals and sets. I countered by telling ABC that the extent of access had been misrepresented: they would not be allowed to photograph principals. Thanks but no thanks, said ABC. Cancelled.

Before the proprietor could make yet another peremptory move, Spiotta met privately with him and explained to him that the completion bond process was at the present moment stalled. Such a bond would guarantee us the finances to complete the film. Should we not be allowed to complete our work on the rented property peacefully and without interference and should his actions this week be viewed by the courts as a factor in our not getting a completion bond, the extent of the man's culpability might be a financial burden he would not want to bear.

That was it.

No more problems that day or the next. I only wish Spiotta could have spoken with the proprietor earlier. We didn't wrap Friday until mid-afternoon, certainly not the early wrap that had been hoped for. The proprietor invited us to have drinks on the house, directing a special invitation to me. I was busy and couldn't accept. Would I have? Probably. It would have been interesting, now that I knew I was seeing the last of him. The next day there was talk of going back there for a day of re-shoots. I screamed when I heard it. Wiser heads prevailed. The scene was shot elsewhere.

* * *

My problem with the proprietor was a sideshow accompanying the big show in the main tent, the making (or non-making) of the movie and a murder mystery without a murderer (or so we thought then: one of Evans's nebulous associates will in time be proved to have popped off another). Certainly the experience on *The Cotton Club* was murder to those involved and most emphatically a mystery. Something I've come in on in the middle of. I don't know the suspects. I don't know the victims. I'm not alone in that: nobody does. We're engaged in a collective quest for clues. Just when we begin to think ourselves the victim, we realize, no, we're the suspect, an equation that can quickly be reversed and often is.

When I arrived at the location the first day of shooting, I had no call sheet. We weren't shooting from a schedule. Richard Gere hadn't shown up. Francis Coppola was in effect vamping till ready. I pushed my way into a room that was dressed as a speakeasy. Smoke is ubiquitous, both from smoke pots ("harmless chemicals") and from the cigarettes sprouting stalagmite-like from the hands of extras pressed into service to help manufacture the free-floating carcinogenic atmosphere. Because of the murkiness of smoke and lighting and the clutter of people milling and things being moved about, I couldn't see much. You can't stand still in such circumstances. Not for long. You're always in somebody's way. You try to be alert with contingency plans, an inch this way, an inch that, an almost imperceptible changing of body positions, watching that you don't trip, that you aren't braced against a precarious object that might fall or rattle, or that you don't otherwise precipitate something embarrassing while cameras are rolling, something that would spoil a take, something that would announce to the company the klutz that you are. You're busy making sure you're out of camera range, that you aren't standing in the tracks of a dolly that would allow a mobile camera to be pulled back onto you, that you aren't standing underneath a boom or cherry-picker that might monitor every breath or expletive or cough—God help you if you cough—or descend on you from above like capricious and uncaring fate. You try to stay out of danger's way: the trouble is that danger's way is a crisscrossing labyrinth and you're never certain of the path.

The camera is on male extras playing musicians at the far end of the room against a background of tall mirrored panels representing the walls of the restroom to which they have retired for a reefer break. I have no idea in what context this scene is supposed to fit. No one I speak to knows. There is no script. It is mad improv time. Coppola is directing from his head.

He wears a white lightweight hat, Panama-styled with a black band, pulled over his forehead. He will wear it often during production, even, as now, in close space with high temperatures. What one sees of his face are the lips and the horn-rimmed glasses and ever-alert, eyes that reflect the mental rollercoaster going on behind them. His beard envelops his face like a blanket. He watches to the left of him, to the right, behind, at a distant wall, the movement of a curtain, a strange face, an intruder, something that might hurt him that he can hurt back or even hurt first. He doesn't want surprises. The Cotton Club set will be full of them. When we get to

Astoria Studios, often he will retreat from the smoky mayhem of the set to the solitude of his video van, his Silverfish, which is parked inside the studio just off the set. There he will work, review videotapes of the work in progress, and relax, sometimes by cooking in his take-it-wherever-he-goes kitchen.

Francis says something particularly outrageous, and a female production assistant who is fond of him says, "I think Francis had something a lot stronger than veal Marsala for lunch."

"Don't you think he's just high on the movie?" I venture. An arched eyebrow is her response.

But the movie *was* his wine, his dope, his veal Marsala. Because he was high on it: sometimes he would seem to be skipping; and when he did, the whole set skipped with him. The movie was being directed by a glorious manic Muppet. He wore a tie that first day, as he often would: a tie with an incongruous pattern and color against a shirt that defiantly did its own clashingly different thing. A viewfinder hung like a pendant from his neck to his waist. Nobody introduced us. At the first opportunity, I did so myself. He shook my hand and said politely, "A pleasure." I asked for his preferred pronunciation of his name, which pleased him. "It's COPE-a-la, not Ca-POE-la," he said.

Later that morning I sat with Novella Nelson while she was eating breakfast. She told me she was playing Madame Queen, who at the time I didn't know from drag or Victoria. I apologized for not knowing who the character was and explained that I had only begun working that day. She was happy to fill me in.

"She was Madame St. Clair and they called her 'Madame Queen' because she was the queen of the Harlem numbers. She ran the numbers bank in Harlem until Dutch Schultz and the white mobs moved uptown to take over the rackets." She added that Diana Ross was also going to play Madame Queen in another movie that had just been announced. "But I'm beating her to the punch," she said proudly.

Novella Nelson's strong Negroid features bespoke dignity, beauty, royalty. With her tight-against-the-head rivulets of rough wheat-ended black hair, with her pride and bearing, she *looked* queenly, whether an African tribal queen or a Harlem numbers queen. She answered my questions circumspectly; and I got the feeling that while she was ready to like me, she first had to come to trust me, and that would take time. I sensed in her something bruised, whether racially or professionally or something else I couldn't know. Diana Ross might eventually portray the Madame in another movie, but I would have wagered that Novella Nelson would turn out to be more like the original. The lady clearly had the strength and the wariness to run a racket. Her role barely exists in the final cut of the film, and I still consider that a great loss.

Nelson had sung on nine different occasions at Reno Sweeney's, a once popular but now defunct Village nightclub. She had played on Broadway in the musical *Purlie* as well as in *Caesar and Cleopatra* with Rex Harrison and Elizabeth Ashley. She had also appeared on Broadway, in Los Angeles, and in London in the Elizabeth Taylor/Maureen Stapleton company of *The Little Foxes*. She had directed *Nigger Nightmare* in workshop at the Public Theater for Joseph Papp, who responded to it so strongly that he invited her to become artistic consultant for the New York Shakespeare Theater.

She had cut an album in 1970. "It's a collector's item now," she said. "A friend of mine found one and tried to buy it. They wanted a hundred dollars for it. I told him, 'Give me fifty, I'll sell you one of mine!'"

Nelson was called away for fittings, and I moved over to sit with Larry Fishburne, a tall, good-looking young black man who had appeared in two earlier movies directed by Coppola, *Apocalypse Now* (the young sailor in the boat) and *Rumble Fish* (the now-you-see-him, now-you-don't dapper, cloaked "friend" of Matt Dillon).

"The character I play, Bumpy Rhodes, obvious to anyone who knows Harlem history—" (which, of course, I didn't really, but I was here to learn) "—is supposed to suggest, if not represent, Bumpy Johnson, who worked for Madame Queen . . ."

Hearing Nelson and Fishburne talk about the characters they would be playing, no matter how sketchily seen in the movie itself, was helping me get a feel for the fabric of Coppola's and Kennedy's research if not their narrative line. In retrospect I realized that at this point no one was sure about the narrative line, not even the authors.

As Larry Fishburne and I talked and I was scribbling notes, I became aware that Fred Roos and Francis Coppola had entered the room and were standing directly behind us. I had been discovered, as it were, working, which wouldn't hurt. Fred interjected, "Tom, have you met Francis yet?" Both Coppola and I assured him that we had met.

Francis spent time talking with others in the room, devoting special attention to costume designer Milena Canonero and Lonette McKee, who was being fitted in a dress and hat for a musical number. I had not met either of the women. Francis rhapsodized about Lonette. "Isn't she a cutie? I think she looks a little

Italiana. Don't *you* think she looks a little Italian? You look just like my mother," he told her.

When Coppola and Roos moved away, Lonette knelt by my chair, touched my arm warmly, and said, "Oh, I've been wanting to meet you . . ."

The Cotton Club was her big break in movies, and of course she wanted to make sure her participation in it would be well publicized. I explained the policy as it had been laid out to me about publicity during production: current preparation for future use. I could see the disappointment in her face: she wanted something now as well. But for press coverage that is not part of the orchestrated publicity campaign for the project, an actor usually must have a personal publicity representative. I usually advise an actor in the position of McKee during the production of *The Cotton Club* that it's not worth the expense or the bother. I knew that with the first wave of orchestrated publicity for the film, McKee's name and likeness would be prominently featured (and it was). If McKee were not happy with the press attention being given her at the time of the movie's release, then she might consider hiring a personal press representative on a limited basis.

In the coming weeks, it did not help Lonette's feelings to read item after item about the film in the gossip columns that featured Coppola, Gere, and the Hines brothers (little of it emanating from me) and nothing about herself, who had the fourth-billed role in the film.

On Broadway, Lonette had appeared in a Houston Grand Opera production of *Show Boat* and had received a Tony nomination for her portrayal of Julie, a woman who, very like her role as Lila Rose in *The Cotton Club*, is part white and part black and can "pass," if she chooses to, and in both cases does choose to pass as white for a while. Lila Rose is in love with a man (Gregory Hines) whose pigmentation is deeper than hers, and if she chooses to continue to pass, she's going to have to pass her love by.

In my biography of McKee, I wrote:

The original and many of the succeeding Cotton Club showgirls like Lila Rose had to be "high yaller" in skin tone, or else they couldn't work at the Cotton Club. Skin coloring was not applicable to the men who played there, however. If they could sing, dance, play an instrument, crack a joke or were otherwise talented and there was a spot for them, they could play the Cotton Club no matter what their color.

Says McKee, "It was almost incumbent of a girl like Lila Rose, with her talent and coloring, to 'pass' at that time. To pass meant she could work on Broadway, the road, white shows."

There were also showgirls, the histories of the time and the club tell us, who were white who passed for black in several Cotton Club lineups. The color line was breached on both ends.

On the second day of shooting, Richard Gere showed up on location. Just to visit, not to work. It wouldn't be until the end of the week that the company's problems with him would be resolved. It was about the money, naturally. It usually is. When the truth surfaced, we learned that he was getting a flat $1.5 million plus $125,000 for every week that he worked beyond October 29 (which would be an additional eight weeks. While I don't know about Richard, I certainly made more money on this film than on any I've ever worked, thanks to the extended schedule). Richard also sold his ten percent of the gross to Robert Evans for another $1.5 million, bringing his total to nearly $4 million. Reasonably good money in those days.

I was in an armchair enclave in the holding room talking with James Remar (who was playing Dutch Schultz), Julian Beck (Sol Weinstein, Schultz's henchman and bodyguard), and special makeup man Dick Smith when I noticed the gaffer in the green Lacoste shirt, the Gere wannabe, standing behind one of our chairs listening to our conversation. This time he caught me just gabbing and not singing to myself. He smiled at me. With a small shock I realized, hey! This really *is* Richard Gere! It was as if we had already met and had a history. We were easy with each other. He would become far more accessible to me that I had been led to believe he would, in part because of what would turn out to be the happy accident of my office at the studio, his dressing room, and James Remar's dressing room being all part of the same suite and blessedly isolated from everyone else. When I told him I hadn't recognized him earlier, he seemed pleased. He said, "I had a feeling you didn't." He liked his new look. It enabled him to eat out anonymously again, at least for a while.

James Remar was thirty years old, the same age Dutch Schultz was when he died. Remar normally looked younger, his hair rich and full, flowing blond tones. Now he had a period cut with one inch shaved from his hairline. Makeup would give him a broken nose. A "plumper" fattened his cheeks. The dental insert was the same one worn by Marlon Brando in *The Godfather*, for whom Dick Smith had designed and executed it.

The next morning I had breakfast with Jimmy Remar in the first floor dining area. I was embarrassed that I wasn't completely familiar with his previous credits; all the time I would have normally devoted to research had been taken up with trying to get the job. At least I had seen him on Broadway in *Bent*. He had played Wolf, the gay Nazi found naked in the bed of the central character, played by Richard Gere, with whom he has spent the night tricking. He is then murdered by storm troopers. Remar was terrific in the role, great-looking too. Made an enormous impression on the audience.

He talked frankly about his acting ordeal the afternoon before. The scene (one set in a magistrate's court that didn't make it into the final cut of the film) was shot in an inordinately hot room in the building's top floor. The scene did not go well. The director, already heated to the boiling point by two days of extreme frustration, was in a foul mood. Remar had to play a winter scene in a wool suit and vest with an overcoat and hat during the hottest part of the afternoon on one of the hottest days of the year. On top of that he was burdened with latex and body padding. His greatest burden had been the anxious realization that his performance wasn't pleasing Francis. With machine gun rapidity, Francis kept firing the same directive at him. "Over." "Over!" "And over!" Faster and faster. Sweat poured from Jimmy's face. At every brief break, makeup rushed forward to repair the damage. To little avail. Julian Beck, also in the scene and dressed for winter, fared better because he wasn't central to the action and his perspiration could more easily be mopped. And that wasn't him Coppola was yelling at.

Francis's brutal direction of Remar followed a temper tantrum earlier that afternoon at the end of the shooting of the Hoofers' Club scene, just before the company had moved upstairs to the courtroom set. The Hoofers' Club was an exciting set to be on. Some of the greatest tap dancers in New York (make that the world!) were in the scene. Older men, retired and semi-retired, tap-dancing wonders. When the scene began, smoke pots going full blast for atmosphere, the dancers cut loose, their tapping feet making a smoke of their own. They really set the stage on fire.

With this scene finished, there was nothing in readiness for Coppola to shoot next. Because of Gere's unavailability until details of his contract could be worked out, the script had been scrutinized for scenes that might be filmed without him and filmed *now*. Yet every time Francis settled on a scene, he was discouraged by the assistant director, the production designer, or the costume designer. Matters were complicated: because this being a period film and because the current script having become available only the day before, scenes could not be picked at random and thrown before the camera. Period cars might be needed. Costumes had to be considered. Actors had to be located and brought to the set. Makeup. This was not available. That was impossible. Not at this particular location.

Whereupon Francis blew the first of his quickly ignitable fuses.

"The trouble is," he exploded, "I'm ahead of production! I'm too fast for you guys!" In other words, they couldn't punt. Francis wanted a crew of punters able to respond on a dime and a doorknob to tactical changes dictated by emergency.

A lot of folks thought it was the set-up for a lot of mass firings. James Remar took the heat for the general unpreparedness, the genesis of which all were trying to understand. I feared that Jimmy would be part of the mass firing, if not leading the parade. Hey, what with my big ears and stealth, I had just overheard a conversation between Barrie Osborne and a couple of suits about maybe bringing in Mickey Rourke in Gere's role and Robert De Niro in Remar's. Mickey Rourke! All this sotto voce talk about Rourke. I couldn't understand it. What was the attraction?

The idea of doing a film about the Cotton Club had its antecedents in Robert Altman's desire to work with black talent in a Nashville-like musical epic involving one of the Harlem music centers such as the Apollo Theater or the Cotton Club. Altman had raised the possibility with Robert Evans when directing *Popeye* for Evans. Evans put *The Cotton Club* into development and hired Mario Puzo of *The Godfather* fame to write the screenplay. After Robert Altman dropped out of the project, Sylvester Stallone was for a brief period penciled in as director and star. When he dropped out, Evans announced that he himself would direct the film.

"Which was a joke," said a person close to Evans. "He couldn't direct himself out of bed most mornings, or afternoons either, for that matter. He's a night person." He also tried to write the screenplay, propped up in bed, a production secretary assigned to transcribe his thoughts later said. "'He strode into the room,'" she recalled him dictating, then stopping cold, stumped, unable to envision toward what the character should be striding. "'He *strode* into the room . . .'"

Realizing that his script efforts were hopeless, in early 1983 he sent an SOS to Francis Coppola. Did Francis know a good script doctor? Hardly an ingenuous query. His Puzo material was "a sick child," he told Francis. It needed a good doctor. Francis told him he was the best script doctor he knew. Coppola had directed three films in a row, two of which had been released to less than enthusiastic notices and business (*One from the Heart* and *The Outsiders*) and the third (*Rumble Fish*) to meet with a like reception after playing the New York Film Festival in the fall of 1983. He was deeply in debt, had a lien on his house in Napa, California, and could clearly see in the offing the loss of his precious Zoetrope Studio.

Francis told Evans, "Send me what you've got." He would read Puzo's script as a courtesy, without fee, and advise Evans on how it might be changed. Evans sent two Puzo scripts, the second and fourth drafts. Francis found them beyond tinkering with. He proposed to write a new script from scratch and to deliver it in two weeks, and Evans would pay him $500,000. He would drop his own plans to direct *The Pope of Greenwich Village*.

He asked Evans to send him his research material. Evans sent him sixty-one books. Francis quickly read them, marked passages that interested him, organized them, and had those pages run through an optical scanner (only twelve of them in the world at that time) and then through a Xerox Star word processor. After his (and his assistant's) manipulations, it came out with prose dialogue arranged in screenplay form. It had the look of a humongous screenplay, totally formless and unshaped. Using color-coded pages to differentiate source material, Francis constructed a first draft screenplay from his mass. It took him three weeks, not two.

Now he needed a collaborator.

William Kennedy's involvement was the result of his having written a novel about Legs Diamond, another Prohibition era gangster. *Legs* is one of the research books Evans is said to have sent to Coppola. The question as to who sent it remains clouded. Gere said he did. Sylbert claims he did. Kennedy said they both did. Someone else insisted that Mickey Rourke did. (Mickey Rourke again!) Maybe they all did.

When I read *Legs*, I could see why it captured everyone's imagination. Terrific book. "This is what we should be filming," Gere said to me one day. The characters are viable and vivid. It is like a 1930s gangster movie lifted above its genre by style, tone, and erudition, evocative of its period, the same period as *The Cotton Club*. Dialogue with the wallop of a pistol-whip.

During production we had five different scripts, the first dated August 16, 1983, the last December 8. Scenes shifted like sands. The reorganizing and rewriting could never have been done without a word processor, nor without Coppola's assistant, a slight, bright young woman with an ascetic look named Anahid Nazarian, hired by Coppola three films back to bring her library science and computer expertise to the problem of cataloging the many video cassettes he accumulated during the course of shooting and editing a film. On *The Cotton Club* she received the credit of "systems librarian."

Monday, August 29. Red-letter day. Gere is working!

The Empire Diner, Twenty-third and Tenth.

I didn't recognize him when he walked past. Overcoat, hat, hair falling over his forehead, stubble on his face. I thought he was an extra. Mark Burchard, Gere's dresser who was to become one of my most trusted and devoted messengers of information, whispered in my ear, "We have our star."

It rained off and off, with filming frequently interrupted. To our surprise, we weren't bothered by freelance photographers, the usual bane of our exteriors work. There was a network—contacts within the licensing bureau of the mayor's office, for instance—that fed news about movie companies to enterprising freelancers. Photographers working for newspapers would naturally have the same sources. I surmised that the word out on the street was that Gere wasn't working. After all, gossip column scoop was that he was out of the film. Still, Coppola was hot news, wasn't he? But by day's end at least one pushy paparazzo would find us.

Ahead of himself yet again, Coppola dragged a scene out of nowhere to shoot, a screen test of the character that Gere plays. Nobody had expected it, nobody had prepared for it. It took wardrobe and makeup an hour to prepare Gere. He had to be transformed from a bum-like musician into a suave lounge-lizard type (think George Raft). The shoes pure patent leather, the hair even more so, slick enough you could slide off it. Bring on the tuxedo.

The delay was blamed on the presence in the star's trailer of a man brought in by costume designer Milena Canonero to "design" makeup. Just design it. The execution of the design would have to be left to union members. The man wasn't allowed to touch actors.

"He was brought in primarily for the women," Chris Cronyn told me. "He became a problem. Always, begging your pardon, prancing about, getting in the way of makeup and hair and wardrobe trying to get their jobs done. We had enough problems with Milena in that respect, always trying to get it perfect. Who doesn't want to get it perfect? Too often it was nitpicking perfection not only unnecessary but slowing us down too much. This makeup consultant of hers was another weight we didn't need."

We speculated that the consultant had been imported from Europe and that maybe Milena had worked with him on Stanley Kubrick's *Barry Lyndon*, where the makeup was such an important component of lighting and costuming.

Since he wasn't allowed to touch Gere, he had brought a pointer with him. He would point to Gere's face while our head makeup man, Joe Cuervo, worked on him. Touching Gere's face with the pointer, he told Cuervo, "You must *sculpt* the face." He moved the pointer from spot to spot on Gere's face like it was a blackboard on which was written an algebraic equation.

"He was *very* grand," Burchard told me. "'Here—and here—and here,' he'd say. 'Sculpt.'

"He had no idea he was being so obnoxious. Richard's face turned red. Not from makeup, from anger. And Joe's just as red. At the same instant they both turned to glare at him. A drop-dead look. The guy almost did. You could see it was only then that he realized what he'd been doing, poking the star all over the face with a stick."

The makeup designer ran from the trailer. He never went near Gere again. Gere refused to let him. Ultimately wardrobe and makeup gave Milena an ultimatum: either the man went or they did.

It was still raining. Umbrellas and canvas were up. The shooting area, the exterior of an apartment building on the corner of Twenty-third and Tenth, was further marked off and blocked from view of the passers-by with rigging and black drapes and large black screens (called gobos). But still Gere was visible to the public in part of the scene.

A paparazzo found us. Gere was his quarry. Production assistants held up huge light cards to block the photographer's line of fire.

"Quiet!"

"We're shooting!"

The paparazzo lifted his camera and flashed repeatedly, ruining the shot. After a scuffle, a cop led him away. He kept shouting, "False arrest!" But he had his shot, both Gere and Coppola, Gere holding an automatic pistol. It was featured in the next day's *New York Post*. Actually, a pretty good shot, considering the circumstances under which it was taken, not bad at all. Lloyd Leipsig, Orion's director of publicity, was delighted with it. "Now the world knows Gere is working," he remarked.

Coppola had fun with the scene, playing the off-camera voice of the director directing Gere, Dixie Dwyer, in his screen test. He played it period and played it Germanic, parodying Hollywood's imported directors in the late twenties. His accent was intentionally terrible and Teutonic, his mouth full of linguistic dumplings. He shouted staccato directions at Dixie Dwyer. It was comedic, in character, cadenced with make-believe anger. Not like what had been thrown at last week's hapless James Remar.

The bogus von Sternberg asked the cornet player cum movie star about Bix Beiderbecke.

"Vicks who?" Gere extemporized, mocking the accent, pretending ignorance or hearing loss.

At least one camera should have been on Coppola. Von Sternberg had an off-camera tantrum. He threw his earphones to the ground and stomped around in a classic display of legendary beret-and-megaphone temperament.

The scene shot that day never made it into the movie. It was re-filmed later at the studio.

Earlier in the day, assistant director Bob Girolami stopped me in the drizzle on Tenth Avenue to tell me he was thinking about firing stills photographer Adger Cowans and wanted to know what I thought about it. Apparently Cowans had "rudely" pushed aside director of photography Stephen Goldblatt while cameras were rolling in order to get a still shot, something you just don't do. Girolami wanted to replace Cowans with another stills photographer, a woman who just happened to be a personal friend of mine and with whom I worked easily. It would be tricky, however, firing a photographer whose work I had yet to see (although the "pushing" incident was grounds for dismissal). I was also concerned about the ramifications of replacing a black male photographer with a white woman on a film that had many extras and several principals who were black. (At that time we were at a stage of evolving terminology: Negro, colored, African-American, black. The last seemed to be becoming the preferred designation.) I told Girolami I'd first have to talk with Fred Roos. Girolami said he had already talked with him and Roos had said talk with me. Okay, I said, Roos and I will talk.

Fred Roos had told me during my interview that it would be my responsibility to see that we had top quality stills and plenty of them. On the first day of shooting I had asked Adger Cowans to let me see his work as soon as possible. It should have been possible the next day. His exposed film representing the first day's shoot should have been dropped off at the lab by Teamsters that same evening. Contact sheets of the black-and-white film should have come to either Adger or me the following day (the processing of color film, usually done at a different lab, might take a day or two longer). I had granted Adger the privilege of checking his shots before I saw them in order to eliminate those he didn't like before giving them to me for review and distribution: it suited me just fine to have him identify the obviously flawed shots, saving me time and eyestrain. But here we were a week later talking about firing a man whose work I hadn't yet seen. "Not back from the lab yet," he kept telling me. Now, under pressure, I called Portugallo, his lab, and said that I wanted all of Adger's work printed immediately and sent by special messenger to me on location that day. The lab checked: their work was current and Adger had been receiving contact sheets daily since last Tuesday.

I was too angry to confront Adger immediately. I had never before had a stills photographer hide stills from me. Before I got to Adger, Fred Roos got to me. The first thing he wanted to know was how Adger's work looked. I told him I hadn't seen anything yet and explained the situation. Had I worked with him before? No, but I had heard he was fired from his last job because of absenteeism.

"His work is supposed to be terrific," said Roos. "Let's wait. If his pictures are good, we won't want to let him go."

A stack of Adger's black-and-white contact sheets arrived from the lab that afternoon. They were some of the best unit stills I had ever seen. When I met with Adger I told him so. The high quality of his work would count for something. I feared, however, that a personality irritating to so many key people would probably count for more.

Adger was beginning to sense the tide of opinion rising against him. He promised that he would have all the color shots for me to see first thing next morning. He thought the color might be a little grainy: he'd had to push the capabilities of his photographic equipment to the limit because of the dim smoky lighting. The color photographs turned out to be beautiful, if anything even better than the black-and-white. A photographer capable of work of this quality (and there was plenty of it) had to be kept on the job if at all possible.

The following day we were filming in Harlem. I took Adger aside and leveled with him. Because of his actions and attitude (and boy, did he have attitude: so defensive I could see how others might perceive it as offensive), there was hostility to him on the picture. He sensed immediately that the bulk of it was coming from Goldblatt.

"I'm not afraid to say it," he said. "It's racism." He threatened to quit. "I've got money and I don't need this shit." He turned his back on me to gather up his gear and leave.

I grabbed his arm and held on tightly. "Don't you dare quit," I said firmly and sympathetically. "Just calm down."

He looked at me with some surprise. He told me that he didn't know me, and he had thought I wanted to get rid of him too. I told him that if I had been able to see the quality of his work earlier, I might have been in a better position to counteract some of the discontent.

Then he said something that moved me. He told me how vitally important it was for him to work on this picture. It was about an important aspect of the black experience, a film that for the first time he could really put his heart into. It meant almost more than he could tell me, he said, that he remain a part of it. If he had the chance, he would work harder on this and at the same time do better work than he had ever done on anything in his life, but he wasn't going to let anybody use him as a wipe cloth in the process. I said nobody likes to be used as a wipe cloth, thinking as I said it, "Not even Goldblatt."

Adger's pushing the cinematographer aside in the middle of a take was a serious gaffe. I know many DPs who would have fired him on the spot. It was vitally important that I made sure Stephen Goldblatt was aware of the quality of Adger's work. I managed to get him aside during lunch break. The entire block between Lenox and Fifth Avenues on 133rd Street had been blocked off for the company's use. We found a private spot behind some equipment trucks (I didn't want Adger to see us). I let Goldblatt examine the first thirteen contact sheets. He made favorable comments about separate frames, impressed. He handed the contact sheets back to me and said, "While I don't like him, I like his work. He's capturing the look of the movie beautifully." In the coming weeks, although he grumbled occasionally about Adger's manners and attitude, he never again to my knowledge entertained the idea of having him fired.

Goldblatt himself had been a stills photographer in London and was director of photography on a number of films. His work on *The Hunger*, starring Catherine Deneuve and Susan Sarandon, had drawn him to Coppola's attention. Coppola had told him we wanted a similar look for *The Cotton Club*. Goldblatt said that Coppola had told him, "Make it very Jazz Age." Goldblatt interpreted that to mean shadow and smoke. "We're still trying to find just the right style and tone and level of darkness," he said. The level he found, beautiful as it is, did not please the film's disillusioned costumers, set dressers, and art director who complained that the detail and richness of their own work was being sacrificed to the film's "look." They dubbed Goldblatt "The Prince of Darkness."

It was nice, that Tuesday. The rain had abated, and the sun was shining. The street was strewn with straw. There were horse-drawn buggies and wagons, one of them an ice wagon. Period cars, period clothes. The houses that lined the shady street were period already. Nothing needed to be done to them. The residents on the street pulled chairs onto porches for a more civilized, comfortable look at us. Kids and adults followed us like a parade when the mobile camera was following Gregory and Maurice Hines, brothers playing brothers, as they walked past Richard Gere and Nicolas Cage, playing brothers, in the middle of the street near the ice wagon.

I had arrived in the middle of a lull in the activity. (If you have ever watched a movie being filmed you know it is full of lulls.) I looked for coffee. It can usually be found readily, maybe on a table set up in a cordoned-off area of a sidewalk or street. I saw none. Okay, then there was sure to be some in the holding area where staff and extras would be. I was pointed in the direction of a church. I saw a sign reading Church of the People. What I didn't see was another church just beyond it by a few doors, hidden from view by the massive branches of trees that lined the street. I headed for the Church of the People. There were two entrances. To reach either you had to climb ten to fifteen steep steps. Two men were sitting on the steps of a residence just this side of what I took to be one of the church entrances, maybe the parish hall or church offices, I guessed, no doubt where the extras holding area was. I was surprised not to see crew activity. The two men smiled and nodded as I passed them and climbed the steep stairs to the parish house. The front door had curtained windows. How civilized and homey, I thought. I pushed one of the double doors open and entered a hallway. Through an archway I saw velvet-covered Victorian settees, a piano with framed photographs sitting atop it, rocking chairs, and a beautiful Oriental carpet. I was in a private residence, abashed to realize what I had done. I turned to leave. One of the men was slowly and warily climbing the steps to his home. I mumbled an apology and explanation. "Looking for coffee," I said, feeling extremely foolish. The other man, following the situation with interest, said he'd be glad to make me some coffee. I felt even more foolish, although I was grateful for their kind and amused understanding. I told him I'd like nothing more but must decline, I was expected on set. The two gentlemen pointed me in the right direction.

I went a few doors down the street to the correct church, the Church of the Nazarene, where the action was and the coffee. Its exterior would represent the outside of the church/community center of which we had filmed the interior the week before in Brooklyn. Inside the building, a speakeasy set was being constructed in which Julian Beck's Sol Weinstein would approach Richard Gere's Dixie Dwyer, who was sitting in with black musicians and playing cornet. Beck's entrance into the speakeasy set had been filmed in Brooklyn on the first day of shooting. Richard Sylbert had recreated the speakeasy set rather than have to deal once more with the notorious publicity-seeking proprietor of that earlier location.

Gere was playing his own horn. He was as good as the professionals playing with him. Our star was a bona fide musician. The crew applauded him after the take.

In early drafts of the screenplay, the Gere character was named not Dixie but *Dance* Dwyer, a name that might have been unnecessarily confusing with him being a cornet player and Gregory Hines the dancer. During production, a mischievously smiling Grace Blake passed along to me an unsigned memo on letterhead that read "Jerry Wexler." Wexler, she told me, had once been on board as music supervisor but had been replaced by Bob Wilbur (whose ultimate credit would be "Music Re-creations"). No wonder Wexler was replaced. The memo was a scathing appraisal of one of the earlier scripts:

Dance is presented as a trumpet-playing hoodlum. If the backup behind this was documented and evolved, it would still strain the credulity of the average 12-year-old. But an unknown white trumpet player sitting in ad libitum in Harlem jazz joints is impossible. White musicians were permitted to sit in if they were super stars with great reputation: Bix, Jack Teagarden, Benny Goodman—or they were brought in as unknowns under prestigious auspices: Louise Armstrong or Fats Waller introduces Dance as their protégé: "Hey, mates, this is my man—dig him."

The sentimentalized picture of him sitting on the street curb in Harlem at night disconsolately blowing his horn is indigestible.

Dutch Schultz is portrayed as a patron of the arts who picks up on Dance because he likes his trumpet playing! Dutch the jazz fan! Dutch, the admirer of "jazz dancing"—whatever that is.

Jazz dancing is something done by Alvin Ailey and his troupe or the Dance Theater of Harlem today—in those days it might have been done by Snake Hips Tucker or a Ted Shawn unit. Civilians who did intricate steps on the ballroom floor were not perpetrating "jazz dancing"—and the reference to George Raft as such is off the mark. He was a slick ballroom snake—master of the foxtrot, the tango, and the Peabody.

Dance's extreme sadism versus Vera is beyond the bounds of good taste as well as credibility. Unreal, confected, unworthy.

The attempt at "high-toned" dialogue is pretentious. The attempt at black talk is unreal . . .

But worst of all—where is THE COTTON CLUB? Where are Bill Robinson, Cab, Ethel Waters. (The script has Dance singing TALL TAN AND TERRIFIC to Vera as a love song!) Where are the production numbers, the great late-hour special shows, the glamour of the thrill-seeing whites who come to town looking for their window on the jungle. The archtype [sic] of the club as matrix for a great screen play is, of course, Casablanca. The interplay among Rick, the Fascists, the refugees, the people sitting at tables, makes for a great interweave, tension, and romance. If only Richard Gere were given the chance to be the new Rick—without literally copying of course . . .

If you suggest to the public that you are exposing them to an experience called THE COTTON CLUB—then you must give them Harlem of the period with everything that that suggests, great jazz orchestras, great dancers, great chorus lines, interracial glamour and tensions, the Harlem Renaissance, the Depression. I am as aware as the next fellow that a story line is required—otherwise you would have just a musical revue—but to make an implausible re-do of The Godfather *doesn't get it.*

* * *

Friday night filming was on a Harlem rooftop. The weather had cooled along with personal temperatures, and it was a relatively quiet, pleasant night. I took the subway to Harlem (some people thought that was daring of me). Dinner was served to cast and crew in the basement of the Abyssinian Baptist Church. I sat with wardrobe people Al Craine and Beverly Cycon, friends with whom I had worked on *Easy Money* and other movies. There were No Smoking signs everywhere, but Al and Bev were smoking like two chimneys. I was in awe of the Abyssinian Baptist Church, although where we were it looked like just any other basement. Abyssinian Baptist loomed large and important from a historical standpoint, and I felt like a tourist. One thing about moviemaking: you never know where the job's going to take you, from landmarks to x-marks-the-spot. Abyssinian Baptist and its neighborhood included something of both.

The shoot was on top of a two-story building at 137th Street and Seventh Avenue (Adam Clayton Powell Boulevard). The location was meant to represent the roof of the Cotton Club where Owney Madden kept his pigeons. Principal actors in the scene were James Remar, Fred Gwynn, and Bob Hoskins, playing Owney. Gwynne and Hoskins were working together for the first time. A pigeon coop had been constructed on the roof, and trained pigeons had been brought in. When released, the pigeons could fly to their home base, should they choose to, or just hang around if that is what they wanted to do. Hell, everybody else was improvising, why shouldn't the pigeons? At any rate, we were prepared for fifty takes if necessary, but only eight were needed. Fully half of the birds released by Hoskins did not fly away immediately but hovered about the set. One returned immediately to the roof of the coop. One flapped about the heads of Hoskins and Remar and brushed the hair of Hoskins, who had to improvise lines to cover his amusement as he straightened his hair.

On this first exterior location, we were treated to our first demonstration of Coppola's use of video as an immediate directing device. He remained in the Silverfish video trailer at street level as the actors ran through two rehearsals, which he watched on a monitor from his trailer. His face, likewise, would appear on monitors on the roof as he spoke with the actors and with assistant director Girolami. It was amusing to see the three actors in tuxedos speaking with the video head of Coppola, which appeared upside down on the small monitor that rested in his director's chair. Coppola's voice was disembodied, something like the voice of God, coming as it did through an amplification system that did not attempt to relate it to his image on the monitor.

I sat on the wide, rough ledge of the roof, my pants getting filthy and my hands and I presume my behind becoming patterned from the jagged stone. I met and talked with the stand-ins for both Remar and Hoskins. An open portable elevator lifted equipment and whoever wanted a ride from street to roof. I had chosen to ascend the two stories by the conventional stairway.

Before each shot, the roof was wetted down with hoses as though it had been raining; and before anyone called "Lights . . . Camera . . . Action!" they called "Smoke!" That was the cue to turn on background smoke stacks. When the smoke was billowing and properly lit, then the camera could start rolling.

I had mentioned to Stephen Goldblatt that from the brief scenes I had seen photographed, it looked to me like the style of the film would be muralistic, with the photographic signature perhaps smoke and shadow. He didn't argue with that characterization. He told me that *The Hunger*, which had starred Susan Sarandon, Catherine Deneuve, and David Bowie, was heavily stylized. "No attempt to be realistic. With all due respect to the considerable acting talent involved, there wasn't much acting going on in the movie. It was an exercise in high-style aesthetics. An exercise—which is not what I think film should be at all. I doubt if I'll ever again be required to work that way. It doesn't sit comfortably with me, that style. It represented an extreme form of visualization.

"Francis doesn't want *The Cotton Club* to be realistic. He wants it to be stylized, but to have its own style, and more than style, he wants it to be an actors' film, unlike *The Hunger*. He doesn't want style to intrude, and neither do I. From the first day, and throughout the film, I imagine, Francis and I are collaborating in the process of finding the film's proper style and tone."

Before starting the film, he and Coppola had looked at old motion pictures such as the original *Scarface*. They also watch archival footage, including film actually shot inside the Cotton Club, and a lot of the five-to-ten-minute musical films of the late twenties and thirties. "These things had a specific look. The acts were photographed straight on, shot in a very realistic style."

When we wrapped from that rooftop at about one o'clock in the morning, Francis told us, "Thank you for a lovely evening." I got a ride back into lower Manhattan with script supervisor B. J. Bjorkman, who had had as hectic a first week as I, in her case trying to deal with continuity. She had worked with Coppola before, and she said, "I've never seen him like this. I've never seen anything like *this*." Within a few weeks, her increasing vocalizing of her complaints about lack of script continuity ("I can't make heads or tails out of this mess!") was to lead to lack of job continuity for her. She was replaced by Lynn Lewis Lovett.

* * *

On a list of cast and crew for *The Cotton Club* dated August 17, 1983, five days before principal photography was to begin, the top six people and their positions were director, Francis Coppola; producer, Robert Evans; co-producer, Milt Forman; executive producer, Dyson Lovell; associate producer, Melissa Prophet; and production manager, David Golden. By the time the film wrapped, only two of these, Coppola and Evans remained, Evans in title only. In a beautifully reproduced color brochure on the film circulated in the summer of 1984, Dyson Lovell, Milt Forman, and Melissa Prophet were still credited although all three had been fired on Sunday, September 25, 1983, in a sweep of key people from the film. But! And a mighty big But! Being under contract to Robert Evans, they were still entitled to credit.

A *New York* magazine piece by Michael Daly would later contend, "Melissa Prophet was often the sole representative of the producers at the studio."

Oh?

She did not have an office at Astoria. Nor to my knowledge, had I ever seen her. Grace Blake told me, "But I'm sure you did. She must have visited the studio at least ten times. She always came with an entourage, either in Evans's limousine or someone else's. She was usually with Evans's people. She was always dressed nicely. Designer jeans, expensive blouses, jewelry. She became friendly with Lisa. Lisa hung out with her some."

I thought she meant Lisa Persky, who played Mrs. Dutch Schultz in the film. No, not that Lisa. Lisa Rubinstein worked for Grace in the production office as receptionist. Her principal job was to answer the telephone, which she did very well. She was invariably pleasant, a rarity in a receptionist, especially one taking calls for a movie in production. She struck me as self-effacing. I somehow couldn't picture Lisa Rubenstein "hanging out" with Melissa Prophet, who had been an actress (and for all I knew still was). A former Miss California, she had played a tennis groupie in the Robert Evans film *Players.* She evidently received associate producer credit as a reward from Evans for having persuaded her friend Adnan Khashoggi, an Arab arms dealer, to invest heavily in the film. If Lisa Rubenstein liked the lady, I'm sure I would too. And Richard Gere would certainly not hang out with some slouch. She had been with him the night of the famous pissing incident.

Finances aside, from my perspective the show was run by two guys, Barrie Osborne and Fred Roos, both acting with an authority bestowed on them by a consortium of "partners," as they were known colloquially by the crew. The Partners, a.k.a. the Las Vegas money. Initially there were two of them, brothers,

Ed and Fred Doumani, and then came another, Joseph Cusumano.

"Another investor joined us yesterday," Richard Sylbert told me. "With five million dollars and five million questions."

Joey Cusumano turned out to be a love, but then all of them did (although Coppola's disposition was not helped any by their presence). The Cusumano brothers became involved with the production on a day-to-day basis, rooting themselves in the studio and taking over offices of the dispossessed. In August 1984, Robert Evans would relinquish to the Doumanis his remaining interest in the film. The guess was that they and Cusumano would be given some titular producer credit: other productions have found ways to dip repeatedly into the producer-credit barrel, and we were confident that ours would also. As it turned out, Fred and Ed Doumani decided against screen credit (smart of them, some thought), and Joey Cusumano would be credited along with Barrie Osborne as line producer. Fred Roos graduated from casting consultant to co-producer, along with Sylvio Tabet (whoever that is: another person I never met or to my knowledge saw).

My production notes, which were endlessly rewritten by Orion's publicity staff as the film neared its release date, were awfully evasive in the matter of credits. There was a long list of the departed that might or might not have to be accounted for. There was also, in my attempt to characterize the film, a reference to Brechtian theater, a reflection of the film as I thought Coppola at the time of production saw it. That of course went. Fast. I was thinking in terms of tone and of who this copy was intended for. As advertising copy, a reference to Brecht would not sell two tickets; but in copy that a reviewer would read after seeing the film, it might suggest an avenue of approach toward an evaluation of the film, provided of course that the final cut of the film *did* reflect something Brechtian and that neither Coppola nor the distributor minded this being underscored.

The place is Harlem. The time: the Jazz Age. Life may have been Folies Bergère in Paris, a cabaret in Berlin, but in New York City it was the Cotton Club that provided the setting and libretto for an epic Brechtian theatre all America's own . . .

* * *

For a moment in time, the Cotton Club was the most stimulating, successful, notorious nightclub in America. The best black talent in the country tapped there, sang there, shimmied, sang the blues, blew a new kind of jazz in shows as spectacular as any Ziegfeld extravaganza. The audience was composed of stars, socialites, slummers, the elite of the underworld. Uptown was where the action was, and those who came shelled out a staggering five-dollar cover charge for the privilege of pouring their own bootleg booze.

It had a racial policy that gnawed at the emerging consciousness of the nation. The show-stopping stars were black. The showgirls, all under twenty-one, were mulatto (or "high yellow" in the terminology of the day). The audience was white. White only.   The club's directors, designers, and choreographers who used it as a stepping stone to Broadway and Hollywood were all white. Blacks need not, could not, apply, except as performers.

The Cotton Club belonged to Owney Madden, a gangster with a penchant for making peace between rival mobs. He demanded and received impeccable behavior in the club, even from such volatile patrons as Dutch Schultz and Mad Dog Coll, upon whom the character played by Nicolas Cage in the film is based. Simply planning a murder or massacre was acceptable social behavior as long as it was done quietly and with taste and the actual implementation occurred off the premises.

The film is the tale of three families—the white Dwyer family (Richard Gere), the black Williams family (Gregory Hines), and the family of the mob. It tells parallel love stories, one between cornet player Dixie Dwyer and club singer and gangster paramour Vera Cicero (Diane Lane), the other between hoofer and numbers runner Sandman Williams (Gregory Hines), and Lila, a Cotton Club showgirl/singer headed for stardom (Lonette McKee). The lives of these four tie in with those of the leading gangster bootleggers of the time.

The Cotton Club opened in the fall of 1923 in a building on the northeast corner of 142nd Street and Lenox Avenue. It quickly became one of the top four nightclubs in Harlem (the others were Small's Paradise, Barron Wilkins' Exclusive Club, and Connie's Inn). Lady Mountbatten, wife of the English nobleman who was later to become First Lord of the Admiralty, called the Cotton Club "the aristocrat of Harlem." In time the club thought of itself that way. The legend was inscribed on its matchbooks. (Those matchbooks along with Cotton Club ashtrays, swizzle sticks, menus, and programs were reproduced for the film with an authenticity to be noticed only by the cast and crew.) The club closed in 1935 when Harlem was torn with rioting and Mayor

LaGuardia warned white people not to go uptown. Although the Cotton Club management did stage two additional revues in the winter of 1935 and the spring of 1936, in the wake of sharply curtailed tourism the audience was no longer there. The Cotton Club closed its doors at that location and moved downtown to Forty-eighth Street and Broadway, where its winter 1936 show was staged.

* * *

During production of *The Cotton Club*, the Evans faction refused to allow the publicizing of William Kennedy's contribution to the script. They were afraid that Kennedy's name would not excite investor money to the extent that Mario Puzo's name would, even though the Puzo scripts had been discarded by the time Kennedy became involved. Kennedy's stature had not yet been enhanced by his winning both the National Book Critics Circle Award and the Pulitzer Prize for *Ironweed*.

In a conversation with Fred Roos, I mentioned an inquiry from a writer who wanted to do a *Popular Mechanics* piece on Coppola. "Francis loves *Popular Mechanics*," Fred said. "It's the only magazine he reads. He doesn't read movie magazines. You might mention it to Francis."

Shouldn't I mention it to Zarem first?

"Whatever your directives are," he said dryly, trying yet failing to be enigmatic, unable to suppress a grin.

We were shooting in the lobby of the Royalton Hotel on West Forty-fourth Street. In the scene, the desk clerk tells Sandman and Lila, who looks white, that the hotel doesn't accept mixed couples. Lila Rose tells him,

"My mother was white, my father was colored, so what does that make me?" Francis had cleared the lobby for rehearsals. Concerned for his actors in a scene that touched sensitive nerves, he said, "I don't want too many people watching this." I sat in the foyer near the hotel entrance where I could watch a monitor. After rehearsing the scene, Coppola retired to the Silverfish. He paused to acknowledge my station at the monitor. "Our little window on the world," he said pleasantly.

Dan Suhart was one of eleven people listed on the crew sheet as "Coppola's Support Staff." His actual title was "Dialogue Coach," although to my knowledge nobody ever saw him coaching anyone. Whatever his designation, it was apparent to all that he was one of Coppola's three right-hand men along with Fred Roos and Tony Dingman, whose title was the ambiguous "NY/SF Liaison." I would find Suhart invaluable as a reader and advisor of Francis's moods. He could usually be found stationed outside Coppola's Silverfish.

Dan told me that Lillian Ross of the *New Yorker* had called to say that she would be dropping by and that Francis had told him to tell me that it was okay. Ross turned up almost immediately. Dan introduced us. They knew each other from the time of *One from the Heart*, when she had written a long piece about Francis. Dan explained to her that we were filming in a small room under tight circumstances and that it was extremely hot. Francis thought it too problematical a set for her to visit, but if she liked she could wait with me in his van and he would try to get down later to say hello.

She said she would come back in half an hour. The *New Yorker* offices were just across the street. She wanted to do a "Talk of the Town" piece on the film. Coppola sent me a message not to consult or inform

Zarem or Evans. I wondered how I could avoid informing Zarem, if only to protect myself. Coppola's wish to keep the Ross visit quiet was a small but definite early indication of the unsettled and unsettling producer/director relationship.

When Ross returned, she had a white poodle with her. I accompanied her and the dog into the Silverfish where Coppola planned to join us. Ross had already written about the Silverfish in the *New Yorker* and described how Coppola made use of it in his movie-making process. The van was equipped with state-of-the-art electronic equipment that made possible immediate replay and review of material just shot in order to allow the director to decide whether and what additional material might be needed.

Coppola called a technician in the van from the hotel room where he and the cast were working and asked her to play for him the rehearsal footage for the scene due to be shot. Lillian Ross and I watched it in the van while Coppola and his actors watched it on monitors upstairs. The rehearsal tape recalled to both Francis and the actors gestures and bits of business they had come up with for the scene.

Ross had another appointment. She said that she would try to make it by the Plaza Hotel, where we were scheduled to shoot the following day. I mentioned Bobby Zarem's connection with the film and suggested that she coordinate her visit with his agency. She would have none of it. "There's no reason for me to deal with those people," she said. "That would only confuse things. I want to deal with *you*." We exchanged telephone numbers. She asked me to call her the next morning to confirm that we were at the Plaza.

We did in fact shoot at the Plaza for the rest of that week and all of the next, except for Monday, Labor Day. Ross let me know she couldn't make it to the set until the second week. On Friday, I decided it was CYA time (good rule for publicists: there is no such thing as too much covering your ass) despite strong hints from both Fred Roos and Francis Coppola that I circumvent the Zarem/Evans people as much as possible. How the hell was I going to do that? I composed a careful memo to Zarem about Ross's visits and other matters:

Francis says she will do a Talk of the Town on the film. I said that it might interfere with your plans for the film's publicity; he said he could control her, that she had even offered to let him see the piece. She confirmed this to me.

She was supposed to have come again today, but hadn't come by 3 p.m. Francis says he told her to drop by from time to time, especially on days (like now) when we're shooting at the Plaza and it's convenient for her.

Also I've received calls from a Popular Mechanics *contributing writer who wants to do a piece on Francis's videotape approach to directing a film, especially in the case of* The Cotton Club. *Chatting with Francis today, I mentioned this to him and he said, "I'd do anything for* Popular Mechanics." *It seems he devoured the magazine when he was a kid and still does. He told me to talk with Anahid Nazarian who is a research assistant of his. He said she would be able to help the* Popular Mechanics *writer get her story. Please let me know if I should proceed with this . . .*

Zarem called, upset. Robert Evans was annoyed with my having mentioned the *Popular Mechanics* request to Francis. "Why did it even come up?" Evans had wanted to know.

"It was Bob Evans," said Zarem, "who raised the $27,000,000 for *Cotton Club*, not Francis. It's Bob Evans's shop. Since it's Bob Evans's shop you have to defer to him and not to some clerk that he's hired to work in the shop."

Francis Coppola, a clerk!

I passed the story along to some of my messengers of information. They responded, as I had anticipated, with howls of glee.

Looking at Zarem's statement from the vantage point of hindsight, I am struck by the poignancy of it, not the least of which emanates from that $27,000,000 figure. The movie ended up costing more like $57,000,000, with Evans locked out of his own shop even though he was allowed to keep his name on the storefront.

The following week Lillian Ross arrived at the Plaza almost before I did. Dan Suhart got word to me that she and her dog were waiting for me in the Silverfish. A woman technician showed us archival footage of Harlem circa World War I followed by rehearsal tapes, including one of the attempted assassination of Dutch Schultz early in the movie. It was rudimentary, brisk, with the feeling of a silent film. It gave an idea of what Francis had in mind for the movie. Exciting. Then the technician said abruptly that she couldn't show us more, not without Francis's permission. My impression was that she had gotten word from someone that Francis might not want Ross to see this stuff. Ross probably got the same impression. She said she would be back the next day, gathered up her dog, and left. She did come back, but Francis still couldn't see her. She never returned, and we never got our brief moment in "Talk of the Town."

* * *

While the crew was hard at work setting up for a scene to be shot, Richard Gere played an upright piano that stood in the wide Plaza hallway outside the fifth-floor suite where we were shooting. Coppola joined him as vocalist. Every inch of him was Helen Morgan and Helen Kane and The Bearded Lady all rolled up into one. Except for the hassle it would have caused, I almost wished we were doing a documentary. The moment called out for documentation. Gere in tuxedo, Coppola in his fraternity-boy shirt and the tie at odds with it, all the extras and crew milling and mixing in period twenties costumes and eighties denim or whatever, a lazy moment of fun for all of us, listening to a crazy kind of jam session. It gave a lift to the collective spirit, and nobody thought about the downs preceding it or the kindred downs that presciently we knew would follow.

There were complaints about the food served to the crew at the Plaza location. Not about its quality. There just wasn't enough to go around! During the first couple of days of shooting there was plenty. The food was served buffet style in large rooms on the second floor. Servants and attendants were formally attired. There were silver tureens and white tablecloths and flowers. All very lovely. But after Labor Day, persons who arrived early managed just fine, but those coming later would find themselves with reduced or nonexistent portions. "The chicken will be out shortly," you might be informed, so you seated yourself, ate the salad and a couple of rolls that you really didn't want but accepted as part of the contingency, drank the coffee poured for you by the waiters, and waited for the chicken go come out. Sometimes it did, sometimes it didn't. If it did arrive, you had already filled up on the contingencies. Meg Hunnewell, the unit production manager to whom complaints would be directed, blamed people who brought guests to lunch, singling out Adger Cowans as a notorious example. He had invited a woman friend to lunch along with her two teenage children. Meg had cornered Adger in a hallway and admonished him about it. I retain a mental image of them and can still picture the confrontation: his hair a wiry salt-and-pepper, her hair a damp honey echoing her name; Adger lighter-than-air, as if missing some ballast, Meg as weighted as he was weightless, anchored to a reasonableness that he found unreasonable and refused to attach himself to. Meg told him that from now on he would please be so kind as to inform her when he was expecting guests for location lunches so that arrangements could be made. He would also be expected to pay for them. Adger raised his voice in indignation and protest. I heard bandied between them like a shuttlecock the word "attitude." Meg told me later, "He's just asking to be fired, accusing me of attitude! Talk about attitude!"

The manager of the Plaza considerately and professionally did not invite TV news people in to photograph us at work in his "lovely rooms." I could relax somewhat. Not finding it necessary to keep watchful vigil in the lobby, I had the opportunity to get to know some of the actors.

Diane Lane looked nothing like the actress I had seen recently in *The Outsiders*. In that film she was lit and photographed to look more mature than the sixteen-year-old she was. Now she was eighteen. (Her subsequent career in films has proved yet again Coppola's sharp eye for promising talent.) Throughout the production of *The Cotton Club*, she came across as the most chameleon-like of any actress with whom I've ever worked. Initially I attributed her changing look to the plethora of wigs and headpieces she was required to wear, but later I began to suspect that it might come from something in the actress herself. On the main Cotton Club set, crowded with actors and extras in costume as the crew prepared for a take, Diane would pass me or be standing next to me and I wouldn't recognize her. Often it wouldn't be until someone addressed her that I would realize that the young woman I had taken for another pretty costumed extra was in fact Diane. After I began to recognize her more promptly in costume, I found myself embarrassed more than once when a young woman wearing jeans with blond shoulder-length hair flowing would say "Hi" in passing and I'd do a double-take and shout a delayed reply, "Hi, Diane!"

My first glimpse of her was on the Friday of our second day at the Plaza. Milena was shepherding her to Francis, who was having lunch, for his approval of the dress she would be wearing in her first scene, due to be shot that afternoon. Unlike most of the cast, she had not been around for the pre-production rehearsals and improvisations. Only three or four days before joining us she had completed her role in the Walter Hill movie *Streets of Fire*.

During a break that first afternoon, Diane and I chatted in the fifth floor hallway while actors and technicians flowed about us. A cloth, skintight, beaded skullcap covered her neck and ears, framing her face and hiding her hair. She wore it in the series of scenes that comprise the gangster's party to which the Gere character is brought to play piano and accompany Diane.

She expected that her voice would be dubbed. "Unless they've got tin ears, it will be." It wasn't. Coppola told her that her character was "no big deal as a singer," so it wasn't really important that she sing well.

I assumed that her character was modeled loosely on Texas Guinan, a woman and a name very much associated with the era and the milieu that the Cotton Club represents. "That's one of the names they mentioned to me," Diane told me. "Louise Brooks was another. I'm just putting myself into Francis's hands. I've hardly had time to breathe, let alone read about any of these people." Once, standing aimlessly, she noticed me and raised an eyebrow. "I haven't got a clue," she said. "Not a single clue. No idea in the world what I'm doing." She smiled, although she obviously didn't find the situation funny. Richard Gere, on the other hand, had had the pre-production time, the conscientiousness, and the interest to thoroughly research the period and the real-life counterparts of the still-evolving Dixie Dwyer. Diane was having to trust that Vera Cicero would spring vibrantly from Coppola's head, an apparition that he could then help her embody.

If I found Vera Cicero closer in specifics to Texas Guinan than to any of the other names thrown at Diane Lane, I found Dixie Dwyer more akin to George Raft with a residue of Bix Beiderbecke. Texas Guinan and George Raft had known each other, although they had no relationship resembling that of Richard and Diane in the movie. But fiction is like that: it must dare to get the facts wrong in order to get it right. Texas Guinan, like Vera Cicero, was a consort of gangsters, a nightclub owner and mistress of ceremonies who sang. Betty Hutton played her in the 1945 movie *Incendiary Blonde*. A character based on her was featured on Broadway in *Billion Dollar Baby*. George Raft made his first screen appearance in 1929 in *Queen of the Night Clubs*, a movie based loosely on her career. For a period in the late twenties, Raft was an entertainer at El Fey, Guinan's nightclub in New York. Her partner and lover was underworld operator Larry Fay. Raft was busy with romances of his own with stellar entertainers and beauties like Helen Morgan, Winnie Lightner, and Hilda Ferguson, a Ziegfeld Follies girl whom Flo Ziegfeld considered one of the most beautiful ever to have been glorified by him. Raft shared her with Enoch Johnson, one of the ten top racketeers in the country, only "Nucky," as he was called (for brass knuckles), didn't know it. The strain was too great for Raft and he ended the affair. Raft was not the only entertainer to associate with racketeers. Looking back from the vantage point of today, I find the amount of interaction between the entertainment world and the criminal world quite remarkable. Then I realize that if you were an entertainer then, you had to associate with racketeers like Owney Madden and Larry Fay: they owned the nightclubs! And they did have a glamour all their own.

* * *

Bobby Zarem's office was near the Plaza. Bobby asked me to stop by to meet with him and Mark Kane about hiring special photographers and deciding which scenes such a special might profitably cover. Adger, of course, was totally against the idea of having any special photographers; and from my growing appreciation of

Adger's talent, I tended to agree with him. We certainly didn't need any underfoot during the filming at the Plaza Hotel. Scene after scene would be filmed under extremely tight circumstances with limited access, and I was pretty sure neither Coppola nor Gere would approve of the presence of a special photographer.

Zarem wanted a memo from me suggesting from ten to fifteen scenes that would be advantageous for a special to cover: scenes with star value, production value, dramatic value (when I told Richard Gere about the memo, he commented, "There aren't any scenes of dramatic value in the picture"), any scenes that promised to have a visual impact. And Zarem wanted the memo before I left the office.

It is part of the job of the unit publicist sometimes to go through what he knows will be wasted motion: "marking-time moves" I called them. Looking back later, I realize that my feeling at the time was correct. A lot of the dickering about special photographers was marking-time moves. The moves nevertheless had to be made, even if they advanced us only by inches. Zarem seemed eager for a resolution to the matter. He wanted, I believe, something concrete to show Robert Evans—a report, a memo, ideally a victory of some sort, a reminder that he and his office were earning their keep.

The meeting with Bobby and Mark was annoying me. As Bob Evans's publicity handmaidens (and by extension Orion's), they were obliged to dance to Evans's tune. But for me, Evans was a tune weakly defined, in fact, a drowned-out melody. I couldn't, at my distance, sway to it as enthusiastically as Bobby and Mark. I had my own music to listen to. It was right there on the set, emanating in discordant harmony from Coppola and Gere.

Mark made some suggestions as to scenes that might be covered, suggestions that I often thought silly, as no doubt he thought some of my ideas were. Some of our exchanges were quite heated. We can be excused, perhaps, since because of the constantly evolving script, a schedule that changed not daily but hourly, lack of information about physical accessibility to various sets, and no explicit directive from Coppola and Gere as to what either would allow. All I had to go on was my own experience and the trickle-down word that they were both against special photographers.

"What about backstage at the Cotton Club? The Cotton Club preparations?" Mark asked.

"It'll be nothing," I argued. "We'd be wasting our money on special photographers for that. It doesn't include principals."

"Gregory Hines? Isn't he backstage?"

"He's not on the breakdown, and there are other scenes with Hines we'll want to cover. Backstage, it's the chorus girls."

"We want the chorus girls."

"In *performance*. Isn't it more important to have them in performance? Besides, it's going to be tight backstage."

"That's all I ever hear from you. Every scene, how tight it's going to be!"

"That's what I'm told. Anyway, the preparation stuff Adger can get. It's nothing you need to pay a name special for."

Mark and I were sitting on a couch in Zarem's office a few feet from the desk where Zarem sat talking on the telephone. The telephone was an extension of his soul. He held the receiver to his ear with one hand while his other wrung and twisted his long side hair. At moments he attended to and participated in our discussion. More often, between calls, he would drift into reverie, soon to pull himself up and lift the phone and say to one of his assistants "Get me . . ." and soon he would be talking to Bob Evans at the Town House, to Lloyd Leipsig at Orion in L.A., or to Fred Roos at the studio in Astoria.

One thing I realized: the matter of the specials was coming to a head, and I had to take it there. Specifically, to the heads of Coppola and Gere.

Gere seemed increasingly remote to me. I'd had no reason to approach him yet and had no reason to believe that he would not be accessible when I did. Passing each other in the wide plush Plaza hallways, we would acknowledge each other without speaking. I was reluctant to risk displeasing him this early on about a special photographer, especially since I could see for myself the impossibility of having one on these sets with the density of bodies crowded into small inflexible rooms, the roasting-oven degree of heat in them due to the intensity of lighting and high humidity, the added sweaty discomfort of actors in formal (and in the men's cases, woolen) costumes, and the restricted space in which the camera crew and others necessary to the shot would have to work. I did not want to risk endangering a potential trust and rapport between Gere and me by taking an adversary role over an issue on which I thought Richard and I were essentially in agreement. And I did want to leave the door open for serious consideration of a special photographer in more feasible and felicitous surroundings.

After Labor Day the stream of celebrity visitors began. I was introduced to Matt Dillon who was visiting Diane, both of them swishing hands in a large silver bowl of ice water, meltdown from chunks of ice. The bowls of water and ice were provided for actors and crew to cool off with. There were cloths for drying hands and mopping foreheads. I plunged my hands in and swished alongside Diane and Matt as we chatted. Matt had wanted to be in the picture. All his friends were, he said. He felt left out. I had heard Matt being mentioned as a replacement for Gere. As more and more footage shot with Gere piled up, that possibility was ever more remote.

Bobby Zarem, Mark Kane, and Fred Roos were having breakfast in the Edwardian Room. They sent word for me to join them. I'd already eaten, but I realized this was about more than breakfast. They wanted to discuss the twelve photo possibilities I had suggested. Why hadn't I listed the scene in which Dixie undresses the inebriated Vera and puts her to bed, taking off her garters in the process? Fred thought it would provide a better visual than my choice, the love scene in Dixie's bed in his mother's apartment. I explained that the latter would be done at the studio in a controlled setting while the garter-removal scene would be filmed in the bedroom of a private residence at the Apthorp, an apartment complex between Seventy-eighth and Seventy-ninth Streets. There would be barely enough room for the camera crew, possibly not even for Adger.

As though he had not heard a word I said, Bobby reiterated his pronouncement: "A special *must* cover that scene." But even more imminent and more pressing was the Killing of Flynn scene. "It simply has to be covered," he said. "It's vital." He was right about the scene. Visually it would crackle with dynamics, a key shot in a publicity campaign and a natural for inclusion in a magazine layout. But I knew this conversation was pure jerk-off. It simply wasn't going to happen. The room where the scene would be filmed was so small that it would be off-limits to half the crew entitled and expecting to be there. No special photographer was going to be allowed in. Bobby said he appreciated the fact and the difficulty but that he was sure that I could arrange it. "We simply have to have that shot. Make sure everybody is notified, especially Richard. Tell him that Theo Westenberger has been approved by his agent, by his publicity agent, and by the director of publicity of Orion Pictures."

Next morning another powwow in the Edwardian Room. Breakfasting with the usual suspects was Lloyd Leipsig, just in from Los Angeles. Leipsig looked like a rare barbecue. "How nice you look," I said. "Been on vacation?"

"No, we all look like this in California," he said. His hair was stark white, thick. Although trying for a laid-back look, he was still a suit.

Fred Roos said that Francis was against special photographers. Thank you, Fred. While this was nothing new, it was nice to hear it again. Besides, this sounded like a more recent comment on the subject, possibly from within the past few hours. "He thinks they're all gossips. They work three days on your picture and then run off and spread lies about it."

Bobby said, "That *is* a problem. But gossip exists on pictures all the time and there's little you can do about it." He paused and looked at me. He said, his voice tremulous with threatened significance, "Francis *has* to be convinced."

Fred Roos couldn't convince him, and *I* had to?

Bobby threw out the names of several photographers that he would like to see used on the film: Michael Childers, Dana Barrett, Maureen Lambray, John Bryson, and Steve Shapiro. Of these I knew only the last two. When we were alone, Leipsig told me, "Bobby's probably promised a spot on the picture to all of them. He's afraid he'll look bad if he can't come through." I had a brief flash of sympathy in retrospect for Bobby and the frustration he must have felt during breakfast when Leipsig had said, "Perhaps it's better that we put just one special on. So that Francis and Richard will get used to that one person."

That afternoon I talked with Richard Gere and an aide named Rob Gach in a hallway outside the room where Richard would soon be working.

Although it wasn't explicitly stated, I inferred that Gach was an associate of Ed Limato, Gere's agent in the William Morris Agency in Los Angeles. Gach had told me earlier that he'd be glad to help me with anything involving Richard. Gach was on *The Cotton Club* payroll and worked in Dyson Lovell's office alongside Lovell's assistant Jim Kelly, with whom Gach lived in Los Angeles. In New York they shared a sublet.

Gach's duties were nebulous other than his being a conduit to Gere. There had, however, been an attempt to gather more express duties to him, duties already assigned to others, duties that these others resented being wrenched from them in what they saw as an attempt to legitimize and make more secure Gach's tenure on the payroll should push come to shove and various heads fall capriciously to the budgetary ax. (His job was a mid-production casualty; but since he was under contract, he was paid for the full number of weeks that he might have been expected to work and was given screen credit as Assistant to Richard Gere.) David Golden asked Grace Blake if she minded if Rob did the contracts, that is, write day-player contracts. The contracts of principals of course are usually done by studios, lawyers, and agents; but on *The Cotton Club* there were so many dancers, singers, and other day-players that someone in-house had to do them. "It was my job," Grace said, "one of my jobs. It was taken away from me and given to Rob. But then somebody had to teach him how to do that, and I was told to do so. So I did. I also told him that he better keep up with them as we go along. So as to avoid any backlog. So that they can be ready to be signed while the actors are here on the premises working. He didn't do this. When Barrie Osborne came on the picture, I had to tell him, 'We have no contracts.' 'What do you mean?' he said. It was a dangerous situation for us to be in with respect to day-players, and Barrie knew it. When Rob left, the contracts were returned to me where they should have been all along."

I mentioned to Gere and Gach the idea of having a special photographer for the Flynn scene (which we were under the impression would be filmed the next day) and told them that Zarem was already trying to line up a special to cover it. Gere hated the idea. "Have you *been* in that room?" Richard asked me irritably. "Have you been in *any* of these rooms we're shooting in? There's hardly enough room for me. How are we going to get another photographer in?"

He knew that Stephen Goldblatt was opposed but didn't know for sure about Coppola. "Does Francis know about this?" he asked.

"No," I said. "I thought I'd speak to you first."

"Francis doesn't want a special any more than I do. You ask Francis. If Francis insists on having a special photographer there, I'll go along with it. But let me tell you, he won't."

When I told Fred Roos about it, he said sardonically, "Well, Francis is not going to insist on it."

At the end of the day, we got the news that the scene had been postponed until Friday. That night I called Bobby at Elaine's where he had told me he would be. I have rarely found Bobby more engaging than he was that night, speaking to me from a phone taken to him where he sat, playing to the table if not the house. Table full of celebrity clients, no doubt. Not my style but a style that tickled me with pleasure to visualize as Bobby's. Our conversation was affable. I explained Gere's response and told him that the Flynn scene had been postponed. He said, "You've saved my life. I haven't been able to get a photographer for tomorrow." He told me that we would talk in the morning, meanwhile we had to *think*: there had to be some way to convince Francis about special photographers, and if we could convince him maybe he could convince Richard.

The Flynn scene, the depiction of the vicious murder of a gangster rival of Dutch Schultz's, was shot on Friday; and no special photographers were allowed to cover it. There was hardly room for Adger, but he managed to wedge himself in somehow. All members of the crew superfluous to getting the shot done were excluded from the room. Anybody interested could watch the scene from monitors in nearby rooms and hallways, if you could get near one. I was interested. I crowded into a space near a monitor and the wall it faced, against which the operator was sitting with only two or three feet between himself and the monitor.

Those of us trying to watch had to press against one another and crane into the area from the side. I found myself pressed against a guy new to me. He wore a baseball cap pushed back on his head. He was wearing boots and jeans. I figured him for a crew member. He had that look. Nice body, not too tall. Fine reddish blond hair. We fitted against each other just right. It would have been prelude to a pick-up in a bar. We began talking, commenting on the scene. I asked him what he did. I expected him to say gaffer, electrician, maybe a Teamster. "Depends," he said. Oh boy, I thought. Wow. On what? ". . . On when you ask me. Right now I'm directing a movie. It's called *Splash*." He smiled at me, my body pressed against his. "And what do you do?" Well, Ron Howard, it's like this . . .

We were later to encounter one another in another room and he acknowledged me with a shy, friendly, and amused glance.

The day ended with the scene unfinished. It would be months before the company could return to the Plaza to reshoot the entire scene. I felt particularly sorry for the young black actor who played the waiter roughed up in the scene by Dutch Schultz. He had spent hours being prepared with laboriously applied special makeup, tubing, artificial blood (to pour from his nose), latex, and the like and never even got to go before the camera until the company reconvened for reshooting in the spring.

It was a privilege for me to get to meet and work with Julian Beck. I felt like I was in the presence of a big chunk (or, considering Julian's slight frame, a small chunk) of Off-Broadway and Off-Off-Broadway (not to mention New York theatrical) history. In the 1950s, Julian and his wife Judith Malina were the founders and the heart of the Living Theater. Judith visited the set during the shoot at the Plaza. The three of us stood in the busy hallway and talked.

"Judith was at the New School when I met her in 1943," Julian said. "We both wanted to be on Broadway. But Judith said, 'There's no way we're going to get on Broadway. We're going to open our own theater!'"

"Everybody thought we were crazy," said Judith.

"We *were*, darling, and thank God," said Julian with a broad smile for his wife. "I was an actor when I met her, an actor making the rounds, trying to find work, not having much luck. I thought hers was the most sensible idea I'd probably ever heard, our *own* theater!"

Together they sketched the history of their Living Theater.

They first began performing in a space on Wooster Street. They were closed by the police. They moved into a friend's apartment and began mounting plays there. Their next stop was the Cherry Lane Theatre. It was closed by the police because, Julian said, "The owner of most of the buildings on the block found us and our work offensive. They said there were violations. We asked where. 'We'll find them,' the police said. We were doing the first of the gay plays. It was called *The Heroes*, written by John Ashbury, young and just out of college, I've forgotten which, Harvard, I think. A play about the gods. We wore white suits, and there were twenties clothes just like on this movie, and I danced with another male actor. It was a short work with a companion piece whose first word was 'shit.' You just didn't say shit on the stage in those days, and rarely on the street. Not to mention two men dancing together. It was all too much for the people on the block. From there we went uptown, 100th and Broadway, and from there to Fourteenth Street and Sixth Avenue." It was at that last location where their celebrated productions of *The Connection* and *The Brig* were performed. That theater too was eventually closed, this time in 1963 when the Internal Revenue Service seized it for back taxes. The Becks moved to Europe where they found a home base as well as financial backing in Paris.

I thought it was both an anomaly and a stroke of casting genius to have Julian Beck playing vicious gangland killer Sol Weinstein in *The Cotton Club*. He didn't know for sure how he came to get the role, but he believed that Coppola (and perhaps Fred Roos) had seen him onstage in Paris where the Living Theater was currently based and performing.

"I venture to say that he liked what he saw," said Beck, "and when I got the call for this film I couldn't have been more delighted. Although I do think it's somewhat of a casting departure, don't you?"

Julian's hair was thin, long, wispy, normally allowed to swing free. It had been that way for years. Lisa Persky, who grew up on Christopher Street in Greenwich Village, remembered seeing him when she was a kid. "There were a lot of weird looks in the Village then, as there are now, it was the norm. As far as I was concerned, Julian sort of represented the norm."

Julian was pleased that he didn't have to cut his hair for the film, something that almost every other man in the cast had to do to conform to the hairstyles of the period. "I'm simply tying it in a little bun at the base of my skull and leaving it to the camera people to keep out of the way of it."

On Friday, our last scheduled day at the Plaza, Coppola told me that Roos had spoken to him about special photographers. "I'd like something from you about it," he said. "*You* write it and hand it to me." It was an echo of the Zarem office imperative. "Let me have it by Monday, the scenes you want a special to cover. I'll study it and let you know. If I decide to let any specials come on at all, it will be for a limited number of days."

On Monday I gave him a list of seven scenes with the reasoning behind each suggestion, all tightly compressed onto one sheet of paper for a favorable psychological impression, accompanied by a covering letter:

. . . While we seem to be getting good material from our stills photographer . . . we need the insurance of special photography from time to time . . . Particularly, we need a generous supply of color transparencies that capture key elements in the film, important scenes and moments. As Lloyd Leipsig told Bobby, Fred, Mark Kane, and myself, Orion doesn't want to sell the film as just a gangster film, or just an exciting and glamorous Jazz Age period piece, or just a backstage musical film (all of which it will be), but as a love story too, a double love story.

Which is why it is thought to be of the utmost importance that at least one scene between Diane Lane and Richard Gere, in an intimate moment, be made available to an additional photographer. Bobby suggests Theo Westenberger, a woman whose credentials come high. In a conversation I had last week with Jim Watters, entertainment editor of Life *Magazine, he remarked that she was one of the best special photographers around.*

Since Dixie and Vera's love scenes, in shots 95 and 96, will be filmed in Astoria, wouldn't it be possible, despite the sensitive nature of these scenes, for Ms. Westenberger (or another top photographer were she not available) to be allowed to shoot one or both of them without being intrusive? The scenes constitute a tender, emotional high that Orion & Zarem would want to emphasize in their promotion of the film.

Additional scenes that we believe would be invaluable for a special to cover are listed on a separate sheet, along with a brief rationale for these choices. Perhaps you might suggest additional or alternate choices. Thanks . . .

Before delivering the letter and list to Francis, I dropped by the Zarem office to leave photocopies of the documents. Mark Kane suggested that perhaps it would be best that I not give the list to Francis myself but that it come from them retyped on Zarem letterhead and sent by messenger. I'm not falling for that ploy, no way. Uh uh, I told him, Francis said the list was to come from me, moi, myself, and I. I wrote it, I'd deliver it. Who did these Pomeranians think they were dealing with?

After reading my letter, Francis shook his head wistfully. "These people don't understand the madness in making a movie, do they?"

(I recalled Zarem's recently pronounced corollary, "Francis and his people don't understand the long-range sophisticated press campaign, as we do. Lloyd said that Francis and his people ruined *Apocalypse Now* with premature publicity." I didn't see the connection between the present situation and *Apocalypse*, but oh well.)

Francis folded my list and tucked it in a pocket. "Maybe I'll approve a special for two days," he said. *Two* days, and a maybe to boot. Another bad tiding to take back to Zarem. It wasn't as if we hadn't been warned.

That afternoon, Fred Roos told me he had received a letter and list of scenes from the Zarem office, written by Mark Kane, essentially recapping my list and letter. Addressed to Roos, copies were sent to Coppola (in care of Roos), Evans, Zarem, and me. The copies for Roos and Coppola had been sent to the studio by messenger. Evans, you can be sure, got his at the Town House not ten minutes off the typewriter. Mine, it turned out, had been mailed to my home, and I didn't get it until two days later. Mark's letter even included the information about Jim Watters, with no attribution to me. Ross suggested that since Francis already had my list and letter, didn't I think it would only confuse him to be given the one from Mark Kane? Yes, I said, totally concurring. Not only confuse but also alienate. The less we harped on this the better.

* * *

The Apthorp is a large apartment house with a courtyard and entrances on both Broadway and West End Avenue at Seventy-ninth Street. We were locked into the location for one day. When I arrived on Monday morning at the Broadway gate, there was no sign of a movie company. I asked the guard. Am I with the company, he wanted to know. I struggled. What was the name of the company? It popped into my head. "The Totally Independent, Ltd. *Cotton Club* Company." The magic words were spoken, the doors opened. It turned out the crew was camped out on West End Avenue, across the courtyard from where I was admitted. All the vehicles, including Francis's Silverfish, were parked there. The shoot would take place in an apartment above, overlooking West End. I immediately spotted a TV crew. Uh oh, here to film the lovely rooms of the Apthorp, no doubt.

Dan Suhart walked briskly toward me. He'd been looking for me to let me know that this was an Italian TV crew invited by Francis, arranged by Fred Roos. The egg on my face couldn't have been any more visible had it actually been there. Dan explained, "I imagine you weren't told about it because the interview is not about *The Cotton Club*. It's about *The Outsiders*, which is going to open in Italy soon, and *Rumble Fish*." The latter was scheduled to be one of the fall's Lincoln Center Film Festival entries. Dan introduced me to a very charming Cecilia, who spoke a delectable Italian-tinged English. She would be interviewing Francis, Dan told me. And here is John. John will be taping the interview. And here is . . . Inasmuch as they are on the location for *The Cotton Club* and obviously as interested in that film as the other two, I filled them in on aspects of the production. When Francis emerged from his Silverfish and saw the crew gathered about me, drinking in my words of wisdom, he motioned to me, "Are these people ready to talk to me?" Then, as though solicitous of my position vis-à-vis Evans/Zarem, he added, "Or are you handling this?"

Sure I was. Even though the whole thing had been arranged behind my back. I motioned for Cecilia to join us. The crew followed.

Cecilia wanted to talk to Francis inside the van. He demurred. "I want to stay away from that," he said. He leaned against the open tailgate of the prop truck and the interview began. It had to be moved inside the courtyard because of the traffic noise. Francis sat on the rim of a quiescent fountain. Adger took pictures. Obviously with the director down here there was nothing for him to do upstairs. I took notes.

Although he didn't want to be photographed in the Silverfish, Francis didn't mind talking about it. "I think of it as a control booth. Which is what it is. I'm surprised there aren't more of them. This is the only one."

He thinks tape is the future of the industry, he says. He pre-visualizes his films now by taping rehearsals. "As hard as it is now to buy black-and-white film, that's how hard it will be in the future to buy *any* film. In fifteen years, twenty, there won't be any film. Everything will be electronic. And by coincidence, it's what I've been interested in all my life. Electronics. Remote control. You push something here, something goes up there. It's always fascinated me. *Popular Mechanics* remains to this day my favorite magazine. Film is like the horseless carriage. It may stick around as a quaint oddity for a while but it's no longer relevant. Hollywood as we know it is over. They're interested in nothing new. Like the automobile industry. They'll lose the entire thing in a few years."

A line-up of period cars sat on Seventy-ninth Street, never to be used that day. Not only did it rain all afternoon and evening but the bedroom set took an inordinately long time to set up. We had the apartment booked for one day only. The living room was dressed as well as the bedroom and hallway, but only the last two were used. But you never know. It had to be ready in case Coppola should decide to use it. Twenties sheet music on the piano, fringed throw shawls. What a waste. The camera had restricted movement in the bedroom, and I wondered again what was gained by filming here. It could have been done far more easily and cheaply at the studio. Mine not to reason why.

A far greater logistical problem was posed for Adger than at the Flynn scene at the Plaza. It would clearly have been a wasted day for the special photographer that Zarem had called imperative for the shoot. The important thing now was for Adger to get his shots, and he almost didn't. He wasn't allowed in the room. Adger reminded Francis that he would have to freeze Gere and Lane in position either before or after a take if we were to get any stills coverage of this important scene. Francis said, "Okay, let stills in." The assistant director, Henry Bronchtein, checked his watch and said, "A minute and a half." After the time was up, Francis told Adger, "After lunch we'll try to fit you in some place." When shooting resumed after lunch, Adger tried to get into the room. Bronchtein denied him entrance. Adger fought loudly enough for Francis to hear and intervene. Francis found a tight but strategic spot for him.

Bronchtein grumbled apologetically to me, "I really am trying to cooperate with Adger. I know he needs his shots, but we also need *ours*. I was going to get him into the room . . ." Yes, I thought, but *when*.

Nothing is ever handed on a silver platter to anyone on a movie set. It is a place of fierce conflicts and personality clashes and temper tantrums in a pool of dependence and cooperation. Within the confines of the pool, each person splashes for himself, always asking or being asked favors and giving or withholding them. If you think somebody is getting in the way of your job, you scream about it. Or you say, "What the hell," and let it, and maybe yourself, go. Adger, to his credit and to the benefit of the movie, was a highly creditable screamer.

* * *

Tuesday, September 13. At last we were working at the studio. "Working" was something of a euphemism. It took forever for anything to get underway. I was spending half my time running around trying to get acclimated, the other half trying to find Meg Hunnewell. She was supposed to provide me with an office. I had reminded her weekly, it's part of my deal. Now here we were at the beginning of the fourth week and I still had no office, no telephone, and no typewriter (the age of the ubiquitous computer/word processor was not yet on us). I left my belongings in the office Meg shared with David Golden and went in search of her. When I found her, she said, "Give me a couple of hours. I have something more pressing at the moment."

I tried to find the working set. It was in the basement, and it took me half an hour to reach it. I kept running into locked doors and blocked stairways and dead ends. I received directions that were totally confusing if not totally wrong. Nobody seemed to know anything.

There was one elevator in the whole building, a freight elevator with two ways to get on, one a normal elevator door, the other two guillotine blades, one rising from the floor as the other falls from the ceiling. They joined in marriage in the middle, and it looked like they'd love to chop your head right off if you'd only get it in the right position. There were levers you had to operate when you got on and then when you got off. When I first tried to use it, it had been preempted for freight use on an upper floor. Finally when I was able to commandeer it, it stopped at the basement as commanded but refused to open its doors. The warning light was on. You can't get off or on in the basement when the company is shooting. You don't know that? Are you stupid or something? The noise would spoil the shot. But *what* shot: the first shot of the day was still two hours off. Let me off! I returned to the main floor. Somebody conjectured that maybe they're getting wild shots. Wild shots, I ask, of what? Gere and Lane who were scheduled to be in the first shot were not in the building yet. I was determined to get to the basement, if just to satisfy myself that I was able to do so and to find out what was happening.

I found a dark staircase that took me there. The shooting area was darker than the staircase. It was completely hung—swathed is a better word—with black drapes to make it look like night. Period cars had been moved in from the Apthorp location. Next to the car being used in the first shot were parallel tracks on which lights would be mounted to simulate automobile headlights going and coming, approaching and passing our principals, Dixie and Vera, in the back seat of the automobile in which they were riding. The setting-up seemed interminable. I groped my way out of the place. I sought out Meg Hunnewell again. I haunted her office. When finally she appeared, she said, "Come with me. I think I've found the spot for you."

She took me to the Diana Ross Suite.

Or, as we of a more classical bent would call it, the Gloria Swanson Suite.

It sat in grand and imposing isolation from the rest of the building on the right wing on the second floor, on the corner of Thirty-fifth Street and Thirty-fifth Avenue. The entrance to the building on this corner was locked and bolted. It would be opened only once during our stay there, on the night of the wrap party when guests were allowed to enter through it.

There had been two avenue entrances, grand ones connected with a recessed driveway. One could imagine Gloria Swanson's limousine stopping in front of the building and the star, in a leopard coat, stepping out of it and into the building and ascending the not-yet-time-worn marble stairs to her dressing room No other access to it except up these stairs.

The suite had three large rooms, a smaller room, a kitchen, a bathroom, and a carpeted foyer separated from the cold swirled marble of the hallway foyer by a glass wall and doors that could be locked. There was another bathroom just outside the foyer. A sign on the door, undoubtedly left by a Dingbat, read, "Warning—ceiling may fall—enter at your own risk." Not a childish joke. The ceiling *was* ready to fall. Large patches had already fallen. Pipes were exposed, and God help us! Was that *asbestos*?

When you entered the foyer, you had your choice of two doors. The one on the right led first to the kitchen and then into the rest of the suite that Richard Gere occupied, rooms B and C, plus a bath. On the left you passed through an anteroom to reach room A. The anteroom was to be my office. When Paul Newman and Sidney Lumet made *The Verdict* at Astoria, they shared this suite, Newman occupying A and its anteroom and Lumet Gere's section.

"This is where Newman made his popcorn," said Meg.

More recently the room had been the playpen and poop-out of twelve-year-old girls called The Dingbats, one of them Coppola's daughter Sophia. Their poop was still there. Crayon drawings, Crayolas, old clothing, pillows. A small decrepit refrigerator the size of a modest saloon safe. I could use it, Meg told me. It had been Francis's in the Philippines. The room contained other Philippines memorabilia including a hutch, a beautiful piece of furniture, highly incongruous in this setting. The Dingbats' stuff would be moved out, but the hutch would have to stay. I would have to live with it. No place to move it. Nor could I use it for storage since the drawers were nailed shut. The top would be useful for stacking, sorting, and collating. When my desk was moved into the room, it would be placed flush against a floor radiator between the hutch and a built-in cabinet shelf on the other wall. I could sit facing the room's one large window overlooking Thirty-fifth Street. Above the cabinet shelf was a large wall mirror surrounded on three sides by neon tubing.

Room A contained a large solid-looking desk, lots of books, a typewriter, a couch, and a fireplace. "And who's in here?" I asked.

"James Remar will be. William Kennedy's in here now, but he's moving out."

This wasn't going to work. I said so. "Why?" she asked.

"I have to have a room I can lock. I can't lock this room."

"Yes, you can. You and Jimmy will both have keys."

"It's not the same thing. He'll be coming and going. He could forget to lock it."

My concern was more than just whimsical.

"Look," I told her, "I'm going to have in my possession all of Adger's original—in fact our only—color transparencies . . ." Aside from the few I would have duped to send to *Newsweek* or whoever, I was prohibited from letting these transparencies out of my possession. I couldn't turn them over to Orion until after the picture wrapped, nor would Robert Evans be allowed to have them. They represented a large and important budgetary outlay. One of a kind, each of them. A burdensome responsibility.

"We'll get you a file cabinet you can lock."

I was still dubious.

The only air conditioner for this side of the suite was in room A. With the connecting door shut, as I was sure it would often be once Jimmy moved in, it could be sweltering in this space. Summer was still very much with us. Even with the window up as it was that day, it was extremely hot. I was most unhappy. I wanted a bona fide, certifiable office. This anteroom seemed so makeshift, homey in a way, but totally unexpected. Quartered in here with Richard Gere? Not to mention Remar? How is Gere going to like this arrangement? How will Remar? How will I?

"I watched you work at the Plaza," Meg said. "You can work anywhere." She had let me share a makeshift office with her at the hotel. "Once we fix this up for you, you'll be happy." With a smile, she added, "And you'll thank me."

She was absolutely right. I did and I do.

But it took forever to get a desk, even longer to get a telephone. I got the phone when the production office crew got tired of taking the proliferating messages coming in for me. In the meantime I had to make do with Kennedy's desk and telephone since he usually came in late. I looked over his research books, searching for clues. There was *Pigeons and How to Raise Them*, relevant to the film's pigeons-on-the-roof scene. *Swanson on Swanson*. Several books dealing with Harlem and the black experience: *The Fire Next Time* by James Baldwin, *Nigger Heaven* by Carl Van Vechten, *Home to Harlem* by Claude McKay, *Carl Van Vechten and the Irreverent Decades* by Bruce Kellner, and *Minnie the Moocher and Me* by Cab Calloway. Books by Brecht, James Joyce, Duke Ellington, W. H. Auden, Polly Adler, Pauline Kael, Langston Hughes. Books on jazz figures: Satchmo, Eddie Condon, Bix Beiderbecke. *Sometimes I Wonder* by Hoagy Carmichael. *Plutarch's Lives*. *Stranger at the Party* by Helen Lawrenson. *Esquire's 1944 Jazz Book*. *Jazz Masters of the 30s* by Rex Stewart. *Jazz Masters of the 20s* by Richard Hadlock. Books about gangsters: *Gang Rule in New York* by Craig Thompson and Allen Raymond, *George Raft* by Lewis Yablonsky, *No Cover Charge* by Robert Sylvester. *Lena Horne* by Horne and Richard Schickle. *Nietzsche* by Richard Hayman. *The New Testament*.

I realized early that Richard Gere was more of a loner than any actor with whom I had ever worked: no entourage, no aides, no wife bringing baked goods or knitting, no lovers, no friends. There would be little fraternization with James Remar: considering the *Bent* connection, I was surprised. He was said to be engaged to a "Brazilian heiress," as *USA Today* called her. I never saw her, and Richard never mentioned her. His supposed assistant Rob Gach was rarely around. He brought in Gere's toilet articles and would verify that the refrigerator was stocked with Perrier and yogurt, each in large quantities. The actual purchasing and delivering of these items was left to George Shutt, a man hired specifically for that purpose and to clean Richard's suite three mornings a week. Shutt turned out to be a great help to me as well.

Richard spent a lot of time listening to records, studying music, and reading biographies of musicians. He was dedicated to the concept of Dixie Dwyer as first and foremost a jazz musician, the peer of any of his day. This was the part of Dixie Dwyer that was in danger of getting lost in the plot shuffle as the scripts evolved and multiplied, and it was this part of the character that Richard Gere tried desperately to hold on to throughout production.

Richard played piano a lot, and he was good. Meg Hunnewell and I actually moved the piano into place for Richard. We situated other furniture, thinking it would be rearranged later. He left most of it where we put it. I asked Meg why she and I and not Astoria maintenance men were doing all the moving. Meg said, "What have you got to publicize at the moment?" Without a telephone and work space, not much.

When Richard wasn't playing the piano, he was usually practicing cornet. If he wasn't playing an instrument, he usually had old jazz records on his turntable: Bix Beiderbecke, Benny Goodman, Coleman Hawkins, Fletcher Henderson. Except when William Kennedy put in a rare appearance, Richard and I were mostly alone in the suite, each of us doing his separate thing. He looked in on me from time to time, usually when my head was buried in a book (no, not just for fun: for research). He was worried about how Remar would cope with this set-up, Gere with his musical instruments and records and me with my typewriter clacking away.

Okay, back-story.

The Dingbats.

Responsible for the first wave of firings. Quickly rescinded. More likely, simply ignored. Before my time and tenure.

I first heard about it when I received the October 1983 issue of *Film Comment*. Nice interview with Coppola by David Thompson and Linda Gray. I mentioned to Coppola how much I liked it.

"Yes," he replied, "but in that kind of interview they always print exactly what you say, and what you say exactly is not always exactly what you mean."

A provocative variation on "I was misquoted."

In their story, Thompson and Gray wrote, "He pierced his beleaguered greeting with an excited story about having fired a group of secretaries, that afternoon at Astoria Studios, because they had been short-tempered with his daughter, Sophia, and her friends who were trying to help round the place. 'I simply can't abide that kind of nine-to-five attitude. It's not conducive to the kind of filmmaking I believe in.'"

The Dingbats put out primitive but charming newsletters and bulletins. With the blessing and encouragement of Sophia's father, they made the studio their domain. There were those who thought their extension into some areas of that domain intrusive. The result was what Coppola called a row.

Grace Blake recalled it all too well. "He was fresh from rehearsal, after having worked on the script with Bill Kennedy all weekend. Without sleep, I believe." A thirty-five-hour writing session that Kennedy told me about. "He was really tired. The pressure was on to get the script out. He had worked his behind off. My feeling was that he did not like the script."

He handed the script over to David Golden on Monday morning; and Golden, Bob Girolami, and Grace worked out how they were going to handle the copying and distribution of it. It was decided that five copies should be run off immediately. One of these would go straight to a printer/copier who was waiting to receive it to run off mass copies. One copy would go to Evans, two to the Doumani brothers, and one retained in the production office for the use of department heads until they could get copies of their own.

Grace said, "I was going to have my assistants continue making copies to get to the actors as fast as they came off the machine. Everybody was working at fever pitch. Add to which, the agent of two of the tap dancers was sitting at my desk, and I was having to deal with that.

"Sophia and one of the other girls were running around, in and out, adding to the confusion, at which point Sophia said, 'I want to help.'

"'That won't be necessary,' I told her."

There was no physical space where Sophia could work, nor was there any task at the moment at which she and her friend would not be more of a hindrance than a help. Nor did anybody have time to instruct them.

"We weren't running a kindergarten," she said, referring drolly to another of Coppola's quotes in *Film Comment*: "'. . . One of my great frustrations, as with many children, was that I didn't have friends, or that I didn't get to be in school long enough or wasn't able to keep my early friends from kindergarten where I was very happy. Kindergarten was really—and I'm not exaggerating—was five times as good as the rest of this life. It's never gotten back to that. For me it was a magical time . . . and, if anything, I tried to create that again.'"

Grace continued, "Pretty soon the girls were back. Running in, running out. Again they wanted to help. This we didn't need. Things were tense enough as it was. Again I told them 'Thank you very much but we're very busy at this time.' They left. Back in two shakes. 'My father wants a script,' Sophia says. 'He'll get one as soon as we have it,' I tell her.

"I shoo her out. I call Fred Roos's secretary. 'Please don't send the children down here again,' I tell her. 'We'll send the script at soon as it's assembled.'

"No sooner said than here comes Sophia. Now demanding. 'My father wants a script and he wants it now.'

"'When it's ready,' I said."

Then Grace had called Coppola's secretary to tell her that the script would be sent as soon as it was ready and that it was not necessary to keep sending the children for it.

"I'd hardly hung up before Francis was down on us like a tarantella—whirling, yelling, screaming, stomping. It was a real floorshow. His big number was 'How dare you yell at my children!'

"I said, 'I didn't *yell* at your children. I *spoke* to your children. There's a difference, Mr. Coppola.'

"He said, 'How dare you answer me back!' If Francis is the floorshow, I must be the heckler. 'You yelled at my child.'

"The man was beyond reasoning with. I said, 'Mr. Coppola, I have three children of my own. I speak to them. I don't yell at them. To yell at a child is counterproductive. I think to yell at anyone is counterproductive.'

"David tried meekly to defend me, and Francis snapped at him, 'Get out of here! You're fired! You're done!' Meaning me too and everybody who worked for me and David.

"While he was carrying on, I went back to my typewriter, trying to ignore him, trying to finish the dancers' contracts, then I thought, no, I owe him my attention. So I stood and faced him. He continued his tirade. I was as quiet as death.

"It went on. I won't bore you. I was trying to speak to a man who was at the moment unspeakable. You could hear a pin drop anywhere in the office. It was embarrassing, and ugly ugly ugly. Everyone was afraid to breathe.

"I truly felt for Francis. I felt like saying, 'Francis, calm down, you're going to have a heart attack.' He was so damn tired. He wanted to get out of the studio so damn badly. Maybe it was a good out. At any rate, he left and didn't come back that day.

"Stephen Goldblatt was in the next office. He heard it all. After Francis left, he said to me, 'Oh, Grace, I'm so sorry. It could have been me. It could have been anybody.'

"And the dancers' agent sat through it all, stunned.

"I saw him shortly after the incident at a Film Week ceremony at the mayor's office. He was surprised to see me there, I'm sure. Our eyes met but we each quickly broke contact. Later we passed each other in a hallway. Neither of us spoke. At the wrap party we spoke for the first time since the incident. He came over to me and said, 'Thank you.'"

* * *

On Monday, September 26, the first day of the sixth week of production, word came about the firings. This time not "a group of secretaries" fired in a fit of pique who would forget they were fired and continue to work. Another group altogether. News of the firings drifted into the studio like dust and insinuations, to be run into like early morning cobwebs. In annoyance you brushed one aside only to find another in your face. The Sunday Night Massacre we called it. The firings had taken place the night before with telephone calls from Barrie Osborne, acting for Coppola. A toppling of the entire Robert Evans totem pole. The rumors had been rampant for weeks, but still we were all surprised at the extent of it.

Milt Forman was already gone and now executive producer Dyson Lovell would go as well. I regretted his dismissal although I had exchanged maybe five sentences with him since our initial meeting. Still, I felt in him I had a friend in court. On a personal level I was saddened to hear that Meg Hunnewell would go. Melissa Prophet was out (and I hadn't even known she was in). Composer Ralph Burns was dismissed as was choreographer George Faison, a personal friend of Lovell's. Jim Kelly was out because he was Lovell's personal secretary and Rob Gach because he was seen as part of the package.

David Golden was fired a second time, this time for real.

I told Richard Gere that I was holding my breath.

He asked me, "Who hired you, Vicar?"

I gave him the run-down. The rigmarole.

"In other words, you don't know," he said. "Maybe you're safe. But watch it. This is the most homophobic production I've ever been on."

I was surprised by the warning but appreciative of it, in no way offended. But I wondered what I had said, what I had done, to have so signaled to him. Had news of my body rub against Ron Howard at the Plaza gotten around?

(Vicar.

When Gere began calling me "Vicar" and "Reverend Tom," I asked him why.

"I don't know why," he said. "I guess it's because you look like a vicar."

What does a vicar look like? Handsome, dashing, irresistible?

Then Jimmy Remar started calling me that too. I became the vicar of the Diana Ross Suite.)

The firings were primarily political, not for the budgetary and artistic reasons cited. Coppola had been given the tool in his deal with Evans. I'm certain he meant all along to use it. Of course, many of those he fired had been made superfluous now that he had elevated his own support staff in position and power.

Grace thought that David Golden was especially wronged. She feared Chris Cronyn, named production manager in his stead, was unqualified. "Even as location manager, he was a novice. He got the job because of Sylbert who is a friend of his parents." Because of our mutual baptism by fire during the first week of production, Chris and I had become somewhat bonded. When I heard of his promotion, I asked him frankly, "Do you think you're up to it?" Evidently no one else had asked him that. "I hope so," he said modestly.

He got off to a shaky beginning. He called a meeting of department heads in his office. He leaned back with both feet resting in a crossed position on his newly claimed desk, hands clasped behind his head, to tell these people, most of whom had been hired by Golden, all with years of experience in the industry and their respective fields, that they could feel free to come to him with all their problems. The consensus was that it should be the other way around: Chris should come to them for help because they all foresaw his needing it.

They resented his paternalism. The only support they could see behind it was a title.

On my list of particulars presented to David Golden and Milt Forman had been the stipulation that I would be provided with an expense account. I wanted it written into the deal memo, the first and only time I've ever wanted it so specified. On other films on which I've worked, it had been taken for granted, a given, that the unit publicist would have an expense account. The expenses would be accounted for on a weekly basis with petty cash vouchers I turned in, most items accompanied by receipts. Transportation and "entertainment" (restaurants, drinks, and theater) are normal weekly items on a publicist's account. The charges encompass the entertaining—sometimes with a specific goal in mind relative to the project, sometimes not—of press or actors or department heads from the production.

Shortly after Chris took over as production manager, he asked about a twenty dollar item on my petty cash voucher. It was for having pizza and drinks with actor Tom Waits at an unpretentious Village restaurant, a far cry from the usual tab which would have been three or four times as much. Chris said, "Did you have dinner with him, or did you take someone else to dinner to talk about him?"

A third degree over pizza?

"Tom Waits was in London on the day you said you had dinner with him."

Oh, shit.

I'd made a mistake, I said. We'd had the pizza the week before. I'd mislaid the receipt and simply added it to this week's expenses. Chris let it pass.

A friend in accounting, Jim Bigwood (who later would be responsible for getting me a location film in

Louisiana, *A Gathering of Old Men*, what turned out to be my final film job) took me aside a day or so later. "Kurt Wollner found the pizza thing," he said. Wollner had been working on the film so long and so fruitlessly trying to get a completion guarantee that he was evidently now going over all petty cash vouchers with the attention to nuance of a diamond cutter.

"Did you have an agreement with David about an expense account?" Jim asked.

"Of course. It's in my deal memo."

"Could you have a copy of it ready just in case it's needed?" he asked

"Chris should have a copy," I said. "It would be in David's files."

"For your own protection," said Jim. "There's so much we can't find."

It sounded like the firings might not be over.

* * *

William Kennedy's desk, typewriter, and books had been cleared out of the office. The couch remained as did the telephone, which I continued using since mine had yet to be installed. With Meg gone, I wondered if it ever would be. Although the room hadn't yet been set up for occupancy by Remar, he and his buddy Tony Dingman had begun using it. He would close the door between my room and his, not to exclude me so much as to give me privacy. Besides, the three of us hadn't developed a rapport yet. Certainly it wasn't to hide anything from me. The door had a loosely curtained glass window, and anything going on that couldn't be smelled could be seen clearly in outline if anyone cared to look.

Once when Jimmy and Tony left the room to go to the set, I went in to use the telephone. There was a distinct odor of marijuana. It was a high just to be in the heady atmosphere. There was a knock on the door. It was Richard in his tuxedo costume and his patent leather hair. He walked over to me where I stood in the far corner with the phone in my hand. With each step his smile got more knowing. He raised his head and sniffed. "This is something I didn't know about you."

I put my hand over the phone and said, "Remar was just in here."

"That's your excuse."

He asked me if I had a key to his room. I didn't, of course. "Maybe you ought to have one," he said.

His door was locked and he couldn't get in. He went in search of Jim Skotchdopole, the rosy-cheeked production assistant assigned to him. They returned together and unlocked the door, and Richard took possession of the key. He suggested that I be the keeper of the key. "That way you can come in whenever you please, use the kitchen, whatever. The refrigerator's stocked. Help yourself. I can't begin to eat and drink it all."

I said that it wouldn't do any good for me to keep it. I was in and out as often as he was.

"It has to be kept in here someplace," he said. "Where can we hide it?" He decided that the ledge over my doorsill would be a good place.

Skotch thought that location was too precarious and suggested that we hide it under the carpet. He raised a flap to show us, and I knelt to place it there. Richard grinned at us. "The problem is, I go up, I don't go down."

I glanced at Skotch. He didn't crack a smile and wasn't about to. He was as poker-faced as Buster Keaton at his sternest. I fear I was less so, and no doubt my cheeks grew rosier than Skotch's. But I let it lie there. Along with the key.

The incident reminded me of the retort of a young actor of some renown featured in a film on which I worked in the early 1970s. Cast and crew stayed in the same hotel, which had three floors. I got on the elevator on the second floor. He was the only person on it and had just come back from location on his way to his suite on the third floor. The elevator ascended. "Oh, I was going down!" I said, startled. The actor said slyly, "As long as you're going down, why don't you come up?"

As in the armed services (I'd had four years of naval duty), there was verbal as well as pantomimed homosexual horseplay from time to time on set. Except for the occasional repartee with Remar, some of which might be so interpreted and which Coppola conceivably might have overheard, I hadn't participated in any of it. I remember once in front of Francis a young good-looking grip was kissed near the mouth by another who then told him, "Oh, I forgot to tell you—I got herpes." The other shot back, "And I forgot to tell you—I got AIDS!" (Grim humor. AIDS had been with us publicly only about two years then.) The neon-pink-costumed dancers who played the Berry Brothers—Benny Clory, Ivory Wheeler, and Bernard Manners—referred campily to their tall tan and terrific selves as the Pink Faggots. They brought humor to the set with gay-alluding shenanigans.

I spoke with a woman production assistant about two men, both said to be gay, who had been fired. Rumor had it that the firing was in part because they were homosexual, the inference being that Francis was homophobic. The production assistant didn't think that was the case, nor did I. She cited an actor in a featured role in our film. "Francis gets along with him beautifully, and he is flamboyantly, unrepentantly gay," she said. "Yes," I replied, "maybe he can deal with someone that open about it. But how about somebody more circumspect?" She named another actor in the film very conspicuously married but openly if circumspectly gay. "Francis has no trouble with him either. They get along great." She thought that Francis might be threatened by gay people on the staff if he thought they were ganged up against him in a political way. His paranoia might have read something like that into a number of production situations, she thought, but those had seemingly been resolved.

More damning perhaps, she wondered if Francis was capable of dealing with anyone on a mature level. "And look at his attraction to children, or his staged attraction to them. I'm not sure how genuine it is. He'll see a child on set and make a point of going up to her, for it's usually a her, and speaking to her."

I thought back to Coppola's *Film Comment* interview and his remarks about the joys of kindergarten.

Gay Thomas!

It was the custom of the Cotton Club to designate Sunday night as Celebrity Night in honor of show biz stars who went there on their night off, and the movie included just such a scene. The master of ceremonies was played by Tom Waits. Megaphone to his mouth, he introduced the stars as a spotlight picked them out where they sat, usually at ringside.

"Over here we have Fannie Brice . . . James Cagney . . . Joan Crawford . . . Tallulah Bankhead . . . Babe Ruth."

There were lookalikes for all of them. Dixie Dwyer, now a movie star, was to be the last celebrity introduced, but Gere was not on set for this part of the sequence. With what happened, I was glad he wasn't there.

Only one side of the club set was being photographed. I sat at a table on a raised platform to left of the stage. The camera and crew were positioned on the dance floor. An actor named Tucker Smallwood sat with me, a black man who looked jazzy indeed although of a different Jazz Age than that depicted in the film. He wore tight leather outfits when not working. As Kid Griffin, the club's maitre d', he wore black tie.

Coppola was on the stage instructing Waits in the proper flourish for introducing a particular celebrity, showing him where to look for each one. Glancing toward Tucker and me, he whispered to Waits. Waits, as instructed, gestured in our direction and said into his megaphone, "And down here we have Gay Thomas!"

Tucker Smallwood whirled out of his chair and joined a group of female dancers sitting at a table in shadows to our rear. Suddenly I was alone, Tom Waits looking at me, everyone looking at me, at the frozen smile on my face, at my red face. The cameraman, the soundman, the script supervisor glanced at me anxiously, askance, as confused as Tom Waits was. I was riveted to my seat, pinned there by all the eyes upon me. I couldn't whirl out of my chair like Tucker. Too late for that. Why hadn't I whirled with him, I wondered. There was nothing to do but sit there glued to my seat, sickly smiling. I couldn't image why Francis had done this. I wondered if perhaps there had been a real Gay Thomas during this period, a Dorothy Kilgallen type, a journalist, a socialite. I was kidding myself. Seeing the reaction, the people looking at me, Francis looked too. I read in his face something tentatively apologetic, concerned, as if to say, "Hey, you misunderstood me, can I take it back?"

Both at the time of the incident and later, I felt waves of sympathy directed toward me. The incident had clearly been viewed as a slap at me and it stung. No one ever referred to it in my presence. No doubt it was seen as part of the fabric of Francis's current behavior. He was likely to do anything, people said. Crew whose names I didn't know and who would normally pass me without acknowledgment made a point of being friendly, of saying hello.

Yet maybe I was hasty in my reading of the matter. Francis did manage to get off the hook on this one, but I didn't learn about it until a week or so later. I don't think some of the crew who witnessed the incident ever heard about it. I doubt if Tom Waits did.

I was meeting with Milena Canonero in the wardrobe room. I had asked her to give me a list of five showgirls who she thought could best model clothing in a photo session we had planned. She was busy when I arrived, so I chatted with key wardrobe man Al Craine. I told him about my new celebrity status and the name that went with it. "Oh, that's very funny," he said. Funny, Al? I didn't think it funny at all.

"Well, of course I wasn't there," Al apologized.

Milena beckoned me over and handed me the list of showgirls. The name at the top of the list was Gay Thomas. My first thought was that Milena had heard the story and written the name in as a joke. She had not. There was a real, honest-to-goodness Gay Thomas!

Milena showed me a picture of her. "Isn't she gorgeous?" said Milena. Indeed she was. But if I the publicist hadn't known of her existence, at least her name, certainly the crew outside of wardrobe couldn't have.

When Tucker Smallwood whirled from my table, was it to stand with the real Gay Thomas rather than sit with the bogus one? For there in the shadows behind me, she must have stood and bowed or maybe waved. Whatever, there were evidently few who saw her do it. Else why was everyone looking at *me*? Had I outed myself by circumstance and assumption?

The real Gay Thomas and I became friends. I never told her how I had almost usurped her identity

When I next saw Francis after the incident, he sought me out with his eyes, compelling me to look at him. When I did, he nodded. The smile may only have been in his eyes but it was decidedly there.

* * *

It was Wednesday, September 28, two days after the firings. A man materialized at my office door to say, "You can have a phone in half an hour *if* we can get in next door." The wires needed were in Richard's bedroom closet. I didn't want to reveal our key's hiding place and didn't have to. The door was unlocked. Richard returned while the workman was there and made a quick change and quick exit, clicking his fingers at me as we went, "You're going to get a phone!" He thought it a scandalous joke that the publicist didn't have one yet.

Later that day a buzzing fly tested my endurance. I chased it about the room and was embarrassed when Richard caught me at it. "The vicar is dancing!" he exclaimed.

That night when I got home, there was a message on my answering machine. Call Liz Smith. Oh shit. About the firings, I supposed. Her assistant noted that they had been unable to reach me at the studio.

I was prohibited from dealing with Liz. Even though she printed three or four items about the film every week, they were mostly derogatory.

Don't ask.

(Well, okay, ask. It seemed to involve a simmering nasty feud between Liz Smith and Bobby Zarem.

Richard later asked, "You know what it's about, don't you?"

Sure. It was the giggle of New York entertainment and media circles. Zarem had spent a bundle printing and mailing—to an extensive and choice industry list—wedding invitations announcing the betrothal of Liz Smith to another woman.

Liz is reputed to have hired detectives who confirmed that Zarem did it. In an unwise fit of pixie maliciousness, one supposed, perhaps miffed at the short-shrifting of his clients in Liz's column.

As for the bogus nuptials, Richard said, "I got an invitation myself. If I can find it, I'll show it to you.")

Not dealing with Liz Smith was nothing new to me. I was fortunate on other jobs to have the services of New York's premier column planter, Mike Hall. If I had wanted Liz to have anything, I gave it to Mike.

Before getting back to Liz, I met with Fred Roos. "I think it's a matter of courtesy to return calls," he said. "I know about Zarem's quarrel with Liz Smith, if that's what's bothering you. Return the call. Bobby doesn't have to know. By taking it out on Francis, Liz is taking it out on Bobby. Which is not fair to Francis.

Francis has been put in an untenable position, made to be the whipping boy because of a feud totally unrelated to him, blamed for every excessive expenditure on this movie, and for everything else. Yes, I would say, call her."

All Liz wanted to know was Dyson Lovell's title. "We simply want to identify him correctly," her assistant told me. "We're printing a nice item about him, and when you write about someone in connection with a film you have to identify him." Obviously she hadn't heard about the firings yet. Dyson Lovell, for all we knew at that point, might well end up without a title.

If Liz hadn't heard about the firings yet, both *Variety* and *Hollywood Reporter* had. I got calls from them next day. My new telephone went into overdrive. I fudged as best I could, but the fudge refused to set. The word was out, and one by one the axed began to talk.

Francis the whipping boy.

I think everybody connected with the movie but me called Liz Smith or other columnists. Among the derogatory items was one imputing a romantic interest on Coppola's part in Diane Lane. Francis was angry and hurt. Not at me. I think he knew that I'd had nothing to do with it. Diane took it in stride, playfully hitting out at me as I passed. A prop man was particularly indignant. (Crew members were fond of and protective of Diane.) "It's so unfair," he said, and wanted me to "do something." Like what? "Call her, demand a retraction." It would only make matters worse, I told him, as well as give the item some credence. Diane's father, Bert Lane, did call Liz Smith and called me later to say that he had. "And what did she say?" I asked. "She sort of laughed," he said. "She said she was sorry she had gotten it wrong."

Still no press allowed on set, of course, but it was difficult keeping track of and identifying strangers on the set. They began to appear with greater frequency. But who were these people? Some obviously were friends of Francis's: Cher, William Friedkin, Bud Yorkin, Martin Scorsese. But how easy it would be for press to sneak into the building. There was a side door on Thirty-fifth Avenue down from where the original main entrance had been. A guard was posted, but he could be easily distracted. We wore yellow passes encased in plastic pinned to shirt or lapel. I was not about to pierce certain fabric with it and often kept mine in my pocket and flashed it when I had to. We came and went through this door, making our way along with a throng of accountants, secretaries, and other clerical and fiscal staff. Anyone with a bit of audacity and bounce could brazen through easily.

Bob Girolami caught a guy with a camera case on the fringes of the Cotton Club set. He was mingling with the crew and extras, camera poised and ready. When he was questioned, he claimed to be a friend of Robert Evans. Those were not necessarily the magic words, but if true he could not be unceremoniously kicked out of the studio. Girolami said, "Fine, come with me, we'll call Bob Evans." The man ran for the exit.

More and more extras were brandishing Kodaks. With the work light as low as it was, their pictures couldn't have amounted to much. It was petty to quibble, but still it was a no-no. A black male stand-in for an important actor took offense when I asked him to put his camera away. Rudely, he said nothing. He continued to hold the camera in his lap, not looking at me. I kept an eye on him from a distance until I had to leave the set. I asked an assistant director to see that the guy didn't use the camera. The next day the stand-in cornered me. He was angry. "You think I'm not intelligent enough to hear what you're saying? You think I'm not bright, maybe? You asked me not to take any picture. I didn't. Then you insult me by speaking to the AD. You think I didn't know what you were doing? The minute you left, he came over to me and told me the same thing you did. *I do not have to be told twice. I do have ears.*"

And a mouth.

I could understand his anger. I said I was sorry if I had offended him, and I tried to explain to him that there were union rules. It was necessary to pay stand-by union photographer wages should stills be taken on the set by anyone other than the contracted stills photographer. Far-fetched as it might seem, I told him, he might conceivably have been construed as one and the information passed on to the union.

Maurice Hines, Sr. (father to Gregory and Maurice Jr.) and a black casting woman overheard us talking. Both later asked me about it and both sided with me. The casting woman told me that the stand-in was already close to being fired for insubordination.

"Don't fire him on my account," I pleaded. "It's all right now. I don't want to cause him any trouble." Besides, perhaps I hadn't handled it as well as I should. In retrospect, I wished I had just ignored it.

Cameras continued to proliferate among the cast and crew. One day, out of a line of eight showgirls, four of them had cameras, snapping away for their scrapbooks. I continued to remind one and all that none of these photos was to be published. Word reached me that black newspapers and magazines had been contacted by one of our technicians who had said he could supply them with all the pictures of the Cotton Club set that they wanted. I found out who he was. He was not in a position to photograph much that would be worth anything to anybody, and we never saw him with a camera. We said nothing, and nothing came of it.

One day I saw a well-dressed attractive woman on the set taking notes. I asked her about it. She was a friend of William Kennedy's, she said. The notes were for her "souvenir." I explained our press policy and asked that her souvenir not be published while we were in production.

Shortly before David Golden left the production, the front desk called him. They wanted to know if it was okay for a TV crew to come inside. He told them he couldn't give them the okay, it would have to come from me.

Carol Jenkins and an NBC-TV crew were outside the building. Jenkins, a young black woman, was a welcome and engaging fixture of the local evening news. She had a sense of humor and a personality as gorgeous as her smile. I told her what she already knew, no press allowed on set. "When the policy changes, you'll be the first to know."

She had the sweet benign look of a dog to whom you deny a bone who doesn't mind because behind your back she's already eaten it. She said, "We're doing a three-part series on *The Cotton Club*."

Oh? "What material are you using?"

"Talking to dancers. As they leave the building. Or we take them outside here."

That sounded ominous. I had a practiced ear for nuance. Sounded like they were coming *into* the building and taking the dancers outside. Coming into the building with cameras. The question was, what had they got on tape?

When the three-part series aired some time later, sure enough, there was Carol herself—dancing, yet!— with Maurice Hines, Jr., in one of the studio's basement rehearsal rooms. The Jenkins-Hines duo was delightful to watch, but she had no permission from the company to be there. I was starting to suspect that Kaufman-Astoria Studios wanted publicity for itself. Shades of the Brooklyn proprietor on the first week's shoot.

The studio administration of Kaufman-Astoria was represented by a woman named Liz Allen, who denied complicity in allowing the NBC crew into the building. She reminded me that she had called to my attention two *Washington Post* interlopers when they had walked into the building with one of our casting directors who thought it might be fun if her friend, a journalist, did a story on casting from the angle of extras and featured players. A number of the players had worked in theater and their names were known in theatrical circles even though their screen time in *The Cotton Club* would be negligible. The journalists were politely evicted, the casting director lightly admonished.

Even without sneaking in by the side door, it was quite easy for anyone to get into the building. Any visitor whose entry had been approved by a *Cotton Club* executive or department head could stop at the desk and get an entry pass, and department heads were as prevalent as freckles on a farm boy. Hell, *I* was a department head. I rarely granted anyone access to the building, but I must have been the exception.

And really! Who is going to stop you if you are a beautiful and easily recognizable woman such as Carol

Jenkins, escorted by the popular and ebullient actor-dancer Maurice Hines?

Okay, so maybe Liz Allen was off the hook on that one. She wasn't off the hook for *Calendar Magazine*, the Sunday feature of the *Los Angeles Times*. She brought a *Calendar* reporter, Lee Grant, to the studio in my absence. She told me about it later and said that Lee would be doing a story about Astoria Studios. Oh, sure. Like the TV crews who would have been photographing only the proprietor's "beautiful rooms" in Brooklyn and paying no attention to *The Cotton Club* shooting taking place right in front of their noses. Lee Grant was collecting material on *The Cotton Club* for a story that would be written by Dale Pollock. Grant even had access to Coppola, an incident that was later to result in heated phone calls, memos, letters, and arguments involving myself, Allen, and Barrie Osborne.

The *Calendar* story appeared in the December 4, 1983 issue. "The set has been closed to the press," the story read, "except for brief visits by *Calendar* reporters and a photographer." We privileged few, right? It left me wide open for criticism and complaint from reporters who wondered why their requests to visit the set had not been honored. Could I say to them, "They snuck in"? I could and I did.

Also from *Calendar*:

". . . Gossip has flowed from the Kaufman-Astoria Studios like bathtub gin at the Cotton Club—tales of cast and crew members not being paid . . ." (True) ". . . of one long weekend when key crew members were fired . . ." (Right on the money) ". . . of 'a friend' of the financiers getting $100,000 for speaking one line as a hatcheck girl . . ." (Actually she got $7,500, which ain't bad).

Michael Daly in his post-production exposé in *New York Magazine* reported that the hatcheck girl was paid $25,000. I'd heard a rumor of $75,000. The $100,000 figure had been printed in a Liz Smith column:

ANOTHER BIT OF FLUFF FROM THE COTTON CLUB
Now here's a goodie and I'll give it to you in the spirit of rollicking rumor and juvenile apocrypha. It seems one of the major backers of the movie "Cotton Club" is a fellow who has invested millions of perfectly pressed and starched dollars in the project now filming here. "The Man," as we shall call him, is invariably around on the Astoria set watching over his investment. Also present is his girlfriend, an attractive young woman we shall call "Rita," because that is not her name.

"The Man" wanted producer Robert Evans and director Francis Ford Coppola to put "Rita" into the movie. So she became a "Cotton Club" cigarette girl, with one line of dialogue. After the day's work "as an actress." Our "Rita" appeared at the production office asking when and how she would be paid. Told she'd receive the standard fee for bit players, Rita said, "Oh. No, that's not right. I have a contract signed by Robert Evans." And so, the rumor goes, indeed she does. The contract calls for Rita to receive—are you sitting down— $100,000 for her one line and one day of work, plus 2% of the gross profits of the movie!

It has been confirmed that "The Man" and "Rita" do really exist and in the context stated. And "Rita" did do her work. One insider on the movie says, "Nobody has seen 'Rita's' contract, if it exists, but nobody doubts that it might!"

A wonderful tale. I don't know what we did before we had "Cotton Club" to entertain us. And again, I hear the footage shot so far is just terrific.

At a mid-production party and screening for cast and crew and invited guests at the studio on October 14, we are able to see Rita in action in a scene with Lisa Persky, who as Mrs. Dutch Schultz suspects that this cigarette girl is fucking her husband. As if to the Bette Davis manor and manner born, she snarls challenge and invective. Pure fire. Knowing all the footage available on the scene from the dailies, I was annoyed that the sequence as edited favored the cigarette girl. I told Lisa, "Don't worry, when it's re-edited they'll throw it to you."

"If they don't throw it out," Lisa said. "It was all improvised anyway—for *her* benefit."

* * *

News of the firings had spread like spilled ink. People couldn't figure out who was the most stained, those fired or those who remained. The telephone was rarely quiet. Everyone wanted to know how far the stain had spread, if it was still spreading, and why the spill in the first place. I told the callers they would have to speak with Mark Kane at the Zarem office and contentedly and perhaps smugly hung up. The Zarem office wanted to be involved. *Let* them be involved. Mark Burchard, coming through with wardrobe for Jimmy Remar, said snidely but approvingly, "Mean."

I decided it wasn't so bad having an outside agency on the film. Fuck 'em.

I really got a kick out of Mark Burchard. If Richard Sylbert's trademark was his safari jacket, Mark's was his ever-on-his-head tennis cap. Mark was an actor with the respected Goodman Theater in Chicago and a member of Actors Equity. He told me that he got into costuming by accident. When he got to New York and couldn't find work, he heard they were hiring "spear carriers" at the Metropolitan Opera. Yes, but they only paid three dollars a day and no rehearsal pay. He couldn't live on that, so he decided to check with the head costumer at the opera house to see if he could find some sort of apprentice work. When he came up to the costumer, the costumer mistook Mark for someone else and started yelling at him. "Where have you *been*? I've been looking for you for two weeks!"

"The guy never showed up," said Mark, "and when I did, I was put right to work. The costumer gave me a bolt of material and showed me a pattern and said 'Cut it,' and then he just left me with it. He wanted it in two hours. He had two assistants. They saw the look on my face and asked 'What's wrong?' I confessed to them that I didn't know a thing about costuming other than what an actor picks up on the run, and I was going to have to wing it. They both thought it was a hoot. Whenever I needed help or advice, I'd sneak meetings with them in corners and hallways just like in spy movies."

Onwards and upwards with the arts. The guys must have taught him well, because he was great at what he did. Milena certainly wouldn't have put up with him if he wasn't.

Remar was holding regular open house next door in his room, having wardrobe discussions and fittings and generally a high old time. He and his guests treated the unfolding public relations trauma as entertainment. Each time I hung up the phone, some ribald badinage ensued.

Mine was not an office that could harbor secrets, not unless I went beyond it to make clandestine phone calls or waited for the area to clear, which blissfully it often did. Jimmy was friendly with Coppola's son Gian-Carlo, whom we called Gio. He worked as director of montage and second unit. Gio was in and out of Jimmy's room, sometimes with a woman friend, more often alone. I couldn't help but wonder if he wasn't a conduit to his father. If so, I thought it could only be helpful. One day he was having lunch with Jimmy, and Jimmy asked me if I had any salt and pepper. They were settling down to sandwiches and French fries and needed the seasoning. I knew there was a salt shaker in Richard's kitchen. They watched me as I got the key from under the carpet, went into Richard's suite, and returned with salt and pepper shakers. I told Jimmy he could keep them since Richard had another set. When I put the key back under the carpet, Jimmy said, grinning diabolically, "You *don't* have to find another hiding place, you know."

I thought to myself, wait till Francis hears that I've got a key to Richard's room. A chilling thought.

One day when I came back from lunch, Jimmy told me, "Your phone's been ringing off the hook." He wondered if I might unplug the phone when I knew I was going to be gone for some time. (Sure.) When he wasn't working or partying, he slept on a cot just the other side of my mirror. He referred to it as "sleeping beside the Vicar." Of course it turned out that unplugging the phone didn't do all that much good. When I returned to my anteroom office, I would usually find that someone—most likely Mark Burchard or Jimmy's makeup man—had been at my desk, plugged in the phone to use it, and (naturally) left it plugged in. Luckily, nothing seemed to disturb Jimmy once he fell asleep. Exhausted by the long daily application of special body and facial makeup and by the artistic development of the nasty character he was portraying, he was able to sleep through anything. Richard and I learned we had no cause to worry about noise from typewriters or musical instruments.

In one of his trips to Jimmy's room, Mark Burchard told us about a woman who had slipped past security. She was trying to "get" to Richard. Burchard described her to me and added, "Be careful if you see her. She might try to get you too." Jimmy said he'd protect me if she appeared. (She didn't. She was apprehended and escorted away by the police.)

Jimmy was in my office looking at contact sheets of himself, admiring himself in my mirror, and studying the contrast between how he really looked and how he looked in his *Cotton Club* drag. He really did find it a drag, especially the plumper and the shaved hairline.

"You look like Edward G. Robinson," I said, pointing to a specific frame on a contact sheet.

"I know that's a compliment," he said, "but don't depress me." He wanted to know what I was going to write about him.

I picked up a ballpoint pen. "Whatever you want me to." Might as well have fun with this.

"Say that I'm a mercurial personality."

"That's good," I said, and wrote it down.

"Say," he dictated, "that I'm magnetic."

I wrote that down too and said, "How about scintillating?"

He motioned for me to write it down. "Also put sexually insatiable."

"In a press kit?"

"Write it down anyway, Vicar. For your own information."

I looked at him. He said, "C'mon, Reverend Tom, you have to be writing a book about all this. You'll need adjectives to describe me." He spelled insatiable for me. I already had it down. I knew insatiable as well as he did.

"Say that I'm horny."

I laughed. "Oh, come on."

"It might come in handy on a press junket for people to have this information."

His special makeup team, John Caglione and Arlette Greenfield, had entered and were waiting to transform beauty into beast. He motioned them away. He would be with them in a minute.

"Aren't you horny?" he asked me.

In the other room I could hear Caglione and Greenfield giggling. Remar frequently went off on kicks like this.

"Not as horny as you," I replied.

"I've noticed that. Why not?"

I had noticed AIDS, that's why not. I wondered if he had.

"I used to be," I said lamely, not exactly brilliant repartee. I hated that it sounded like an excuse. Besides, I'll bet my testosterone could dance on the ceiling with his any day. Better yet, on the floor.

"What happened?" he pressed.

"I became a publicist, that's what."

It got lamer and lamer.

"Don't use that as an excuse. You're not publicizing anything on *this* movie. You're not publicizing *me*." He went in to the makeup people, gesturing to my pad of adjectives. "Put that on the wall where I can find it. I'll be wanting to add to it."

I did. I taped it to the wall. From time to time we would add another adjective or so.

On a later occasion I overheard a conversation Remar was having with Caglione and Greenfield while they worked on him. They were talking about religion, Mormons, God.

"To me," Jimmy said, "God is my cock."

"May I quote you on that?" I said, standing at the doorway, pen and pad in hand.

"Say that I made my Broadway debut as God. You could hear it all over the audience—'God! The cock!'"

"It was a revelation," I said in the same grand manner.

"I heard you the night you saw *Bent*," he said. "'I have seen the light!' you screamed."

Caglione put a stop to it. "Get out of here," he pleaded with me, "or we'll never get him ready in time."

One of my greatest disappointments in working on *The Cotton Club* was that I was unable to place with Liz Smith an item about James Remar. I sent her before and after shots of him, as he looked with all his hair and without the padding and as he looked after the makeup transformation. Liz's assistant, Clare St. Pugh, kept reassuring me that Liz was going to use it. He kept bringing the item and Remar's pictures to the top of her stack, but repeatedly they got buried again.

Sorry, Jimmy. I did try.

I received instructions from Robert Evans that I was to give a number of transparencies to Mark Damon of PSO to be used at an upcoming MIFED film convention held annually in Milan.

Who was Mark Damon?

What was PSO?

Producers Sales Organization had foreign distribution rights on the film. (Nice if someone had bothered to tell me.) Orion had the domestic rights. Mark Damon *was* PSO. Like Evans, he too was a former actor. Most charming and personable, it turned out.

I took a selection of slides to Damon at Zarem's office. He selected twenty-eight. I wasn't about to yield up the original transparencies. I gave originals to no one. I would never have seen them again. I insisted on duplicates for every submission, regardless of the expense. The originals, if lost or damaged, could not be replaced. I sent the slides as a rush order to the color lab with the information that I'd send them a purchase order when I got back to the studio. We were to be charged a whopping $8.50 per slide rather than the usual $4.25. Of course it would have to be me and not Zarem or Damon who explained this exorbitance to Chris Cronyn and to accounting.

I cautioned Damon that Richard Gere had absolute kill rights, and Zarem confirmed it, "Tightly defined by contract."

Richard had not seen all these transparencies. Even those he had already approved, he said, he wanted to have a new look at before he would allow publication. I wouldn't be able to show him Damon's choices until the next day. Damon said that Gere's kills could be phoned to him in California and he would himself pull them from the twenty-eight.

Richard killed seven of them and was not at all happy that I had let someone have pictures of him that he had not yet seen, let alone approved. He was even unhappier with Evans and Zarem for pressuring me to do so.

But on the whole he was remarkably gracious about it. At least to me.

* * *

On Friday, September 23, the Cotton Club extras started working, and wow! What an operation! And what bitching, too. About *Milena*. The money she is costing the production. Nobody sitting on her. All those extras being costumed and made up and hair cut just for her to *look* at. They're taking photographs of each extra. In costume. A page per person. Special photographers. Adger has no time. The numbers of extras are legion: people everywhere, elegant black people in twenties finery; white people tuxedoed, gowned, coiffed, patrons of the Cotton Club.

Rows of dressing rooms, four or five people in each one. Rows of makeup and hair-styling rooms, three or four people working in each room. Long rectangular collapsible tables set up in the basement hallways, outside the rows of rooms. Mirrors on them, slanted, resting against the dressing room walls. Behind the rows of rooms, folding chairs have been set up. Beyond those are multitudinous rehearsal spaces.

The basement is the holding area for the extras, and I suppose for the dancers too, or maybe they have their own dressing areas in this labyrinth. There are fifty-two dancers on the picture, including Mario Van Peebles who has a couple of specialty numbers with Priscilla Baskerville ("Creole Love Song") and the dancing girls. There are ten hoofers and a number of specialty acts.

Mixed in with all this is a set representing the Ubangi Club, where Dixie Dwyer endears himself to Dutch Schultz by saving his life and another set depicting a radio shop and exterior of the Cotton Club. Gregory Hines and Tom Waits are playing a scene on a narrow flight of stairs built between the basement and the Astoria main stage that duplicates the stairway passage to the Cotton Club.

I even find a screening room I didn't know was there. It is sequestered one-half floor off the main stage, and it is with some shock that Richard and I find out later that it actually opens into his rooms though a narrow passageway and short flight of stairs. An unnerving discovery.

The lot of the extra on such a movie is a hard one.

Sit. Sit. Wait. Wait. Sit. Wait. Wait.

There were two groups of white extras, one for what we called Cotton Club One (the first floorshow extended sequence featured in the film), the other for Cotton Club Two. It took about a month to film the first sequence, a little less for the other. Smaller numbers of white extras were needed as background for two other clubs, the Bamville and the Ubangi, because the showgirls, musicians, and dancers there were predominately black. The Vera's Club scene used only white extras. The extras would all be made up and costumed, and then they would sit, either in holding areas (divided by the geographical position in which the extra would be situated in the Cotton Club) or at assigned tables on the set (and sit, and sit, and sit, for they had to be in place and ready for whenever a sequence would be shot). Because of the films logistics, they were constantly being moved about; and they came to think of themselves as cattle. Moved from holding area to set, from set to commissary, from commissary back to holding area, in packs. To walk among them in their attire and to eavesdrop on their wisecracks was like being in an old MGM or Paramount drawing room comedy. I still have this picture of a group of them in tuxedos and evening gowns being led from the main stage, the leader as always a production assistant with a walkie-talkie. They weren't moving as briskly as the PA would like: it was difficult moving briskly in a mass such as that. The PA had a number of lesser persons assisting her. They were like cattle dogs, verbally prodding, barking at the elegantly dressed herd. A few of the extras began lowing. Others picked it up. Soon it sounded as if I was caught in the middle of a mournful *Red River* cattle drive.

One frustrated woman pinned an open letter on the bulletin board. Other copies she passed among her peers. One found its way to me:

Dear Abby, I know you will think I'm a psycho, but the truth is I have been stuck here in this dungeon for 4 weeks with the Stepford Wife, a windmill, a dancer who is half man and half woman, a yenta, the Queen of England, a kleptomaniac, the Statue of Liberty, and Richard Gere . . .

(Most of these allusions escaped me.)

. . . The scary part of all this is that it's true. They make me get up at 4:30 every morning, and they don't let me rest until 8:00 at night. They have dressed me as a flapper and have led me to believe that it's 1929. They make me inhale poisonous gases, and feed me terrible tasting starchy food. They keep telling me that they will let me rest for a week before they make

me do all this again, but at the end of every day they tell me just one more day. I don't know what to do. I am so exhausted, and I don't know what daylight looks like anymore. Please give me some advice on how to escape this torture.

    Signed, Extra

    P.S. But I want to be a star!

Posted in the wardrobe area is a memo for extras: ". . . Get help in getting undressed. The clothes are antiques . . . You will have to be smocked before you eat . . . Wear no personal jewelry."

Gwen Verdon and Allen Garfield (a.k.a. Allen Goorwitz) told me about an unprovoked act of violence by a black extra against a white one. Gwen had heard that the black extra had a black belt in judo, and the white one, a successful model, was the son of the late actor Lex Barker. Apparently the attacker had a history of sudden and inexplicable violence. "He was fired immediately," Gwen said, "which they say surprised him. I guess he thought he'd be acclaimed, patted on the back. 'Look what I did to Whitey.' Get some publicity. He wanted to be a model so he attacks a model."

"Which made perfect sense. To *him,*" said Garfield.

We speculated about who the mother of the injured Barker might be. Anita Ekberg? Lana Turner? Arlene Dahl? (None of the above, it turned out, but an Irene Lambert whom Barker married in 1959 and with whom Barker had a son, Christopher. The right age for the extra.)

Asides like this keep us going. We gather and we gossip.

I was terribly excited about being able to work with Gwen Verdon, and I think she was excited about playing the mother of Richard Gere and Nicolas Cage. I noticed quickly and commented to Gwen about the "family resemblance" I saw in her, Gere, and Cage. They looked as if they could very well have been mother and sons. In early drafts of the script, Tish Dwyer was a piano teacher, but once Verdon was cast it followed as night the day that she should become a dance instructor, working at home, teaching pre-pubescent boys the social graces of the dance floor.

The way the script kept changing, I was hoping that Verdon's role might be stretched somewhat to allow her to dance. "Even though she's a dancing teacher, it's not a dancing role," she said, "although I do have one lovely moment with Richard on the dance floor of the Cotton Club."

Most of Gwen Verdon's Broadway shows had been realized in collaboration with director/choreographer Bob Fosse, from whom she was divorced but with whom she remained friends. Together they had done *Damn Yankees, New Girl in Town, Redhead, Sweet Charity,* and then in 1975, *Chicago,* in which she co-starred with Chita Rivera and played Roxie Hart, a role Ginger Rogers had played in the earlier film version of her story. (In an interesting turn of events, Richard Gere would play the male lead in the later movie version of that musical.)

Verdon had no idea why Coppola had chosen her to be Tish Dwyer. "I only knew, small part or no, the chance to work with Francis Coppola was something I wasn't going to say 'no' to." He had looked at a made-for-TV film she had done called *Legs* (no relation to Kennedy's novel or to Jack "Legs" Diamond). "Maybe you saw it, it was about Radio City Music Hall and we shot it there. But I've done other things for television. I've done segments of *M*A*S*H*. I think Francis looked at some of those. Actually, I started in television Straight acting. Maybe that's where I'm headed now, after a long sidetrack. Oh, and before that I'd done nightclubs, and in the forties I had an act with Jack Cole."

She and Cole had worked some pretty sleazy joints, and the milieu of the Cotton Club was not exactly foreign to her. She became Cole's assistant as choreographer for movies, and she was teaching Jane Russell and Marilyn Monroe the "Little Girls from Little Rock" number for *Gentlemen Prefer Blondes* when she was given the chance to fly back to New York to audition for Cole Porter's *Can-Can*. The rest is theater history.

We were standing to the rear of the Cotton Club set. A back wall had been removed to facilitate the shooting of a production number as seen from Owney Madden's left rear corner table. They were ready for the take. We watched in silence. Wonderful. They did it again. The song was "Barbecue Bess," sung by Sydney Goldsmith. Not much of it made it into the movie, like so many other numbers didn't, not in their entirety, anyway. There is yet another *Cotton Club* in musical outtakes waiting to be put together. We had the cream of the black actor, singer, dancer, and choreographer crop working at the peak of their craft on this movie, and so much of their work has never been seen other than by those who watched it filmed or saw the rushes. What a terrific DVD it would make. Hey, Francis, when will we get *The Cotton Club Redux?*

Gwen and I talked about how relatively little racial tension there seemed to be on the movie. I did mention the black actor who reacted racially when I asked him to put away his camera. Then of course there was Adger, ready to cry racism if Stephen Goldblatt looked at him cross-eyed or any other way.

"I was brought up on charges once," Gwen told me. "I was a dance captain, rehearsing black dancers who made the charge. I was giving orders just like I'd give to any dancer, white or black. They charged discrimination.

"Bob and I broke the rule that black and white dancers could not dance together. In *Damn Yankees* in 1954, then again in 1957 in the movie, I did a dance where I touched the top of a black dancer's head. I was told, 'You can't touch him.' On *Broadway*! But I did it."

Wait a minute. I take it back. About racial tension. I forgot about Nicolas Cage.

Cage's convincing portrayal of Richard Gere's racist thug brother, Vincent, did not endear himself to many black people on the film, certainly not in our early days on the Cotton Club set.

Nicolas Cage was an unknown quantity to most of them. They didn't see him as an actor but as a piece of shit. He came across as a piece of shit. He had made only a few pictures by the time he started work on *The Cotton Club*. Only *Valley Girls* had been released, while waiting in the wings were *Racing with the Moon* and *Rumble Fish*.

His real name was Coppola. His father was Francis's brother. I once asked him how it was he hadn't been in his uncle's film *The Outsiders*, in which so many other rising young male actors of his generation had appeared. He smiled sheepishly. "I was sick."

In the audience's introduction to the Cotton Club, the Dwyer family—Richard Gere, Gwen Verdon, Nicolas Cage, and Jennifer Grey (Nick's wife)—enters the club and is escorted to a table while a floorshow is in progress. Because of Vince Dwyer's surly attitude, maitre d' Kid Griffin, played by Tucker Smallwood, seats the foursome at the worst table in the house, back near the kitchen. As scripted, there is a bristling exchange between Kid Griffin and Vince. Not scripted but improvised by Cage were the racial epithets thrown not only at Kid Griffin but at blacks in general, including the beautiful showgirls in the middle of their performance. At the first camera break there was threatened mutiny. The showgirls refused to continue dancing, movie or no movie. Some jerk yelling "Nigger!" at them.

Tucker Smallwood told me, "The thing is, I think he's getting off on it." Later, after getting to know Cage better, he changed his opinion. "I think I was wrong. It's part of his performance. But he's so powerful, you don't realize that it's all the character. It's still hard to take."

Smallwood and the assistant directors worked together to assure the showgirls and dancers that in the milieu and period being recreated, an obnoxious person like Vince Dwyer might very well, in his anger and frustration at being seated at a bad table, go around shouting racial and other slurs. Even his embarrassed brother is not able to control him.

After he finished *The Cotton Club*, Cage went on to make *Birdy*. Our own Mark Burchard worked as dresser on that film, and he told me that Nick came across totally different. A cameraman on both films confirmed it. "You wouldn't have known he was the same person," Burchard said. "Sweet, considerate, polite. Everybody loved him. Nicolas said to me, 'I was not very nice on *The Cotton Club*, was I?'"

Burchard answered him back. "Would you believe 'asshole'?"

Nicolas was nineteen when he did *The Cotton Club*. His Vincent Dwyer was a terribly nasty character. Nicolas got into character early in the production and stayed there. In my personal contact with him, I found him polite, if distracted and remote.

Early in production, Fred Roos told me, "Nick's going to be an important star. You must make sure we have good pictures of him, good copy, good placement of his name in all releases and production notes." I started paying the boy more serious attention.

Once talking to me about the character Vince, Nicolas told me," He's so maniacally up, he's almost in outer space. At times I have to hold my head to keep it from hitting the ceiling. The guy's an empty balloon with a lot of unsuspected and unfocused energy. As mad as they come."

It was a relief to learn that Nicolas Cage wasn't.

* * *

I arrived at the studio one hot day to find the tempers and temperature on set even hotter. Richard Gere and Diane Lane were playing what we called the "Dada" love scene, also known as "Man Ray Madness," crazy lights playing about their faces and bodies. Adger Cowans (not to mention everybody else) was out of sorts. Adger told me first, and then Rob Gach confirmed it: Adger was not being allowed to cover the scene.

"Maybe it's because of what happened yesterday," Rob commented.

"What happened yesterday?" I braced myself for the revelation.

"The girl got upset," said Rob.

Girl? What a peculiar way to refer to Diane Lane.

"No, the other girl."

It took me a moment. Jennifer Grey.

Bob Girolami amplified. "I think Francis was as much at fault as Adger. Francis hadn't prepared Jennifer that he wanted her and Nick nude. It was a snap decision. You know Francis. Suddenly, 'Off with your clothes,' you know. Adger's on set, just doing his job, shooting away with a mechanized camera, motor buzzing. Jennifer got kind of hysterical. Nick, as naked as she was, tried to protect her, and all the while there's Adger moving in on them clicking away . . ."

He told me to tell Adger that he had just spoken with Francis. Francis had agreed to get him on set for the Man Ray Madness if he thought that Richard and Diane were sufficiently relaxed about it.

When Girolami left, Adger sidled up to me and said, "Whatever they're saying about me, it isn't true." Then he decided to hell with it, he was going home, he wouldn't be allowed to shoot anyway, it's the same old shit. He motioned to his son and assistant, Eden. Adger's boxes of film equipment were sitting on the edge of the set, Eden there to guard them. Adger said, "I only wish that they'd bring special photographers in here in droves. That would really drive them nuts." He and Eden charged out with his equipment.

If Adger seriously intended to go home, it would be a major gaffe, especially now that Coppola was prepared to intercede on his behalf. Girolami tracked him down via walkie-talkie in the production office, but by the time I got there he was gone. I heard the cry, "New set-up!" What did that mean, a new scene? I was frantic to find Adger. Finally I caught up with him and got him back to the set.

Francis's hair was wet from perspiration. The temperature was eighty-seven degrees outside and humid. Under the lights in the close confinement of the set, it must have been twenty degrees hotter. The focus puller told me, "It's like working in hell."

I approached Francis directly and asked about the stills.

"They're very uptight," he said of Richard and Diane. "I don't know what's wrong. I'll see what I can do."

Richard was in a white body-fitting period piece tank top that he wears in the scene. He was adjusting his tuxedo trousers and suspenders. I asked him about Adger's covering the scene. No, he said. Too hot. Too crowded. Diane's not in a receptive mood.

I told him that I guess we'd just have to do it like Kubrick does, get stills from frames of film. Not ideal for us but better than nothing.

Richard gave me his friendly, twisted smile and said, "While that is a 'no,' it is not, Reverend Tom, a definite 'no.'"

I thanked him, smile for smile.

Two hurdles out of the way. Now Diane. It turned out she was a peach. She had no problem with it, she said, as long as Richard and Francis didn't.

Adger was allowed in after the last take. He only got a few frames. Richard and Diane stayed in place on the bed, a sheet covering all but their shoulders, arms, and heads. The kaleidoscopic lighting gave a zebra-like effect to everything, including skin, and the photographs did not turn out well. Richard killed every one. Rightly so.

Fred Roos called me at home that night to let me know that Nicolas and Jennifer had protested to the

Screen Actors Guild about Adger's shooting them in the nude. They wanted the negatives.

That news meant I had to stop by the lab the next morning on my way to work. I looked at the color transparencies of Adger's supposed indiscretion. They looked perfectly all right to me, nothing untoward, nothing to get excited about. The black and whites would be sent to me later in the day by messenger.

When I got to the studio, I went directly to Nicholas Cage's assigned space in Dreary Lane, the row of dressing rooms that housed him, Lonette McKee, Bob Hoskins, Allen Garfield, makeup, hair, and various and sundry. When he looked at the transparencies, he said he had no problem with them. I showed him more of Adger's work. He pronounced it excellent, just as Richard had when he first saw Adger's work. I felt gratified for Adger.

Jennifer Grey liked the transparencies too. There were only two that were in the slightest questionable. One showed a part of a nipple above a pulled-up sheet. The other showed her lying on top of Cage with the outline of a breast visible. I gave both of them to her.

I was surprised to find out that she was the daughter of Joel Grey, whom I had known slightly through a friend. She had gotten this role because she had read and acted it in the pre-visualization taped rehearsals when Jennifer Jason Leigh, originally cast, was unavailable. Leigh remained out, Grey remained in. "And I couldn't have been happier," she said, cuddling the kitten which served her as a prop in the film and which, at her request, was given to her by the prop men when its scenes had been completed.

When the black and whites arrived and we looked at them, there were no problems. The supposed indiscretion was just that—supposed.

As a result of the flap, Barrie Osborne sent a memo to casting directors Gretchen Rennell and Lois Planco, with copies to Coppola, Roos, Girolami, Bronchtein, Adger, and me:

Please note the following nudity provisions in the SAG Basic Agreement, Paragraph 43, Page 40:

A) The Producer's representative will notify the actor (or his representative) of any nudity or sex acts expected in the role (if known by management at the time) prior to the first interview or audition.

B) During any production involving nudity or sex acts, the set shall be closed to all persons having no business purpose in connection with the production.

C) No still photography of nudity or sex acts will be authorized by the Producer to be made without consent of the actor.

D) The appearance of an actor in a nude or sex scene or the doubling of an actor in such a scene shall be conditioned upon his or her prior written consent. Such consent may be obtained by letter or other writing prior to a commitment or written contract being made or executed. If an actor has agreed to appear in such scenes and then withdraws his consent, Producer shall have the right to double, but consent may not be withdrawn as to film already photographed. Producer shall also have the right to double children of tender years (infants) in nude scenes (not in sex scenes).

Bob Girolami must provide me with a list of all upcoming nude scenes or potential nude scenes, so that I

can advise casting in accordance with sub-paragraphs A and D.
        BARRIE M. OSBORNE

* * *

Janet Pett, Robert Evans's secretary, worked out of his townhouse, also called the Crisis Center. So far, whenever Evans wanted to contact me, he did so through Zarem or Janet Pett. I never saw Robert Evans until the night of the wrap party. I asked an astonished Fred Roos if that man over there were he. It was. He popped in. A few photographs. Popped out.

I was in the production office. Grace Blake said, "May I give you a call?" At that time I still didn't have a phone, and I thought she was making a joke about it. "This call," she said, handing me the receiver. It was Pett. She told me about Jason Squire, author of *The Movie Business Book*, a collection of essays on the film business to which Evans had contributed. Mr. Squire was in New York and wanted to visit the set. Would Mr. Coppola consent to it? Could I arrange it? I wrote a note about the request to give to Francis. As I slipped it into his hand, I told him about its content. "Is he a good guy?" asked Francis, not breaking stride on his way to another set-up. "Well, he's put together this very reputable book of essays," I said, assuming that it *was* reputable and that it *was* a book of essays. Francis seemed in a good mood. "Sure, let him come," he said, "just so long as it's to hang around. No interviews."

Jason Squire visited on Thursday September 22. At an appropriate moment I told Francis he was on the set and asked him to say hello when he got the chance. Francis said he would and maybe an hour later did so.

"How do you like the buffet?" Squire asked Francis.

The buffet, the "French hours," as it was called, had gone into effect less than a week before. Highly touted and encouraged by Robert Evans, a continual buffet was set up near the set, starting with elegant breakfast foods and lots of pastries and finger foods with other goodies added as the day wore on. The idea was that cast and crew might eat whenever they were hungry and had a moment and not have to stop production, thus providing eight continuous working hours per day (the actually working hours in France were seven and out, I was told). A caterer had been flown in from Los Angeles to supervise the project and get it underway. The food was quite good.

"Do you mean the quality of it, or the idea?" Francis asked. He thought that although it might work well on a small personal film, it was not working on a large project like *The Cotton Club.* It would be even more ineffective when the big Cotton Club production numbers were being filmed with hundreds of extras milling about who had to be fed. "I understood that I'd be getting ten hours of working time a day with this, and I'm only getting eight. You can't do a picture like this on eight hours a day. And you can't sit down and relax with it. You eat makeshift and sit makeshift, if you can even find a place."

Squire was disappointed and said so. He loved the idea of the French hours. Coppola said he did too, but the reality was it simply wasn't working. Whereupon he walked away from us and immediately put into motion the rescinding of it.

Bud Yorkin had produced and William Friedkin had directed the unreleased *The Deal of the Century* co-starring Gregory Hines. They were disappointed that Gregory wasn't working the day they visited the set. They watched Francis direct Gwen Verdon and then Richard Gere in scenes. Then Francis took his guests to the third floor where special effects were being shot by the second unit under the direction of Gian-Carlo Coppola. In the small darkened room, a small crew and cameras were focused on a water tank that looked incomplete without goldfish. The water was being electrically charged to simulate peaks and swells of a storm at sea with lightning added at appropriate intervals. Terrific stuff, but what, I asked myself, was a storm at sea doing in *The Cotton Club*? Had rumrunners been added to the script? Maybe, I suggested to my attentive self, it was to be a visual backdrop for either "Stormy Weather" or "Ill Wind." Better not to ask questions. Just listen. Maybe something will drop. That's why I was tagging along on this junket, ostensibly welcome, if uninvited. Coppola seemed pleased that I was there, and Friedkin was especially gracious. Coppola told his guests the reasons for his having done two successive films in Oklahoma: "I wanted to get away . . . freedom . . . brink of financial disaster . . ." Friedkin was wearing an army-green quasi-safari jacket, new and tailored. (What was this thing with safari jackets? The new uniform for directors?) Coppola mused, "I used to wear a jacket like that." He looked down at Friedkin's waist and said, "Billy, you used to be thin as a rail." Friedkin and Yorkin were smoking cigars (yes, just what we needed: more smoke in the studio). Despite a Hirschfeld caricature of Coppola depicting him with a cigarette that appeared in the *New York Times*, I don't recall seeing him smoke anything at all during the production.

When I first met Tom Waits, I found his gravelly voice mildly off-putting. Gradually I found myself charmed by him. At the time I didn't really know his work except as songwriter/singer for Coppola's *One from the Heart* and actor in *Rumble Fish*. In *The Cotton Club* he played Irving Stark, the club's stage manager. I wondered if Tom Waits knew of a 1930s character actor named Ned Sparks whose delivery was invariably deadpan and who was rarely without a cigar dangling from the corner of his mouth. In the accumulating bits and pieces that were incorporated into Stark's character, I could tell that someone on the film knew Ned Sparks, and I think I know who. I think it was no accident that Ned Sparks's stage manager worked on *42nd Street* while Waits's Stark worked way uptown on 142nd Street!

During our first conversation, Waits kept shifting from one foot to the other. The prop man brought him a box of cigars. "Treat them with respect," he said. "They cost eighty-five cents apiece."

Waits selected a cigar from the box and studied it. "What a shame, I don't smoke. I don't know where to begin with this. Somebody's going to have to show me what to do."

"Francis will," said the prop man. "Keep the box. You'll need them for retakes."

"Maybe you can use those you don't smoke to make friends," I said.

One of Waits's eyebrows seemed perpetually cocked. He arched it even higher, sizing me up. "Yeah, that's *one* way, I guess."

He plainly didn't know what to make of me. That made two of us. I frequently didn't know what to make of myself either.

Milena Canonero came up to him with her assistant costume designer and began fussing with him. The assistant carried a box of period dress handkerchiefs from which Milena selected one for the breast pocket of Tom's jacket, to be worn in his first scene. "Treat this with respect," she began. It was beginning to sound like the film's Rodney Dangerfield mantra.

Rightfully so, and well might she repeat it.

The pilferage on the picture was far-reaching and particularly endemic to wardrobe. Despite security, there were many thefts. Some things turned up missing not only in the final inventory but throughout production. Milena had borrowed her husband's unique and very expensive period-looking wristwatch for a featured actor to wear. It disappeared. The actor said it must have been lost or stolen. "Stolen, yes," said Milena, "the question is, by whom!" A woman extra was suspected of walking away with expensive shoes. She swore she left them with a wardrobe assistant. The assistant swore she hadn't. A photograph had been taken of the extra with Richard Gere. When I told him about the incident, he joked, "Tear that picture up. I can't be seen with a thief." During our last week on location in Harlem an entire rack of "irreplaceable" men's jackets had disappeared.

There were complaints and grumblings about Milena from disgruntled associates and underlings. "It's not that she changes her mind," one said, "it's that she never makes it up. She doesn't delegate responsibility. She spends three hours on a fitting for each *extra*. She's into everything, including props. She tells props what she wants not just for the principals but for the extras too. She's driving everyone nuts. Watch out, she'll be into publicity next."

Milena Canonero was born in Turin, Italy, and educated in a French convent. The nuns must have found in her something pretty and petite that they could make over. The petite prettiness remained. She would have made a beautiful nun with her shy little-girl demeanor, a decided asset in the service of piety. Likewise, the degree of her obsession with perfection would not be out of place in a religious order. On a movie set, perfection is the great unobtainable. (Then again, she *had* worked with Stanley Kubrick on *A Clockwork Orange* and *Barry Lyndon*.) Conscientiousness is one thing, but Canonero inhabited a stratum somewhere above that. She considered herself an artist and not a costumer. She saw detail in her mind's eye, which was her artist's eye. She strove to realize through that eye and that detail a total perfect composition of elements, her canvas not only wardrobe but makeup and hair and props and, where feasible, production design as well. She aspired to total artistic control, and that extended to directing. To be left to another time, another place, another picture. On *The Cotton Club* she exercised total control of her designated and appropriated domain. The control was not deeded to her so much as confiscated by her in the vacuum of control that she moved in to fill.

I would have thought that this consolidation of departments under her stewardship would have brought her into conflict with David Golden. Grace Blake said, "Oh, no, David was always one of her staunchest defenders. When people would come in complaining about her, the huge sums she was spending, he'd say, 'Nobody is telling this woman what they want. We have no script, we have no director . . .' (This was B.C., before Coppola) '. . . She's working strictly from research, imagination, and intuition. Who of you is doing as well?'"

Robert Evans had given her carte blanche. If he had not, she certainly would not have blanched at taking the cart. For a long period, she and production designer Richard Sylbert held the reins of creative power on a directorless and directionless production. Milena's demands and requirements pitted her against the demands and requirements of others, most notably assistant directors Girolami and Bronchtein, neither of whom she had high professional regard for and with whom she often quarreled.

Her notorious fight with Bob Girolami was heard by anyone with a walkie-talkie or within hearing distance of one. Milena's almost unnatural obsession with perfection brought her into perpetual conflict with Girolami and crew. It was their job to get the shot. She wanted the shot as well, but not until it looked just like she wanted it to. They wanted it now. She wanted it perfect. From their point of view, she was a disaster.

Mark Burchard said to me, "It is the only film I've ever seen where the wardrobe department had at least a dozen walkie-talkies, spread out over several floors. We had five wardrobe locations inside the studio in addition to all the other places where somebody always has to be." He continued on about the big fight:

"Milena wanted something changed on the set. She had a wardrobe person with a walkie-talkie on set. They were ready to get a shot. Milena told the wardrobe person to hold it up until she could make a change. You see, Milena didn't really care whether they got the shot that day or not, just as long as it looked right when they did get it. Bobby told the assistant to tell Milena that they were shooting *now*. Whether she was ready or not.

Milena's voice came back over the walkie-talkie, 'Well, you can tell Bob—*fucking*—Girolami *he* can WAIT!' Now this was blasted all over the building in every walkie-talkie that was open, and you can bet all of them were. Bobby of course heard it. He took the walkie-talkie and said, 'What is this about Bob—fucking—Girolami?'

"'Fuck you,' she said.

"'Fuck you,' he said.

"'Fuck you,' she said."

On my first day at the studio, immediately following my interview with Fred Roos, I had stumbled on a quarrel between Canonero and Girolami and Bronchtein. I had worked with both of the men before, and now I was hoping to be introduced to Milena. When I perceived the tension, I quickly backed away. (Another good rule for the unit publicist: if you stumble on conflict, run! If it can be blamed on you, it will!)

Milena's delays provoked Coppola, but it was always Girolami and Bronchtein who took the brunt of his anger. Coppola wanted to shoot a scene in which chorus girls were in the background. Girolami called wardrobe and then spoke to Francis. "It'll be a few minutes. The girls aren't quite ready."

Coppola, taxed to the brink of endurance by other matters, snapped. "When I ask for something, I either want *it* or I want no answer."

Girolami was perplexed. "What?"

"Every time I ask for something," said Francis, his pitch rising, "I get this fucking lip!"

The room was filled with actors, extras, and technicians, most of whom stopped whatever they were doing to listen to the exchange. Bronchtein, softly placating, tried to interject something. Coppola was having none of it. "I want it done! I want no response."

Girolami repeated lamely, "The girls aren't ready."

"Do it without the girls."

Since the camera was to be focused on actors with the girls seen peripherally, this could hardly be done with the present camera set-up. Fortunately, word had gotten through to Milena about the crisis. The girls were sent to the set ready or not.

Because of her language proficiency, Milena had dubbed the French and Italian versions of three of Stanley Kubrick's films: *Paths of Glory, A Clockwork Orange,* and *Barry Lyndon,* the first having been shown in France after a long period when it had been banned.

"It was a job I loved," she told me. "Because I'm interested in films, period. I like costumes because they're part of the general play. But they just happen to be the way that right now I'm allowed to work in films. I like to be useful to a director in whatever way I can. I like to supervise makeup and hair because I think that's part of costuming."

She had been accused of profligacy: custom-made shoes from London and Rome, antique beaded frocks scouted from private sources all over the world, showgirl costumes made in France. She placed mind-bogglingly large orders for costumes costing thousands of dollars at a time when it was not clear how or even if they would be used, at a time when the script was fluid, which is to say, formless. Even nonexistent.

"It's true," she said with an engaging laugh. "We didn't know what we were doing, but we were being paid to do something spectacular, Dick (Sylbert) and I, so we did it." She said, concerning the old costumes purchased or rented, "After one wearing, some of these dresses will split and we will have to repair them. We put a mount under the garment to preserve the beading as much as possible. Some of these dresses truly are priceless."

Despite their bitching, her team seemed to love her. At the end of production, they lavished gifts on her. The lady had energy, which I commented on to her once and which she reciprocated by commenting favorably on mine. We seemed constantly to be passing one another in the labyrinth that was Kaufman-Astoria Studios. If she thought me ubiquitous, I thought her more so.

Milena wore chic designer jumpsuits of neutral and earth shades. To this she would add adornments, perhaps loops of encircling leather or cloth. From these might dangle a walkie-talkie. These colorful loops and her boots made her look like a West Fifty-fourth Street desperado in search of strobe lights and a hideaway disco whose music matched the pulse of the light and the night. From loops and elsewhere she hung ties or scarves. In her travels about the set and the vast caverns of the studio, she evaluated the costume of this or that actor. When she found the right person and context for a tie or scarf, there it went, replacing one that the actor already wore, the bit thus replaced then becoming part of her garb until she found another person upon whom it must be endowed. And all the while she was accomplishing at least ten other tasks. She circulated at the studio as if it were a party, which for her it often was, even with a lot of rude people present.

Arlene Coffey from wardrobe told me about a scarf that she had been wearing one day. "Milena complimented me on it three or four times in passing, then asked if she could have it. The scarf meant something to me, and I said no. She kept asking in that charming way of hers. How can you resist that accent? So

I thought, well, if she wants it so much, why not give it to her as a goodwill gesture. I did, and she was delighted. About a week later I was rummaging through a bin of clothing we were preparing for the bombing of the Bamville Club, clothes that had to be torn and bloodied. And there was my scarf! I yanked it out and hid it and never wore it again anywhere near Milena."

Mark Burchard told me, "You can't break her concentration. Richard mooned her once—but you were there, weren't you?"

I assured him I wasn't. "I don't think Richard would have been quite so frisky with me in the room."

"Oh, because you're a vicar."

"No, because I might take it as an invitation."

"Not with Milena in the room, I hope."

(Repartee comes easily for a vicar. So does wish-fulfillment fantasy, an addiction in our calling. Richard did do a fresh-out-of-the-shower number on me once, Sally Rand with a towel. Big towel, unfortunately. But lots of leg, a touch of crotch. A tease and a pose. But what is a vicar to do under such circumstances but remain primly seated, prayer-book in hand?)

"Tell me," I encouraged Mark. Not that it took much encouragement.

"Well, as you know, Richard has this very decided sense of humor. Milena comes in to check out his wardrobe for the next day. I thought you were there. I guess it was just me, Milena, and one of her assistants. Richard is dressed only in his period boxer shorts. He asks Milena to wait in the next room. Then he pulls down his shorts, bends over with his behind to the door, and calls her in.

"The assistant is mortified, turns every color you can think of. But it didn't faze Milena. 'Hmmm, not as fat as Marshall's,' that's her husband. She brushes right past a sight most women and a good percentage of men in America would have paid money for. Her mind was on that clothes rack."

Milena's single-mindedness on occasion had blind spots. Early in production, she made significant costume goofs from which a guardian angel saved her. At least her assistants attributed her good fortune to a guardian angel. Late in production, her angel started napping.

Mark tried to warn her. She had told him she was designing and having made in London new suits for Dutch and his gang to wear at the Palace Chop House where the men go after they've been thrown out of the Cotton Club. "Oh, but you can't do that," Mark said. "The scene *has* to be synchronized with the Cotton Club. They *have* to be wearing the same tuxedos." He suggested that she take a look at the script again. Francis would be intercutting the Cotton Club scene where the hit is being set up with the Palace Chop House where the hit occurs and then back to the Cotton Club where the success of the hit is being celebrated. It was imperative that the men be assassinated in the tuxedos they were wearing when they left the Cotton Club.

Milena didn't need to look at the script. "Oh, no," she said with confidence, "they'd have plenty of time to go home and take showers and change."

The lady would not be convinced. Mark quit trying. The suits were made at a cost of about $24,000.

When it came time to shoot the scene, Coppola walked onto the set and saw his actors in costumes that were alien to him and to the moment. "Where are the tuxedos?" he asked in disbelief.

Milena then explained to him about the showers.

Coppola's face was something you really didn't want to look at. It turned purple in a gathering fury of incredulity. As if a tornado were spiraling upward inside him. As if bricks were falling on him while he, like Oliver Hardy, was standing there patiently waiting to be beaned just one more time. You wondered if in his dazed state he might topple over, and if so, in which direction. A face that purple might splatter. You wanted to move briskly away from him and distance yourself from the fury that you saw to be on a short fuse indeed, but you didn't want to call attention to yourself. Or you could wait and be blown to smithereens along with everybody else.

He exploded in expletives. A heart attack refusing to happen, he stormed out of the bar on Twenty-third Street where we were shooting. Before he got to his van, Milena, like a child unable to let go of an exploding skyrocket, her hand already badly scorched, ran after him to continue the fight in the street. He called her a dumb cunt and she replied in kind and dissolved in tears. The back-and-forth insults briefly took on the aspect of the name-calling litany that had characterized her fight with Bob Girolami.

"If this had happened during the first three weeks of production," Mark whispered to me, "we'd have had costumes by Theoni V. Aldridge."

Fortunately Mark had foreseen disaster and had prepared for it. The men's tuxedo costumes were on the wardrobe truck in perfect condition, sorted by actor, ready to be put on immediately. Jimmy Remar and the other actors were dressed and ready to play their assassination scene within fifteen minutes.

* * *

From the *New York Post*, "Page Six," Tuesday, October 4, 1983:

COPPOLA A NO-SHOW, STRANDS 300 ON FILM

No movie set is without its occasional crisis, but Cotton Club *seems to be harvesting more than its share.*

Yesterday the situation reached its tensest moments since the project got rolling the last week in August, with a cast and crew of some 300 people waiting out a frustrating, filmless shift at the Kaufman-Astoria Studios in Queens.

Movie sources tell us that director Francis Coppola, who's apparently been working without a signed-and-sealed contract, never appeared to order the start of the day's production.

One actor who'd been signed to appear in the film, and preferred to remain anonymous, told PAGE SIX:

"Coppola decided to stay home because they haven't settled his contract and haven't paid him. When the limo went to fetch him, he decided not to go . . . We came in at 6 a.m. and stayed until 3 p.m., waiting, hoping. No work got done at all. Finally, an assistant director told us to go home and call our agents to find out when we should come back."

And until that point, another actor told us, "Everyone sat around in a state of confusion."

Will the $35 million film, which stars Richard Gere, Diane Lane, and Gregory and Maurice Hines, be back on track tomorrow? Will Francis Coppola occupy the director's seat?

Don't ask producer Bob Evans. The high-powered promotional campaign surrounding his picture got a head start last winter with a press conference heralding an historic agreement by a group of motion picture craft unions to cut overtime costs.

Since then the picture—and Evans—have reaped a bountiful crop of press coverage, with every hiring, firing, and studio move duly documented.

But yesterday, Evans emitted only sounds of silence on the subject of Cotton Club. *"He's in negotiations," with Coppola, is all Evans' spokesman Bobby Zarem would say. Our attempts to reach Coppola for comment were also unsuccessful.*

Richard Johnson, the author of the story, called me that day and asked if I had seen it. "One hundred percent accurate," he crowed. As well he might. It was right on the button considering what we knew at the moment, except that Francis hadn't stayed home. He had flown to England. Few knew that. I laughed in appreciative acknowledgment of the reporter's coup but told him I had no comment.

He asked who Fred Roos was. The name had been given to him as a person he might call. I told him who Roos was but said I doubted that he would be able to tell him much more than I. Call the Zarem office, I suggested.

He replied with a touch of plaintiveness. "They can be utterly useless at times." I found that rather amusing. He was relieved to find in me at least a willing listener. He said, "Nothing is happening today, is it?"

"You know that already, don't you?"

"Yeah."

Plenty was happening, just not in the way Richard Johnson meant. We had kept ourselves busy with the unimportant, thinking Francis would return momentarily.

Johnson tried to pump me. He'd heard rumors that Coppola was unhappy with Richard Gere's performance. I said that wasn't true at all and that the picture was looking marvelous as was Gere in the leading roll. Both in looks and in performance, I hastened to add.

Johnson's source indicated that some three hundred cast and crew members were waiting around for Coppola's return. A more accurate estimate would have been five hundred.

Hollywood Reporter that day and the day before had carried stories not about the no-show but about the firings. On Wednesday Francis's disappearance would be reported in both the *Reporter* and *Variety*.

Monday's *Reporter* quoted David Golden about the firings. Tuesday's contained a rebuttal by Robert Evans with regard to Dyson Lovell. He said that Lovell's contract was being renegotiated and that with the exception of Golden no one had been fired, the "departures" merely reflecting the completion of a term of employment by the departees. Beautiful stuff. I all but memorized it, knowing I could use it later.

I had come to work the morning of the big shuffle-off to find people talking in hushed groups, the chill of death in the air. I was quickly filled in on the reason for it. Our dim view of the matter grew even dimmer when the railings were removed from around Francis's Silverfish, an ominous act that I viewed as symbolic. In effect Francis was making the point that his departure was serious and that his demands had to be taken seriously. When the laborious process of moving the van out of the building began, it looked even more serious. Of course, Francis was guarding against its seizure in any kind of counter-pressure that might be brought to bear against him. Naturally there was a television crew outside the studio to shoot the removal.

On Tuesday, October 4, rumors abounded. There was talk of our going into hiatus for two weeks with only heads of departments (that would include me) remaining on salary.

It appeared likely that a replacement director would be brought in.

"Herb Ross has been called . . ."

"Bob Fosse is meeting with Evans . . ."

Then we heard the shocker: Francis had taken the negative of already-shot footage with him and was holding it as hostage.

"But he wouldn't have access to it, would he?" I argued.

"Not normally" said one of the electricians, "but what is normal about this movie? He had to have been planning this. He simply pulled a fast one. Evans pays up or he doesn't get the negative."

In every studio gathering and especially around the tables of the commissary in the studio basement, there was wild conjecture liberally laced with laughter. It was a hoot. None of us had ever seen anything like this.

An apologetic letter from Coppola was distributed to his actors. In it he regretted putting them through the strain and uncertainty of the past few days and offered them an analogy by way of an anecdote about the great electrical engineer Nikola Tesla and industrialist and inventor Thomas Edison:

. . . When he first arrived in America the young Tesla was drawn immediately to Edison's lab where the engineers were working desperately on a new dynamo

that the Edison Company was supposed to deliver the next morning. The work was going badly and there was no hope of making the delivery. Tesla remarked that he thought he could get it going and Edison replies that if he could by the delivery date he would give Tesla $35,000 in cash. Penniless, literally off the boat from Yugoslavia, Tesla rolled up his sleeves, worked all night, and the next morning the dynamo was running perfectly. Edison made his crucial delivery but when Tesla asked for his payment now that the work was done, Edison replied, "Tesla, you don't understand our American humor."

Many times I've worked through the night and we have completed the first half of the movie and like the dynamo it runs beautifully. But when our employers are asked for the deal that they offered to entice me to do this work they seem to feel that it's not necessary to live up to those agreements . . .

Richard Gere didn't come in. George Shutt asked me to help him clean out Richard's refrigerator. That is, let's have a snack. He cut a cantaloupe. We shared that and some morning cocoa. The various cheeses were going bad. We cut a small hunk from one square and left the rest untouched. "I was told how much Richard liked cheese," he said. "Evidently not."

On Wednesday we heard that it had all been settled and that Francis was returning from London on the Concorde. He had missed an earlier flight. He would touch down at Kennedy at about three o'clock in the afternoon. Actors were called in or put on Will Notify. Filming would resume immediately. It would presumably be a late day for us. No one had expected work to resume so soon, and many weren't prepared for it.

James Remar had been disco dancing into the early hours and was bleary-eyed and irritable when he reported to work. He had expected to sleep all day.

Three-thirty p.m. We were expecting Francis any minute. Someone said he was in the building. Someone else said he wasn't. I got a call from Barrie Osborne. An NBC-TV News local team headed by our old friend Carol Jenkins had been cruising around the outside of the building from time to time during the crisis and was now parked at the entrance. That was fine, Barrie said, just as long as they stayed there and didn't begin driving around the building again and spot Francis coming in through another entrance. The Concorde had landed and a limousine had picked Francis up. He was on the way to the studio and would not want to talk to the press. Barrie asked me to be the diversionary measure: if I spoke with the TV people and kept them occupied, Francis could be smuggled in undetected.

Now, dear reader, "to speak with the TV people" is to my mind to speak on camera. How would you have interpreted it? Later I would find myself greeted with an incredulous "You spoke on *camera*?" as though I had committed a sin just a few shades short of cardinal. Yes, Virginia, I did. There was Carol Jenkins and a camera and a microphone and I blathered away.

Carol Jenkins was good at her job. She immediately put me at ease. I opened up like a blossom after an April shower, but always careful not to let the stamen show. See how much I'm revealing to you so you can't see what I'm hiding? Good trick if you can get away with it, and I was not all that practiced. The camera started rolling and I relaxed into it like its lover. The questions were mostly about the firings. Those were easy to handle. I had Bob Evans's comments in the *Reporter* memorized and simply reprised them in my own words.

I made light of the story that Francis was said to have taken the negative with him. "I've heard that story too," I said. "I got calls about it at home last night." I laughed and added, "It makes a wonderful story and I almost wish it were true, but how could he have gotten hold of it? The negative is kept in a vault."

"Is he in the building now?" Carol asked.

"Oh, yes," I said positively, hoping that it might be true, that Francis just that moment *had* stepped into the building.

"You've seen him?"

I hated being put in such a position. I told her I had not.

"Then how do you know he's in the building?"

"I was told he was."

Not so big a fib. After all, I was told that he soon *would* be in the building. What's a tiny change of tense? See, children, what one lie can lead you to . . .

Carol Jenkins made it all so easy. With her irrepressible smile, she gave me the impression that she was having as good a time talking with me as she had dancing with Maurice Hines. However, it was hot. Perspiration was pouring from me. I knew that with one misbegotten word this interview could become my last identification with the film. I was wearing a shirt that hadn't been pressed and looked it. I kept thinking about the smart shirt I had almost worn today. What perversity had made me change my mind! And my hair! It was wilting down my forehead.

As we talked, the Silverfish was moved back into the building, a visual underscoring of the upbeat tenor of my spiel. The cameras trained on it, and I said a few words about the significance of its return.

The interview was over.

When I got back to my office, I called Bobby Zarem to tell him what I had done and why. He received the news with genuine horror.

"*You* are not the spokesman for this picture," he said. "You should not have done that no matter *who* asked you to. This is serious, but maybe we can ride with it so long as Evans doesn't know. Whatever you do, don't tell Bob!"

Hardly likely, that. I'd never met Evans nor spoken with him. I tried to calm Bobby's fears and emphasized how innocent, how affirmative my words had been. Perhaps they were, said Bobby, but Bob Evans would view them as another grave mistake, the first being that I was quoted in this morning's *Hollywood Reporter*. Evans didn't like it. Evans wanted all information on the film to come from him or Bobby.

"What am I to do? They call *me*!"

"You refer them to us."

"I do."

"But you speak to them first."

"In referring them to you I have to speak to them."

It was becoming an Abbott and Costello routine.

"That's not all you're doing, Tom! Otherwise they wouldn't be quoting you. This is an extremely sensitive matter and Bob wants it handled only through us. Evans is the spokesperson for this picture, if he chooses to be. I know how difficult this is for you, but please try!"

When the chewing out by Zarem was over, James Remar (who had been trying to sleep but had failed to close the door) was wide awake and eager to know what was going on. I told him about Evans's irritation with me about a quote in that morning's *Hollywood Reporter*. As we were talking, a messenger turned up with the copy I'd sent for.

Sure enough. There it was. I saw what the flap was about.

"Sources close to the production . . ."

"Sources close to Evans . . ."

The writer obviously could not go on in this unidentified-source vein too long without naming an actual person to whom she had spoken. Since I was a source seemingly close to no one, I had been elected to be so named, making it appear to the incautious reader that information in the story other than that specifically attributed to me might have come from me. Tricky, Ms. Mary Reinholz. Tricky indeed.

She had been a real bulldozer when she called me, running roughshod over my objections about speaking with her and my attempts to refer her to the Zarem Office. I told her, "Zarem has the information you want. *I* don't."

"Is he at the studio?" she asked pointedly.

"No."

"Are you at the studio?"

"Yes."

"Since I assume he gets his information about the set and studio from you, you're the one I want to talk to."

"I have nothing to tell you."

"Is Francis working today or isn't he? That's all I want to know."

"He isn't. Now I really can't speak with you any longer."

Here's what Ms. Reinholz did with it:

NEW YORK – Major hassles, to put it mildly, are brewing on the production of "Cotton Club," the root of which involves a power struggle between producer Robert Evans and Director Francis Coppola and has resulted in an apparent work stoppage on the film.

The major issue, still unresolved as of yesterday, reportedly involved demands by Coppola that Evans, according to sources close to production, is unwilling to meet. One report alluded to Coppola apparently not having been paid for his services, although this was denied by a source close to Evans. In any event, Coppola refused to show up on the set yesterday for the second day in a row, according to unit publicist Tom Miller, in an apparent attempt to gain leverage over Evans regarding his demands . . .

It went on and on, a long piece. While Jimmy was reading it, I got a call from Reinholz pressuring me for more information. Again I urged her to call Zarem.

"All I want to know," she said, "is Coppola back?"

By that time we'd heard that he was. I said tersely, "Thank God, Francis is back."

When I hung up, I said, "They'll probably hang me for that."

Jimmy looked at me with sympathy. "What a shitty thing they're doing to you. You don't deserve this."

My sentiments exactly. His words were sweet to my ears.

The phone rang again.

It was Janet Pett. "Tom, Robert Evans wants to talk to you." I put my hand over the mouthpiece and told Jimmy, "Evans."

"Christ," he said. We went into his room to give me privacy but left the door open. During my conversation with Evans, he paced back and forth between our two rooms.

Until then, I had never spoken to Robert Evans, never met the man, and never even seen him. I certainly knew of him by reputation. When Joanne Woodward heard that I might be working on *The Cotton Club*, she told me gravely, "Oh, you don't want to work for Robert Evans."

"Hi, Bob," I said. Casually. Like we'd been dining together the previous night. I felt like a sixties Las Vegas janitor being called by Howard Hughes.

His voice was resonant, nice, practiced, but filled with a note of urgency. "Tom," he said, "I just want to warn you—do not talk to the press about any of this. I'm in a very sensitive position vis-à-vis Francis at the moment . . ."

He went on to say that he didn't want anything said, even though said in innocence, that might tip some very shaky scales that could conceivably destroy a new understanding he had reached with Coppola. There was something about a new contract, as yet unsigned, but I didn't attend to the details that closely. My mind was buzzing with other matters that concerned me more: should I tell him about my being interviewed by Carol Jenkins. Better he find out sooner than later, I reasoned, and better from me than anyone else. Not heeding Bobby Zarem's warning, I told him what I had done and tried to tell him why.

He wouldn't let me finish.

"You've got to kill it!" he cried.

"I'll call her now," I said. "Maybe I can even reach her outside. Perhaps she's still here." I tried to sound as reasonable as I could: *Look, see, we'll simply stop the piece, no sweat, Bob.* As if I thought I had a hope in hell of doing so. I was sweating like a fat man in a sauna and must have smelled to high heaven. Remar was now in the room with me, standing right behind me. I didn't dare look at him. I had to keep my head. I sensed his agitation, and I felt that if I looked at him I'd lose it.

"Tell her, it's your job!" Evans said. "Tell her if that story runs, you're through!"

Was I to tell Jenkins that, I wondered, or was Robert Evans telling *me*? I decided it was probably the latter.

He continued. "You've *got* to kill that story!"

No way could I kill that story. I was a cooked goose. "I'm sure I can," I said, gurgling like a man going under. "Don't worry about it, Bob."

His voice escalated to new decibels. Remar heard him as clearly as I. "You've probably blown the whole movie!" he screamed. "My deal with Francis is down the drain! He'll walk and we're done for!"

Now I began to appreciate what Zarem had been going through. Thank God I didn't have to deal with this man every day. His reaching to my level of the scapegoat barrel struck me as a little much: he was claiming that the reprised words of the producer uttered by a publicist on copycat detail on a local TV news spot could in some way endanger the completion of the movie.

Again I tried to impress on him the innocence and innocuousness of my comments to Carol Jenkins, all merely quotes from himself in Tuesday's *Reporter*. All done so that Francis could sneak undetected into the studio by a side door.

He switched gears. He became conversational. It was like talking to another person. "Does Bobby know about this?" he asked. I told him that Bobby did.

"What did he say?" There was a note of impishness, an anticipatory pleasure, in the question. Actually, I thought Zarem might come around to my position, but I didn't think Evans wanted to hear that.

"He was furious."

Evans chuckled. He obviously liked the idea of Zarem being furious. He spoke in an even friendlier tone. "Tom, see what you can do. That story must not run. Understand me?"

How could I not.

"Don't worry about a thing, Bob," I said. All part of the act and part of the job. What job? After the story ran I would have no job. My days on the film were numbered. Hanging up the receiver, I told Remar so.

"He can't fire you," Remar said. "Francis does the firing here, not Evans. Tell Francis. I'm serious. You've got to tell Francis."

Dan Suhart had witnessed my interview and when it was over told me, "You did very well." Prop man Bob Wilson had also been watching and had similarly complimented me. I didn't think it would turn out so bad, and I only wished that Evans had waited to see the finished piece before making his dire pronouncement.

I'm sure Carol Jenkins had not believed what I was saying any more than I did. That no one except David Golden had been fired and that other departees had left only because their jobs had been completed was complete bullshit. But Evans's bullshit, not mine. If this was the approved crap, what could they expect of me but to smile and shovel it.

I called Jenkins's office at NBC. She was away on assignment. I told her assistant who I was and stated my problem. As instructed by Bob Evans, I told her that I had given Jenkins "incorrect information." I stood to be fired if the piece ran. "Tell Carol, please don't run it."

The assistant said it would be extremely unlikely that the story could be killed. (Surprise.) "They just don't do things like that around here. But I *will* tell her."

Then I called Zarem. If I thought Evans had been hysterical, it was because I hadn't yet made the acquaintance of real hysteria. Zarem introduced me to it.

"I *told* you not to tell Bob!" he screamed.

I explained in detail what had transpired with Evans. "All right," he said, much calmer, "don't worry. It's not the end of the world. I'll fix it."

I had never realized Bobby Zarem could be so comforting. Fix it? I believed he could.

Richard Gere stopped by on the way to his room. "What does the press have to say about all this?" he asked. I told him about the ongoing crisis. He repeated Remar's advice in Remar's presence. "Tell Francis as soon as possible."

Richard went on in a mocking vein. "'Spokesman for the movie.' He wants *his* name in the paper. He wants *himself* on television, not you. Bobby wasn't hired to get *your* name in the *Hollywood Reporter*. He was hired to get Bob Evans's name there. What a joke." He walked toward the door and reiterated his advice. "Tell Francis."

Finally, at the end of the day, I was able to speak with Francis. I told him the whole story.

He said, echoing Remar's encouraging words but not quite so encouraging in the way he put it, "Don't worry about it. If anybody fires you, it'll be me."

I guess something in my face made him realize how it sounded. He added, "I hear you handled yourself very well. Again, don't worry about it. And thank you."

When I returned to my office to lock up, I got a call from Bobby Zarem telling me he had reached Carol Jenkins and she had consented to hold the story in return for an interview with Evans. Evans had agreed to do so.

Thank God. The crisis was over. Time now for a celebratory dinner with a friend.

Fast forward through the next day to Friday morning. I was walking past the main Cotton Club set. Suddenly throngs of people converged on me, acknowledging me, smiling. A technician whose name I didn't know said, "Saw you last night on TV. Terrific."

Choreographers Henry and Ellie LeTang and a couple of showgirls enthused, "Oh, here's the star of the movie! You were wonderful on TV last night!"

What a sinking feeling to hear you were wonderful on TV last night and not know anything about it. It didn't help to think that I might be fired because of it, despite Coppola's assurances.

"Last night?" I said dumbly, still trying to process the information.

"It was so funny."

"Funny?"

They finally realized that I hadn't seen it. They described it to me with some relish. "They kept cutting from what you were saying to Carol Jenkins who kept repeating, 'Misinformation.' It was hilarious."

I felt sick at my stomach.

"First she said they'd had a call from you, saying that you'd be fired if they used your interview. Then she said that you'd said that you had given them misinformation. So after everything you said, she said 'Misinformation.' It was real cute."

Another showgirl piped up. "Just darling."

I'll just bet.

I got to a phone as soon as possible and called my friend Jonathan. "This may be my last day on the movie," I said. "I'm waiting for the call." At that moment my buzzer sounded to alert me of an incoming call held for me at the switchboard. "There it is now," I said. "I'll call you back."

"What happened!" cried my friend.

"They ran the fucking thing. Last night. My TV interview. They made a joke of it. I've got to go."

I took the other call. Bobby Zarem.

"How do you feel?" he asked. I thought it was a civilized way of easing into the bad news. Sort of like, if you're not feeling bad now, just wait!

"Not too well," I said. "I heard I was on TV last night."

"Oh, that was all right," he said. "It was fine." I couldn't believe it. "Bob was worried that if it had run on Wednesday night, it could throw a monkey into his deal with Francis. But by Thursday night there was no problem. In fact, Bob kind of liked it. He thought it was funny!"

* * *

Francis's absence and the concomitant hiatus generated dizzy spinoffs.

The payroll was payable every Wednesday morning. On the Wednesday of my infamous television interview, no payroll. Chris Cronyn told department heads that the company was under no obligation to pay the employees because production had ceased when the director walked. It went over like Jesus in long johns. Grace Blake summed it up: "Ludicrous. The paychecks we didn't get today were for *last* week. And the company's financial obligation to its crew has not been lessened by the fact that Francis didn't show up for work. The cast and crew *had*."

Cronyn was scorned and savaged and made to see the error of his ways. The crown of thorns was removed when the paychecks finally arrived. They were reduced by a certain amount so that those who chose could get that much of their salary in cash on the spot. But because of the company's perceived financial precariousness, the crew refused to work until the checks had been converted into cash. Vans had to be provided to take people to the bank on which the checks were drawn. Then the vans returned to the studio for another load of crew. The process took over two hours. Not everyone took advantage of the cash-now offer. If they had, the later checks would have bounced, an accountant told me. Money would not have been in the bank to cover them until the next day. From that day until the end of production, it was nip and tuck. Will my paycheck arrive or will it not? Is there money in the bank to cover it or is there not? Too often, said the accountant, there wasn't. "And believe me, it was scary!"

In addition, and only in part because of Cronyn's ill-considered interpretation of present liability, the crew issued an ultimatum to the producers. A bond would have to be posted to cover the payroll for a two-week period so that they would be guaranteed money due them, as wardrobe assistant Arlene Coffey put it, "the *next* time it happens." Crew members began to doubt that the picture would ever be completed. "The spirit has gone out of all of us," said Arlene.

Someone in payroll told me, "It almost did happen again. And if it had, I would have quit. I would never have been about to take it a second time—the hostility, accusations, agony, humiliation—of not being able to pay people, many of whom I'd come to consider friends, the money due them."

That afternoon Coppola made a historic gesture.

He called everyone together on the Cotton Club set and told them that he personally would pay their salaries for any days that the company reneged on its obligation to them.

A gaffer said, "I'll continue working for Francis but I won't take his money. He's had a hard enough time getting his own."

A prop man said, "He's out of his bean. He obviously has no idea what one day's salary would amount to. He'd have to mortgage a second house in Napa Valley, which I don't think he has."

I wondered about "the Cronyn mistake." Had it been one? It sounded like a ploy, Cronyn acting, perhaps unwisely on the part of all involved, on behalf of the Doumanis to buy a little time.

I had heard stories of how week after week the Doumanis had shaken their money tree for one more tenacious, yellowing autumn leaf. Somehow there was always one left to fall, although to the naked eye the tree looked bare. They were able to bring in "piddling" sums from friends and associates ranging from $2,500 to $250,000.

No wonder all these strangers had begun showing up at the studio, waddling around like penguins, self-designated private eyes poking into everybody's business and offices and dressing rooms. When challenged, they would identify themselves as investors. Once I came upon two obnoxious investors standing in James Remar's room watching him sleep. After that he became more careful about locking our mutual door.

And no wonder that Robert Evans wanted us to continue the fiction that we were working from a Mario Puzo screenplay, Puzo being the investor lure that William Kennedy was not.

"It was a horror show," an assistant auditor told me, "all these Mickey Mouse checks and calculations, and us trying day after day to find out if we had enough money to cover everything. Which we usually didn't. And if we didn't, trying to figure out what we could fudge on. Or hold back on.

"Richard Gere's check, for instance.

"After the crisis, his management stipulated that his check had to be certified. There were some weeks we couldn't certify it. We only hoped we had the money in the account when it got deposited and tried to clear. Once we didn't, and we pleaded with the bank to make it good and we would make up the difference later that day or the next morning, and then we'd pray that we could make it up. Oh, it was a horror show. We were always just one step ahead of total collapse. You'll never know how close we came to folding."

Yes, I did know.

Toward the end of production, my own paycheck, normally ready by Wednesday noon, didn't get written until Thursday. The next week, Friday. Sort of an accounting system based on the eight-day week. Auditor Tony Trimarco, from whom I would receive the check, was deeply apologetic. An Orion auditor had by now been assigned to oversee an additional investment they had made: all checks had to be signed by her. "She hasn't signed it yet," Tony would tell me forlornly after making a special trip to the auditor's second floor office on my behalf. "I don't know what the problem is," he would say unconvincingly.

We both knew what the problem was.

No money.

However, I was patient.

Others registered protestations at high decibel as if declaiming Shakespeare in a summer amphitheater. They got quicker results than I. The less indignantly demonstrable of us were put on financial hold.

* * *

Newsweek decided to run a photo from the film on their "Newsmakers" page with a brief text. They wanted a shot of Richard Gere and Diane Lane. I sent slides to Zarem for deployment to the magazine, the ones Richard had approved separated from those he had not yet seen. I reminded Mark Zane that nothing of Richard could be published until he had given his approval. Richard had already said that he wouldn't talk to the *Newsweek* writer. He was uncomfortable giving quotes and suggested that Diane do it. Coppola did consent to being interviewed briefly by telephone.

Sure enough, *Newsweek* decided it wanted to run a picture of Richard that he had not seen and approved.

Zarem sent it to me by messenger for Gere's quick approval. Richard looked at it. He didn't like it.

"Why do they think I go through all this, take the time to approve pictures, and then they send out pictures I haven't even seen. How did this happen?"

(How did it happen? *Newsweek* had told Zarem they wanted to see "everything." I had argued against it, to no avail. I was told, "If they pick something Richard hasn't approved yet, we'll just have to ask him to approve it.")

"Well, I won't approve," Richard said. "They're got to be taught a lesson."

I called a surprised Mark Kane to tell him that Richard was disallowing the use of the photo. An equally surprised and disappointed *Newsweek* representative called. "But *why*?" she said. "It's such a darling picture."

I told Richard about it. Maybe it was the "darling" that did it. Or maybe he thought I needed a break. "Okay," he said, "they can use it, but tell Bobby this is the last time."

By then *Newsweek* had selected another photograph similar to their first choice. I didn't like it as much and urged them to go with the first one.

The text accompanying the picture dredged up yet again Coppola's feud with Evans. Did we really need to beat that horse again? None of the affirmative quotes that Coppola had given *Newsweek* were used. Wasted time, wasted breath. The magazine reached the set just one day before the issue of the *Daily News* that contained yet another inflammatory Liz Smith item. The two pieces almost changed the modus operandi, not to mention the operators, of the film's publicity apparatus.

From Liz Smith, November 9:

"COTTON CLUB": QUIET BEFORE THE STORM?
Gird your loins for the coming explosion and fallout between director Francis Ford Coppola and his sometime tempestuous star Richard Gere. Yes, the "Cotton Club" movie set in Astoria, Queens, had been mighty quiet ever since all the shouting stopped after the interrupted production schedule a few weeks ago. Bets are now down by cast and crew that the high tension between director and star will soon blow sky-high. (And, of course, there are the usual on-going rumors that temperament isn't the only thing blowing on this production.)

Interjection and note: Francis Coppola/Francis Ford Coppola. By this time, Coppola had decided to use "Ford" only in producer credits and not use it in director credits. Needless to say, this made for some confusion.

From *Newsweek*, November 14:

If the movie "Cotton Club" comes in on time and near budget, it will be no thanks to the teamwork of producer Robert Evans and director Francis Coppola, who began squabbling shortly after production began. Last month Coppola left the set for three days because of a dispute with Evans. Now the two men, who had teamed up for "The Godfather," say they've resolved their differences, although Coppola doesn't anticipate being "in the situation" of working with Evans again. The tension between them has "hit the nerves of everybody on the set," admits Diane Lane, 18, who costars with Richard Gere in the movie about the legendary nightclub. But Coppola, says Lane, "is holding up fine. He's still cooking pasta."

The Tuesday afternoon when the *Newsweek* story reached the set, Francis fell over a set of steps (used for a dance number) and hurt his chest. He had hit an area near his heart on the edge of the three-foot-high construct. At first, because of how he was sprawled, there was general concern that this leg might be broken. I was standing behind Coppola's wife, Eleanor, the only time I was to see her on the set. Coppola said he was all right and returned to directing the scene.

I went to my office. Shortly afterward, Coppola was brought through it and taken to Remar's room, where he was tended by Remar, Gregory Hines, Tony Dingman, and Tucker Smallwood. Gregory told me, "He's going to be black and blue. He could have been killed. I think he's shook up, scared, impressed by the close call, the mortality of it all."

What nobody told me was that in addition to the physical hurt, Francis had been hurt by the *Newsweek* item. His anger was on slow simmer.

Next morning the Liz Smith item set the tone of the day. My first knowledge of it was when I arrived on set to see a prop man showing it to Richard. I read it over his shoulder. He looked up at me and sighed. "She hates me," he said, adding philosophically, "but it all comes in cycles. They write good things, they write bad. The best thing to do is forget about it."

Tony Dingman told me that Francis had seen the item. "You better be prepared to deal with it," he said. "I've already told him, 'You have to believe that Tom is not responsible for this shit.'"

I felt blessed.

I didn't wait for Francis to come to me. I went to him. His first words were the same as Richard's. "She hates me."

For lunch I picked up a sandwich and a soft drink from a nearby Chinese deli, as I often did. (Sometimes I would pick up a sandwich for Richard, who although a professed vegetarian, would in moments of stress say, "Get me what you're having." Usually a chicken salad sandwich.) I returned via the production office to see if I had any messages. Yes. One. "Francis is looking for you."

I wasn't sure I had heard right. I hoped I hadn't.

"Who?"

"Francis. He was in here. He's looking all over for you. He said he had to see you right away."

I started sweating.

Francis had never "looked for" me before. At least not with any announced sense of urgency. It didn't sound good. I headed for the Silverfish. Tony was out front. He said, almost in a whisper, "Don't let him see you." He went on to explain, "He's in a better mood now. He's sitting in the makeup area with some of the girls. If he sees you, it might set him off again."

In effect, I was being told by one who knew Francis best to hide. I hid.

One of my telephone messages was to call Zarem. I did. I was told that Bobby was at home waiting for my call. When I got him, Bobby said that Francis had been trying to reach him but he hadn't returned the call. He had wanted to find out from me what it was all about. "I don't know," I said, "but I think it's about the Liz Smith thing in this morning's paper, which I know you had no more to do with than I. Whatever it is, they tell me he is pretty hot about it."

Zarem asked me to check it out further and get back to him when I knew something. It looked like there were two of us in hiding.

I called Coppola's office. His secretary, Sara, said, "We've had a call in to Zarem for some time and he hasn't called back, and Francis is annoyed. It's about the *Newsweek* piece. He only talked to that woman because Bobby convinced Fred that he should. He gave her some good quotes and look what she used!"

I gathered that Bobby was being blamed. That was unfair. You put a journalist with a client and it's a crapshoot what they're going to write. You can try to influence the direction and tenor of the piece, but rarely can you set conditions up front on what aspects of the interview the journalist is going to feature or how it is going to be colored. Francis was being far too sensitive about the matter, but I could understand that too. The Evans/Coppola feud had been done to death in the trades and local press. This was simply the case of a national news magazine trying to keep abreast.

I immediately called Bobby and told him what Sara had said. While he was still reluctant to talk with Coppola, he realized that he must. Later when I ran into Coppola on the set, he had calmed down. He said to me, "We've decided to do nothing, to let it lay. We're making the movie and they're not, so fuck 'em."

It sounded to me like he had been contemplating asking for some sort of apology or retraction from *Newsweek* and Zarem had wisely discouraged his doing so.

I asked how he felt. He didn't understand me.

"The fall," I explained.

"With everything else, that's all I needed, right? But I'm okay. Sore, but okay, thanks."

A virtual party gathered in my office to look at the *Newsweek* item, check out photos, and shoot the shit in general: Richard Gere, Diane Lane, Gregory Hines,

James Remar, Tucker Smallwood. Diane, in her long black evening dress, black hat, blond wig, and—what she invariably wore when she came up the stairs from her dressing room to my office—*sneakers*, was a delicious paradox. Eighteen or not, she was more like a twelve-year-old dressed up in her mother's attic clothing, giggling at some of the pictures of her wearing it. Her pimples worried her. (They worried the cinematographer too.) "I've always had good skin," she remarked, frowning at a frame that betrayed her problem. "It has to be the tension, everybody tells me." There was plenty of tension to go around, and she had come onto *The Cotton Club* from *Streets of Fire* with only forty-eight hours in between.

Although the right to kill photographs had not been granted to her by contract, as a courtesy I had allowed her to pull frames that were not to her liking. Actually she pulled only a few, ones that I would have pulled myself. Just to be mean, I asked Richard, "Want to see some great shots of Diane?" Then I showed him her kills. She squealed and started beating at me lightly with her fists, trying to block the photos from being seen.

She said, "I didn't know he was like that, did you?"

Richard said enigmatically, "I suspected he was."

When the others left, Gregory Hines stayed behind. He was concerned about another matter.

"I haven't seen much on my brother and me."

Of course he hadn't. My hands had been tied. I had been desperately trying to get them untied. The *Newsweek* piece—almost in the middle of November and two and a half months into production—was *the first officially sanctioned publicity connected with the film.*

Obviously the piece had brought to the surface another festering sore that I hadn't been aware of but that didn't surprise me unduly.

Gregory Hines was one of the most amiable, warm, delightful people with whom I had ever had the pleasure of working. After my first day at the dailies, I went with Jonathan to dinner on West Forty-sixth Street and then took a Ninth Avenue bus down to the Village. Two stops after we got on, Gregory and his father also got on the bus. We sat together in four back side seats. Gregory lived in the Village not too far from me. His father was staying with him for the duration of the production. His mother had stayed behind in their Las Vegas home but would visit during production. Four young women were sitting opposite us. They couldn't take their eyes off Gregory, and small wonder. His was a personality that wouldn't quit. It radiated from him.

Now he was looking at me wistfully. "Tom, you wouldn't know there was a black person on this picture. I know you didn't do it, and although it's been *bad* press, it's been all white."

It was serious when Gregory took this tone and tack. I heard the alarm, and I was determined that Evans and Coppola should hear it too. And they did: Evans through Zarem, whom I immediately alerted, and Coppola through Fred Roos. They all got the message, and I got the okay from both quarters to go ahead with publicity on the black actors, particularly Gregory and Maurice Hines. I could write my own column items, and those earmarked for Liz Smith I could send directly to her, with copies to Zarem. All others should be sent to Zarem for deployment.

I didn't know how successful I would be at this late date, considering the surfeit of *Cotton Club* mentions in the press and the gleeful enjoyment of the negativity thus far expressed. The favorable reception of new material, particularly upbeat material, would be problematic. Nevertheless, I got Gregory to help me and we went to work.

Liz, November 29:

PICKING COTTON: Yep, they're still picking out in Astoria, Queens, and the other day, the star Richard Gere got so fed up he blew his cool and threw a chair. But only at a wall. Even Gere knows that somehow it is all going to be worth it what with the rumors that the film shot so far is dazzling . . . And, people are talking about the tap routine in the movie by Gregory and Maurice Hines. It is said to be the hottest thing since Fred Astaire and Eleanor Powell tapped to "Begin the Beguine" in "Broadway Melody of 1940." The Hines brothers' pop, Maurice, Sr., is a consultant on "Cotton Club" and Gregory's daughter, Daria, 13, is also in the cast.

Pictures of both Gregory and Maurice ran with the item. An exuberant Gregory hugged me in gratitude. The Gere portion had been phoned in by an anonymous informant, certainly not by me. Francis knew that the Hines story and the photos came from me, and his assumption, I suppose, was that I'd thrown in the Gere item as a bonus and perhaps an inducement for Liz to print the Hines item. Francis remarked coldly to Richard, and Richard repeated to me, "Well, now we know who has the publicist in his pocket, don't we?"

The fact is, I'd been dealing indirectly with Liz Smith for a couple of weeks, with Fred Roos's blessing and without Bobby Zarem's knowledge. It came about through two items in Liz Smith's columns whose content and juxtaposition threw Francis into a funk. Richard Gere's attitude was, "If it's negative, don't show me." On the other hand, the negative acted on Francis like a magnet. You couldn't pull him off it.

The first item, captioned "Coping with Coppola," suggested that Francis had ordered the painting of a big flat depicting a fanciful castle which was then placed so that he could see it from the window of his Silverfish and not have to look at the Cotton Club set, concerning which Liz speculated, ". . . he does like to forget . . . from time to time just for a moment."

The second item was the result of a call from Gere's agent, Ed Limato, who had taken exception to Liz's describing Richard as "sometimes tempestuous." By way of amends, Liz had written, "Gere is actually quite low key, quiet and not the tempestuous type. I didn't express my real vision of him, which is as a strong, silent star who knows what he wants and doesn't suffer fools gladly . . ."

Coppola did not gladly suffer statements that seemed to suggest that he was one of the fools.

Liz continued, "Certainly none of the excesses surrounding the filming of 'Cotton Club' can be laid to Gere's door . . ."

Gere's door. Please note.

Regarding the flat. It was a found object that was hung almost capriciously at the door to Coppola's van, both for fun and to lend a porch effect. To suggest that Francis was trying to block the set from his view was ludicrous. Francis should have laughed it off with a shrug or a vigorous thrust of his middle finger. Instead he had the flat removed and disposed of and the Silverfish reversed in position so that the door opened onto a blank studio wall.

Richard and I had a good laugh about "none of the excesses . . . can be laid to Gere's door" because Francis had recently kicked the door to Richard's suite off its hinges after screaming at Richard, "I'm more powerful than you, and I'm richer than you, and I don't need this shit!"

How Liz missed that incident I'll never know.

I heard about it from Richard Gere and James Remar. I had gone to downtown Manhattan on my lunch hour to get my driver's license renewed. When I got back, I saw Richard's splintered door lying at the entrance to Richard's kitchen. Jimmy said he had been lying on his couch, his door and my doors both open. "Suddenly I hear this splintering crash . . ." he said.

Richard said that he and Coppola had been sequestered in Gere's suite. Yet again Richard had been laying out his objections about the lack of a reliable schedule, the script with its constant changes, and, most recently, the cutting of three of his dramatic scenes, tossed out along with his cornet solo "Them There Eyes" (which I had heard him practicing repeatedly).

Suddenly, Coppola freaked. He walked to the door to make a dramatic and indignant exit, found that he couldn't open the door (Richard had locked it), and rather than wait for Richard to unlock it, gave it a walloping kick. He walked over and through the wreckage.

When the door was replaced, Richard inspected it reverently, touched it for flaws, found none. "Good door," he said, looking at me significantly. Francis would bust a gut if he tried to bust this one down. A portion of the busted (or "bad") door showed Francis's all-too-visible footprint on the broken, splintered wood. Richard had it framed. It hung briefly as a work of art outside the Diana Ross Suite until prudence caused someone to have it removed.

A day or so later Fred Roos asked me, "How would you handle all this if you were doing it on your own?'

If I were the sole publicist.

I thought back to my list of particulars and the proviso about the contingency should the outside PR agency (Zarem) remove itself or be removed from the film. It was no secret that Coppola and Roos would not be disconsolate if Zarem disappeared. It seemed about to come to pass. If I wanted it. At this late date I wasn't sure I did.

Fred's secretary had told me that Francis had wanted to fire Bobby Zarem after the *Newsweek* piece appeared. It was why he had been so eager to find me, to ask me about it. She knew that Fred had been talking to me about the possibility. I got the impression that it pretty much depended on me whether Zarem stayed or left.

I did some quick thinking. Whether Zarem stayed or went didn't mean that he would not continue to be associated with the film. He was under contract to Evans. He would continue to do Evans's bidding. If he stayed on officially, he would continue to be a buffer between Evans and me and might continue to be useful as a buffer in other circumstances as well. And it seemed wise to keep your opponent (if that's what he was) in sight. I tried to express all this to Fred, although perhaps not quite so boldly and bluntly.

Fred mulled a bit, and then moved on.

"The problem is, Richard has Ed Limato to call Liz Smith on his behalf, but Francis has no one." He went on to ask discretely if I thought I might do so without checking with Zarem or Evans.

Sure.

He suggested that I work through publicist Renee Furth's office, at least call her, and she would let Liz Smith and Clare St. Pugh know that they could expect to deal directly with me from then on. I did, and Furth did. My first item, about actor Joe Dallesandro who had appeared in several Andy Warhol films and would be playing Lucky Luciano in ours, went directly into Smith's column.

Later I told Richard about it. "Francis wanted to fire Zarem. Fred talked him out of it."

Richard was incredulous. "*Fred* did? Why?"

"Well, maybe it was me," I said.

I explained what I'd told Roos. Richard listened carefully (he was a great and intense listener) and saw the wisdom of my thinking.

I decided to let Zarem and Kane know about the precariousness of their situation. I got Mark Kane on the phone and didn't really say much, but Mark caught perfectly the nuances of my ellipses. (Another rule for the aspiring publicist: never spell out what you can make clear by hints.) Mark told Bobby. That night, Bobby, evidently having spoken with Evans, called me at home to suggest that it was all right for me to deal directly with Liz on publicity matters relating to Coppola and the black actors. It was a victory of sorts, but I didn't gloat. Not so anyone would notice.

* * *

I went to dailies as often as I could. The dailies were shown at the Technicolor screening room on Forty-fourth Street near Eighth Avenue. The first time I got there, September 1, they were screening the Sandman-Lila love scene filmed the day before at the Royalton. The screening room held about fifty seats in five rows with five more seats at the raised control desk where the director usually sat with the cinematographer and film editor. That night the room was filled with people—I recall seeing Fred Roos, Dyson Lovell, Gregory Hines and his father, Richard Sylbert, and William Kennedy, whom I sat with.

Later on the attendance grew smaller. Sometimes Francis himself didn't show up because he was too busy elsewhere, maybe even rewriting still another draft of the script. At times there would be only the camera people and me. Stephen Goldblatt insisted on seeing his work projected correctly on a proper screen. He couldn't gauge it properly, he said, on tape on a television monitor.

Some directors welcome, or at least tolerate, a publicist at the dailies. Some do not. Brian de Palma prohibited my attending the *Blow Out* dailies, and Andrew Bergman had second thoughts about my being present at the dailies for *So Fine* about halfway through production.

I like to go because it helps me to understand the director's intentions for a film. I wish I could say that it helps me perceive how well he is *realizing* those intentions—and of course it often does. But seeing a film in bits and pieces and the same bits and pieces repeated again and again from different angles and distances is not always an accurate gauge, for me at any rate, of how good a finished product the edited and scored film will be.

Primarily I like to go to the dailies just to keep up. As a film accelerates toward a wrap, I have to be away from the set more and more to produce the required copy and captions. Often contact sheets come to me that will feature the same actors on the same location in different clothing in disparate scenes shot on different days: only by having seen the dailies (usually screened the day after they have been shot) can I succeed in sorting, say, Scene A on page 40 from Scene X on page 84. Sometimes an action appears on the contact sheets and in the slides that leaves me perplexed, it being foreign to anything I've read in the script, something improvised in the moment, perhaps. Of course I can ask someone who was present on the set the day the action was shot—the script supervisor, the photographer—but I rarely have the luxury of having such a person about at the time I want the information. Even if I do manage to ask someone, the answer is often misleading. Another's perception of the action would not necessarily be mine. This need for information was particularly important on *The Cotton Club*.

Too, attending the dailies was a way to become more closely acquainted with co-workers, a way to establish oneself as a member of the team. Going to them meant at least another two hours added to what would be my normal work day (not that I had many normal days on *The Cotton Club*), but to me it was not only professionally but also politically necessary. It was sometimes the only place I could exchange ideas and information with Fred Roos and Francis Coppola.

One night only a few of us were there. Coppola and Goldblatt were sitting at the control desk. In addition to me there were about five others scattered about. I invariably sat on the front row on the far side, away from the entrance. So positioned I felt less obtrusive and also didn't have latecomers stumbling over me while groping for a seat in the dark auditorium. From there I also got an unobstructed view of the screen. That evening we were seeing special effects, second-unit work, specifically stacks of coins diminishing in number or increasing in number, so patently an early thirties expositional movie device that I laughed out loud in appreciation, like catching sight unexpectedly of an old friend. My laughter was shared by a guest of Francis's, a man I didn't know, who was sitting on the row behind me, one seat to my right. We were treated to other devices borrowed from another movie time: a slowly rotating martini glass suspended beneath a similarly rotating upturned shaker pouring a cocktail, and in a triangle in the upper corner the dancing feet of chorus girls.

Francis, who seemed pleased at our reaction to the material, called out to his amused guest, "Marty, we call it all 'homage.'"

His last name was Scorsese.

The next evening we saw more of the diminishing-and-accumulating coin footage, and Richard Sylbert spotted an anachronism, two in fact, a Kennedy half-dollar and a coin with a 1937 date. Talk about sharp eyes! "Somebody ought to give these kids a clue," he said. I suggested that Gio Coppola and his helper girlfriend, Tracy Rheiner, both in their early twenties, probably couldn't get all that many exact-period coins and had settled for what they could get, leaving it to editor Barry Malkin and his assistants to cut away from any coin whose date didn't fit the period. Sylbert snorted: Barry had time to sort out the 1937 half-dollars? They wanted to get this film released before the year 2000!

Richard Gere came often to the dailies, Gregory Hines less so. I saw Lonette McKee there once, Nicolas Cage and Jennifer Grey a few time, Diane Lane never. Richard told me that he had started going to the dailies about four films back because he realized that it did help him with his work. He could be brutally honest about what he saw himself doing on screen.

Richard was not able to be there the night a scene between him and Nicolas Cage was screened.

I told him, "You looked great last night."

"Fuck how I looked, how did I *act?*"

I assured him that his acting was a model of restraint. Richard Sylbert, who was sitting behind me, remarked, "Cage is playing it so high, Richard had no way to top him but to go under him—and Richard is so under he's topped him."

It pleased Gere to hear that.

* * *

Howard "Stretch" Johnson got his nickname because of his height. It would have made him a natural for basketball. Instead he became a chorus dancer and as such danced at the Cotton Club where his sister, Winnie Johnson, was a star. His brother Bobby was also a dancer. Stretch saw all the shows at the Cotton Club between 1931 and 1940 because his family was involved in each of them one way or another. In 1934 he was in the show *Ten Dancing Demons*. Later he appeared in *New Faces of 1936*.

In December 1980 he read that Robert Evans was planning a film based on the Cotton Club. He wrote a letter to Evans with his credentials and expressed a desire to work on the film in some capacity. In August 1981 a series of interviews with him began from which, he said, "A lot of script ideas emerged." The Johnson family may be the genesis of the Williams family in the movie, and even the name of Winnie for the character played by Wynona Smith is the same as that of Johnson's sister. (Of course, Winnie might have come from the name of actress Smith herself!)

Johnson was made a technical consultant on the film and was so listed on the crew sheet. He is listed along with Norma Jean Darden and Maurice Hines, Sr., as research consultant in the film's credits, and he appears briefly as a waiter.

I was sitting with him and Hines, Sr. in the Hines brothers' dressing room. Johnson said, "I kept insisting that it couldn't be just another gangster film. You could see gangsters at any club in New York then. It was not the gangsters that made the Cotton Club unique. What they came uptown to the Cotton Club to see was *black energy.*"

Black energy. It said so much. I made note of it and later put it into my production notes. Hines repeated it, validating it, "Black energy."

"The Cotton Club had so much black energy," said Johnson, "that soon every city in America wanted and got their own Cotton Club. But none could duplicate the original."

"That time will never come back," said Hines, "but I'm so glad I lived to be a part of it."

Hines, a big man himself but nowhere near as tall as Stretch Johnson, had been for some time a distributor for White Rock Soda in Las Vegas and more recently a maitre d' at one of that city's nightclubs. Twenty years ago he had been a drummer as part of an act featuring his sons Gregory and Maurice, Jr. It was called Hines, Hines, and Dad. Gregory had been about fourteen, Maurice a couple of years older. Hines, Sr.'s mother was a Cotton Club showgirl beginning with the second show ever performed there. She visited the set a couple of times, and both times I missed her. Maurice, Jr. said of his grandmother, "She's still alive and beautiful, thank God, and still has the kind of figure a woman would die for."

While black people couldn't go as guests to the Cotton Club, Johnson said they went "everyplace else." One of his favorites was Smalls' Paradise. "We went there all the time. We were afraid to go to bed for fear we'd miss something. Ethel Waters broke a bottle over Pretty Eddie's head? And I wasn't there to see it?! And the ladies! The ladies today don't seem to have the energy we had when we were young. We could dance all night, and all the rest of it too. Today they read books—how to do everything. Even how to screw. You don't have to read books on how to love somebody, you know or you don't know. It comes from the heart. We did it all from the heart then."

At Barron's—Barron Wilkins' Exclusive Club—black people and white people could mingle, as in the Bamville Club in *The Cotton Club*, he told me.

Stretch Johnson was always near the set, often called upon to verify some detail. I once heard Coppola ask him how waiters at the club had held napkins on their arms. Stretch showed him. Much to do with the Cotton Club and Harlem of the period—graphics, pictures, archival film, text—was made available by

Stretch Johnson to various of the film's department heads, all of whom benefitted greatly from it.

* * *

Hinton Battle and Gregg Burge, two great young tap dancers, were set to perform two numbers, "Don't Let the Blues Go to Your Feet" and "Bugle Call Rag." I cleared my schedule to be there. Because the Cotton Club had a thrust stage, duplicated in our set, an unusually large number of extras were required daily. Unlike proscenium theater numbers, which can be photographed separately from audience reaction shots, *The Cotton Club* floorshows had to be performed in the simultaneous presence of audience, extras in full costume and makeup. The logistics were staggering. The strain on makeup and hair and wardrobe, not to mention on the extras themselves, would have taxed a Hercules of extraordinary strength matched evenly with extraordinary patience. Extras would be coiffed in the early morning, rouged, gowned, and tuxedoed. Then they often had to sit around all day on call, unused, doing nothing, bored out of their skulls.

With the Battle/Burge numbers, it was different. These dances would be shot straight on with only a portion of the Cotton Club audience seen on the right side near the kitchen. Only a few extras were needed. The numbers, which were to be interpolated into footage still to be shot, were being done early because of Battle's rehearsal schedule for *The Tap Dance Kid* on Broadway and Burge's scheduled flight to Japan the following day to appear in a production of *Sophisticated Ladies*.

The dance numbers were for the "Cotton Club II" sequence. The show curtain had been changed from the previous view of a plantation porch to a new glittering silver drop. The ice-cream-parlor chairs had been altered with cloth envelopes slipped over their backs. In the "Cotton Club I" sequence, Duke Ellington's orchestra had provided the music. It had been replaced by Cab Calloway's.

Because shots featuring audience were kept to a minimum and carefully worked out, those of us wanting to see the show could have ringside seats. I sat on the right side, not far from one of the playback loudspeakers, pretty much away from most of the other spectators. On the other side of a post from me were Grace Blake and tap choreographer Henry LeTang and his wife. (The film would credit thirteen choreographers in all, Michael Smuin being the principal. Gregory Hines's credit for "tap improvography" was a new one to me.)

Sitting directly across the stage from me were Gwen Verdon, Joel Grey with daughter Jennifer, Bob Hoskins, and Fred Gwynne. Richard Gere slipped into a chair next to me. "Is it safe to sit here?" I assumed he was asking whether the table was out of camera range. Then again, he could have meant, "Will Francis have a shit fit if he sees us together?"

It might as well have been the latter. When Coppola noticed us together, he stopped dead in his tracks. On a dime. Lot's wife turning into a pillar of salt. Here they were, Sodom and Gomorrah, together again. The dark pools of his eyes fixed on us, glaring like the Wrath of God getting ready to unleash His fateful lightning. He stood on the raised platform only a few feet from us, staring, saying nothing, sizing up the import of our being together. It didn't help matters that

Richard continued to sit with me for over an hour. Francis had perceived a conspiracy between star and publicist that was responsible for Gere getting all the good Liz Smith mentions and the director getting nothing but turds. I had been told by persons in Coppola's confidence after the door-kicking episode that Francis thought Richard was using me as a conduit to plant some of the derogatory things being printed about him. I have wondered whether I managed to keep my job primarily due to the intervention on my behalf of Fred Roos and Tony Dingman.

What Richard and I talked about at the table between takes was not Coppola but favorite restaurants. He asked me to write down the names of several of mine that he wanted to try. Between takes, both Battle and Burge came over to tell Richard how much they liked him in *An Officer and a Gentleman*, which many had seen for the first time during its first network airing recently. Burge asked for autographed pictures for his nephews. Richard referred him to me to work out the details, and I was later able to get photographs signed and mailed to Burge.

After Diane Lane had been on the David Letterman show, she had told me what Letterman had asked her. I suggested to her that I thought it best not to tell Richard: it would only disturb him. Lisa Jane Persky, however, didn't know about our little agreement. She stopped by the table where Richard and I were sitting. "Did you see Letterman last night?" she asked Richard. "He asked Diane, 'Does Richard take his clothes off in this?'"

Gere looked at me judgmentally. "I wasn't going to tell you that," I said.

"Oh, but Diane handled it wonderfully," said Lisa, going on to describe Diane's adroit evasiveness.

Richard said, "I used to like David Letterman. Now I think he's an asshole."

Persky cornered me later. "You should have warned me!" (Like when?) "I could wring Richard's neck," she said. "He's so sensitive."

The Burge/Battle routine was like a climb to the top of Mount Everest with no one to know except the few of us who saw it filmed. The dance numbers didn't make it into the final cut of the film. So much wonderful material didn't. Like I've said before, there's a whole other movie out there in outtakes.

During the final take, Gregg Burge stopped, unable to continue, holding his foot in pain. Goldblatt had been filming with two cameras: arguably he had adequate coverage although he told me he didn't. (Richard Sylbert said, "It was enough. You don't want these guys upstaging the Hines brothers.")

The concern at the moment was Burge. How badly hurt was he? He was being attended by a number of his peers, including both Gregory Hines and Arthur Mitchell, director of the Dance Theatre of Harlem, who had recently come in as a choreographer. Mitchell massaged Burge's foot and said he had pulled a tendon and would have to stay off the foot for a few days. Then he would be all right. He could continue his planned trip to Japan and would be ready to dance again in a matter of days. Gregg's warm smile spread into a grateful laugh.

That evening Francis gave his mid-term party and screening, a nice gesture. It began half an hour after wrap in the makeup area. After an hour of partying, we got to see a rough cut of the first assembly of footage of the film. I sat at a table with Diane Lane, Lisa Jane

Persky, and Diane Venora, a wonderful actress who made a brief appearance in the film as Gloria Swanson. I knew her stage work well, and in 1981 she was the female lead in *Wolfen*, one of the best horror movies of modern times. Her co-stars in that film were Albert Finney and our own Gregory Hines. Against the far wall I saw Bobby Zarem, who had been invited, and Mark Kane, who hadn't been invited but for whom I'd left a pass at the door.

Richard had told me to keep my door locked since there would be people wandering about the studio. When I left the office, James Remar was still in his room. I asked him to lock up when he left, but he misunderstood and thought I was going to be returning. When I did get back to the office after the screening, I found a man and a woman making themselves at home, both of them high, the woman combing her hair before my mirror. Later I discovered that a box of transparencies was missing.

That was on Friday night. On Monday morning, Tony Dingman told me of the party's tragic aftermath. A personable young Vietnam War veteran who had been hired by the studio to clean rooms (including Remar's and mine) had attended the party, drunk a few beers, and continued partying afterwards. He had been found dead the next morning. Apparently he had passed out while vomiting into his toilet bowl and had drowned.

* * *

The parade of visitors continued: Ellen Barkin, greeting me with a big kiss (I had worked with her on my previous film, *Harry and Son*), Carol Kane, Sean Penn visiting Nicolas Cage . . .

One day, outside the Silverfish, Tony Dingman said to me, "Guess who's here? De Niro. He's in there with him now."

I wanted to say hello. I waited.

I hadn't seen Robert De Niro since just before he left for Italy to do *1900*. We used to live near each other, me on West Twelfth and Greenwich Avenue, him on Fourteenth Street just west of Seventh Avenue, two blocks away. We'd worked together on *The Gang That Couldn't Shoot Straight*, but I had known him earlier. De Niro and Coppola had a history dating back to *Gang*, which was in production at the same time as *The Godfather*. Al Pacino had been signed to play De Niro's role in *Gang*, and De Niro had been set for a minor role in *Godfather*, a Corleone driver, I seem to remember. When Coppola decided to cast Pacino in *The Godfather*, De Niro was chosen to replace him in *Gang*.

When they were ready for Coppola on set, Dan Suhart lifted the receiver connecting the outside of the van with the interior to inform him so. Francis came out first, followed by De Niro, Gio, and a few others.

"Bobby," I called. Francis, a few paces in front of him, stopped and waited as De Niro turned to me. He knew me immediately.

"You're working on *this*?" he said, pleased and amused.

I was aware of Francis pacing in the background, waiting for him to conclude with me. De Niro was facing me, his back to Coppola.

"What do you think?" he said, gesturing toward Coppola.

"I love him," I said. "Exciting guy to work for."

No lie *there*.

In typical de Niro fashion, he gestured to my hair. His mumbled ellipses went something like this: "It's a little -ummm—ah—up here."

I was letting the gray show. As Richard was. Only I had a lot more to show than Richard.

"A little more salt than pepper?" I said.

"No, I mean the um—ah—Ummmm— "

"Length? I cut it."

He grinned, which I interpreted to mean, "A lot."

Well, I'd known him in the late sixties, early seventies. Back then my hair had tended to be shoulder length.

"You still live in the same place?" he asked.

"Yeah. You ever eat at El Charro?"

Where we would drink margaritas and eat Mexican and Spanish food.

Back and forth, our brilliant repartee. I sensed Francis's impatience to get back to the set. He was reluctant to go without Bobby. He wanted to make his entrance with Bobby. I was holding up production. A circle of people had gathered about us, keeping a respectful distance.

"Well, I just wanted to say hello," I said to De Niro to give him a chance to withdraw.

"Yes, well . . ." Awkward, saying goodbye. ". . . It was nice seeing you."

A few days later I was sitting on the steps leading to the Cotton Club stage with a scantily clad Mario Van Peebles in his "Creole Love Song" costume. Hundreds of extras and actors and crew were milling about, and in the surrounding din it was difficult to carry on a conversation. Mario and I were sitting closer than Siamese twins. I was almost in his lap, my hand on his bare shoulder which felt like satin. He was telling me about his dilemma. He had an important commercial scheduled, and Francis had excused him for one day to shoot it. Now one of his two big production numbers in *The Cotton Club* had been scheduled for that very day. He'd been told by Girolami not to worry about it; they'd use a double and intercut him with footage of Mario so that it would all appear to be Mario. Still, it worried Mario. The use of a double could diminish the potential for any impact he might make in the number. I was patting his shoulder and sympathizing when we were startled to find Francis hovering about us.

"Have you seen my guests?" he asked.

What guests? I didn't have a clue what he was talking about.

"Never mind," he said, "I think I see them."

The guests were Steven Spielberg and George Lucas. I quickly rounded up Adger Cowans and got a photo of the two of them with Francis, not that it did us any good. It was taken under work lights, and the quality was poor.

After chatting with his guests, Francis slid up onto the wooden railing circling the set. Sylbert told him it was okay to do so. Whereupon, crunch! The railing gave way, a post toppled, and Humpty Dumpty might have taken a great fall except for Tony Dingman, who was standing behind him and managed to break his fall.

Robert Evans had had his picture taken at this very same point, his smartly booted foot resting on the railing, his head bowed, one hand supporting what we were meant to see as an anguished forehead, Richard Sylbert standing by in his safari jacket and holding his talismanic pipe. The photograph had been taken on a Saturday when Coppola was supposedly never at the studio. But this Saturday he was, big surprise. I'm told that Evans spoke, Coppola didn't. The picture had accompanied the infamous *Calendar* story and added yet another bit of laughable lore to the continuing entertainment that the production was turning out to be.

Nobody was having more fun with the production than Richard Sylbert, who had a marvelously trenchant sense of humor, usually at someone else's expense. I'll never forget his commenting that Nicolas Cage should get the Yul Brynner Award for Acting for his performance as Vince.

"Yes, he's funny," Richard Gere told me, "but just remember when he's putting somebody else down, he's probably doing the same thing about you to somebody else."

* * *

Joey Cusumano asked me to prepare a souvenir book for investors. He needed nine copies, but I had fifteen made up. I knew I could make judicious and political use of the excess. The art department designed them, and I supplied the copy and twenty-eight 8 x 10 photographs—scene stills and gallery shots, in color and black-and-white. I kept the book secret from everyone. I was able to prepare it in relative privacy since both Gere and Remar were then working on location.

When the finished copies came in, I took one to my favorite Japanese restaurant, Fuji, on West Fifty-sixth Street, to show to my friends Pat, the proprietor, and her daughter, Karen, who waited tables. Jonathan and I were seated at a table in an alcove near the kitchen and restrooms, hidden from most of the rest of the diners. When Karen brought our drinks, I pulled the book out to show her.

I heard a shriek, and there she was all over me, Diane Lane. "It's you!" she said. "I thought it was you when you came in! I made a special trip to the restroom to make sure."

I was delighted and astonished to see her there. I recalled that she lived nearby. I told Karen, "This is our *star*!"

Diane, looking every inch the American teenager, wearing jeans, long blond hair flowing, wasn't having it. "Don't *say* that," she said, clasping her hand over my mouth and imploring. This was one of her favorite restaurants, she said, and she didn't want to be known here as anything other than an appreciative customer.

The souvenir book fascinated her. I told her I was having a few choice frames blown up and would be giving her 8 x 10 glossies. "Which ones?" she asked excitedly. I described head shots of her in various hairstyles. "On, thanks, but I don't want them," she said. "The only pictures I want are of Richard kissing me." She had a crush on her co-star that was charming to see.

She turned to go back to her table to pick up her check.

"You're alone?" I asked.

"Who would I be with," she teased, "since you never ask me?"

There is a particular still of Diane that I enjoy looking at. She is wearing her Louise Brooks wig. Straight hair, bangs, very much the flapper. She and Richard are lying on the floor of the Bamville Club. The two actors have been rehearsing a scene they're about to shoot, the one where Dixie throws Vera to the floor when the bomb meant to kill Dutch Schultz explodes. What the still shows is their reaction to a new script page that has just been handed to them, changes in the scene they are preparing to shoot. Their look is one of utter dismay, Gere looking at the new page, Lane at the camera.

Utter dismay was also the expression on Richard's face when the matter of the insecurity of his suite of rooms had come to light. "The rear vulnerability," Richard called it.

Rock entrepreneur Bill Graham was flown in from California to play the movie producer who evaluates Dixie Dwyer's screen test. The scene was shot in the small theater one-half floor off the main stage, next to a holding area for extras. Because the camera blocked the entrance to the theater, all comings and goings into the screening room had to be made through Richard's suite by way of a tight passageway that led down from his bedroom. The doors to his rooms were thrown wide open, and crew members with no previous reason to visit the area got their first glimpse of our set-up. What really upset Richard was the discovery that his back door was secured only by an easily breakable hook. When the screening room scene was completed, Richard summoned workmen to install a secure lock.

It made me feel more secure too.

One afternoon I walked into my room thinking I was alone. No sign of Richard or Jimmy in their rooms. Then I realized that Richard was standing behind my open door, leaning against the refrigerator, and reading the famous copy of *Calendar* that I'd been keeping on top. Although I had circulated copies around the studio where it had created an excited stir, I hadn't shown it to Richard because of his instruction not to show him anything negative. I didn't know that he would interpret anything in the piece as being negative about him but had decided not to take the risk. Richard continued reading without comment other than a nod in my direction. When he finished, he laid the paper down, also without comment. Pregnant pause. Then he turned to me.

"Well," I offered, "Lloyd Leipsig likes it."

"Figures," said Richard.

"He says, 'We're doing everything right. This is the most want-to-see picture in years.'"

Gere said, cynically but sincerely, "Oh, no doubt about it, it's good publicity."

Jimmy came in with news. "The plug is being pulled. We've got to be out of here by Christmas, no matter what."

Richard looked at me. "Isn't this boring?" He meant the pressure, the uncertainty, the lack of time to bring it all together. "Well, they'll have to do it without me. I won't be free again until the spring."

He was locked into his next movie, *King David*, and wouldn't be available for retakes or reshooting or dubbing until that was completed.

He turned to go to his room. "Want some cheesecake, Reverend?"

Gere had mentioned his fondness for cheesecake to a visiting dignitary who began sending him the most delicious, rich, elegant cheesecakes any of us had ever eaten. And cheesecake wasn't the only goodie available. Lisa Jane Persky had prevailed upon Richard to let her use his kitchen from time to time to make chocolate chip cookies.

"How about it, Fadder," Jimmy said, sounding like one of the Angels with Dirty Faces. "A little cheesecake. C'mon."

The vicar had some but didn't provide any.

* * *

Adger wanted to set up a gallery in which he could take posed black-and-white glamour portraits of the actors in the style of George Hurrell. We found a space off the main stage but in yelling distance accessible only by a precariously twisting, almost free-floating metal ladder. It looked like a rat's nest and probably was.

It was Adger's idea to practice on lesser-billed actors before he tackled Richard. Assuming he even got the chance to tackle Richard. In anticipation of Richard's possible recalcitrance, I began preparing him right away. I left a note in his room explaining the situation. *You've got the look in this movie that personified many of the top male stars of the 1930s, and I think it would be nice to have a gallery type photograph of you like we associate with these stars . . .*

Well, what do you know! He came to me as soon as he read the note. "Sure, Vicar, it's all right with me. How about before this next shot?"

In other words, *now.*

I was caught off guard, Adger more so than I. After much hustling and confusion and clearing it with an army of assistant directors and production assistants, Richard was allowed to ascend to the modest heaven of our hastily assembled rat's nest and sit for Adger's hooded camera. We had makeup, hair, and wardrobe with us. The whole thing had been pulled together in less than forty minutes.

"To me there's nothing more boring than stills," Richard remarked.

At one point he suddenly glanced at me and said, "What are you looking at, Vicar?"

It was to become a refrain during picture-taking sessions. I thought it was just a joke, banter, a running gag. But during the last session photographed by Herb Ritts at an all-night filming at Grand Central Station, Jim Skotchdopole said to me, "Tom, you really do make him nervous. I don't know what it is about you, but I've noticed. Anybody else watching him he doesn't mind. But you, he gets edgy."

I've never managed to figure that one out, but I've wondered if maybe it didn't have something to do with the nickname Vicar.

For the gallery session, Adger had produced one full 8 x 10 contact sheet for each frame shot. When I got the ones of Richard, I saw immediately that they were inferior to similar work Adger had dome with Lonette McKee, Priscilla Baskerville, and Mario Van Peebles in their "Creole Love Song" costumes.

Richard kept pressing me to show the stills to him. He wanted to send one to *Rolling Stone* for the magazine's end-of-the-year issue, and he was looking for a good pose that could be duplicated for autographing and distribution. (As far as the latter was concerned, I convinced him to use a photograph of himself as he normally looked. I would give him names, explain who the people were, and let him know who had made the request for a photograph if it was someone other than the recipient. He patiently autographed more than two hundred of them.) When he finally did see Adger's shots, he said, "Now I see why you hesitated to show them to me. Okay, we'll do them over. I thought he was tighter on me."

He asked me to bring him a book he had seen in my room, *The Image Makers*, which featured glamour photographs of movie stars of the 1930s and 1940s. He studied certain of the pictures, commenting on the lighting and comparing it with Adger's lighting of him. He suggested that Adger's lighting might be as much to blame as the laboratory for having printed the photographs without proper contrast.

He looked at the contact sheets of himself and then lifted his head to look in the mirror. He said wanly, "My face."

I think I laughed, but Richard was serious. I believe that he felt his face was too bland. I thought of something I had recently heard on *The Today Show* in connection with a story on cosmetic surgery for men. "We can't all look like Richard Gere, so why try?" If his face was to be considered bland, then I figured that his body would be considered bland as well. Perhaps the reason he used so much body language in some films, endowing his characters with hyper body movements and tics, was to make up for the blandness that he perceived in himself. Then too, the Richard Gere look that we had come to know invariably involved hair, a sensuous free-flowing lot of it. In our present project, for his Dixie Dwyer the hair was a much lesser feature, the moustache more prominent.

I feel that Richard's performances started to become more restrained about the time of *The Cotton Club*, and I believe that this restraint led critics to discount the importance of his performance to the success of certain films (perfect case in point: *Pretty Woman*). I have wondered if his being in *The Cotton Club* might have been part of this evolution of his acting ability. Just possibly he got more from Francis Coppola than a hard time, suspicion, and a kicked-down door.

I considered having the lab reprint Adger's gallery shots of Richard with more contrast, but I decided first to seek a second opinion, that of cinematographer Stephen Goldblatt. He already knew Adger's work and looked eagerly at my present examples. He said, "Adger's an excellent photographer with *my* lighting. But look at this stuff. He doesn't know how to light."

I told him we were planning on re-shooting Gere. "I'll light it for you," Stephen volunteered.

"How can you," I said. "You're up to your ass."

"I'll do it on a Saturday. A Saturday morning. But they'll have to pay me."

I didn't tell him that this was pure pipe dream. They would have to pay not only Stephen but also Gere, wardrobe, hair, makeup, electricians, props, Adger. I was the only one they wouldn't have to pay. Just thinking about it gave me a headache.

It turned out that we never reshot Gere in the rat's nest studio. For whatever reason, we got evicted. Adger managed to set up a gallery in the cubicle outside Diane Lane's dressing room, and we took actors there when we could grab them.

We actually ended up having two special photographers on the film at various times: Theo Westenberger because of Bobby Zarem, and Herb Ritts because of Richard Gere.

"Herb Ritts is my man," Richard had told me early on. "He goes where I go." At that time I had never heard of Herb Ritts, not yet fully the star he was soon to become. Richard would agree to Westenberger if I would agree to Ritts. I passed the information along to Lloyd

Leipsig at Orion, who thought it was a deal worth making.

Lloyd and Richard did not care for each other, I gathered. Their experience on *Breathless* had left each one soured on the other. Richard felt that he was exploited in the Leipsig-approved posters and artwork. "It looked like a porn movie, the way they sold it," he said. He believed that the exploitation of him by selling him as beefcake was seriously detrimental to his career, and he didn't know what to do about it.

Sitting in a chair with his name on the canvas backrest, Richard looked like a 1930s icon, Ronald Colman, maybe, or Warner Baxter. Tuxedo, fedora, moustache. Personally, I thought the moustache did nothing for him, even diminished him, unlike Clark Gable who without a moustache looked somewhat unfinished. His hair had an appropriate slicked-down look, achieved, he told me, by the early morning application of curlers. The beginning gray in his hair had been touched up.

His new film, *The Honorary Consul*, based on the Graham Greene novel, was being given a new title: *Beyond the Limit*.

"I'm hysterical," he said. "I've been on the phone all morning, with Paramount, with my agent. Wait till you see the newspaper and poster art. It's *Breathless* all over again. My chest is bare and I'm on a bed . . ."

His voice trailed off. A sleazy pattern was developing in the way his films were sold; and to add insult to injury, he was being blamed in the press for his own exploitation.

"And it *is* beyond the limit," he said. "How could all those geniuses come up with a title as nothing as that? In the context of the movie it means nothing. It isn't metaphor. It isn't literal. It isn't anything but meaningless. There are people out there who have read *The Honorary Consul* who might want to see a movie based on it. You're going to lose even them with a title like *Beyond the Limit*. It's disgusting."

(Bob Hoskins, who co-starred in the film along with Michael Caine, later told me that he had seen both the director's original cut and then the studio's version. "They've butchered it," he said. "It's a fine movie and they've fucked it up every way they can.")

Richard was grasping about for a way to better control his image. "Maybe it starts with the stills," he said. "The bed, the bare chest. If they don't have the ammunition, they can't fire it. I hate to do this to you, Tom, or to Adger, but I don't want any pictures of me on a bed or bare-chested."

This was too sweeping a restriction, one I thought impossible to abide by. Carefully I ventured, "Yes, I know, but there are a couple of scenes where . . ."

He interrupted. "For the *movie* these scenes are important. For stills they aren't. If they've got a shot of me on a bed or partially disrobed, they're going to use it. You can't sell *The Cotton Club* that way. I won't approve any pictures of me on a bed or with my clothes off."

Later I had fun with him over this sweeping and impractical pronouncement. I found a color transparency on him fully clothed with his hat on sitting in a chair beside an empty bed. He was looking plaintively at the bed. "I've found a wonderful shot of you," I said, "but there's a problem. You're sitting by a bed. I don't know whether I should show it to you or not." Of course, he insisted on seeing it. He did find it amusing, and he passed it. But either I mislaid it or he appropriated it: in any case, it disappeared. He had already passed a few shots of himself on a bed but clothed. When I had two of them blown up and displayed in my office, he swore he hadn't okayed them. Since I had his initials and personally crossed-out kills on each contact sheet, I was able to prove otherwise. He didn't make an issue of it, and it may have just been his way of kidding me. With his demeanor and dead-pan delivery, you couldn't always be sure.

Theo Westenberger had turned up on Monday, September 26. She told me that Zarem had promised her ten days on the movie, which was news to me. She wanted to shoot Gregory Hines and Lonette McKee off the set. I saw no problem with that, although I would have to get the cooperation of makeup, wardrobe, and hair, not to mention assistant directors. I thought I could manage it. She also said she wanted to get some "good stuff" with Richard Gere. He was immediately suspicious.

"What do you mean by 'good stuff'?"

"An acting scene," I said.

"Tom, I don't have an *acting* scene in the whole movie." He sounded, and looked, weary. He told Theo apologetically, "I hate to sound negative, but that's how it is. Good luck."

Theo and her wasted days.

We would schedule her on a day that looked "good." The shooting schedule would change without warning. She would come in and none of the principal actors would be working after all. Sometimes the scene being shot would not be worth wasting a special photographer's time (and fee) on. Goldblatt couldn't understand our disappointment and frustration: to him the good stuff were the production numbers, the chorus girls, the visuals. Great stuff, even "good" stuff, but in terms of publicity merely gravy. The stars were the meat. Time and fee had been set. Theo was there, we had to pay. It was even worse later with Herb Ritts.

The day that Francis walked looked like it would turn out to be another of Theo's wasted days. I set about quickly to see that it wasn't. I pushed for the special photography set-up for Gregory and Lonette that we hadn't been able to achieve the preceding week. Gregory and Lonette were agreeable. I got everybody in on the act. Everyone was cooperative, especially Milena and the wardrobe department. Theo wanted to set up in the corner against the flats of the Harlem skyline. Night flats were hanging, and Theo thought the day flats preferable. Henry Bronchtein didn't want to change them. He was afraid (hoping!) that Francis would come back and changing the flats would delay shooting. I conferred with Milena about costuming. Since Theo had her own strobe unit and an assistant to operate it, we didn't have to call in our electricians. All other pertinent departments were told what would be happening.

Then came the depressing news: the company would be wrapping after lunch, a development that could conceivably knock the props (as well as makeup, wardrobe, Hines, and McKee) right out from under us. I dashed off a hasty memo to Bronchtein and Girolami:

We hear that the company may wrap after lunch which makes it unfortunate for Theo and what we're trying to get today in the way of special photos.

Would it be possible, if they do wrap, to have one makeup person remain available for Diane Lane, and also for Lonette and Gregory.

All Theo has been able to get thus far (at lunch wrap) is Gregory alone.

Since we understand that wardrobe people will remain two hours later anyway, that would be no problem.

All we need would be a couple of hours, and to have Diane, Lonette, and Gregory alerted to stay.

(We'll also want to get James Remar and Nicolas Cage but that we can do another day, hopefully; Theo certainly doesn't want everybody against the same backdrop anyway.

We were hoping to get Diane Lane posed in the Cotton Club at a table against a mural.)

Diane wasn't available after all. It was ambitious to think that we could photograph her on the same wrapped afternoon as Hines and McKee. It took Diane three hours for makeup, hair, and costuming.

We had been shooting Hines and McKee for half an hour when Jim Skotchdopole, assigned to the session by Bronchtein and Girolami, told me that in another fifteen minutes we would have to relinquish our stars because Gio's second unit needed them. Barrie had approved it, he said.

I blew up.

"Like hell," I said, along with other choice expletives. "I set this up. This is my session. Second unit had no part in setting this up. I arranged for Gregory and Lonette to stay after they'd been wrapped. I arranged for them to be dressed . . ." I nodded to those who were helping with the session and who were sitting just out of camera range: Milena, makeup woman Margaret Sunshine, various wardrobe men and women and hair stylists ". . . and I'll be damned if I let anybody else have them!"

Skotchdopole went to tell Barrie Osborne, who sent him back for me. Together we went to Barrie's office. Fred Roos was with him. I made an impassioned argument.

Fred made the decision. "Let stills have them."

I couldn't blame Gio for trying. Second unit had to scrounge the same as the rest of us. It was their job to shoot whatever actors were available, costumed, made up, in "set pieces" that might be intercut with footage already or still to be shot. But I had scrounged these people first. Good try, Gio.

The material Theo got on that day would receive wide coverage, particularly a striking shot of Gregory Hines dancing against the Harlem night skyline.

On one of her "wasted" days Theo got into a bit of trouble. There was nothing much doing on the set. Theo decided she would shoot in the extras' dressing area and makeup, hair, wardrobe, and rehearsal rooms. The women's wardrobe area was a space partitioned off and surrounded by mobile screens and mirrors. Theo noticed a woman who had stripped before putting on period underwear (Oh yes, even the lacy step-ins were period!) and her artist's eye was caught by a discreet tattoo on the woman's backside. She asked the extra for permission to photograph the tattoo, which the extra granted. With the woman's back to her, surrounded by other women in various stages of period dress, Theo found her composition. But then another extra reacted angrily and called for a production assistant. Although she herself did not figure in Theo's composition, she announced that she would not be party to any "pornography" and threatened to call the union immediately unless Theo and her camera were evicted from women's wardrobe if not from the studio. A young black casting woman, whose sophistication and style I came to admire, was also indignant over Theo's intended shot. She said, "If this got out, can you imagine? It's not the kind of publicity we need right now, on top of everything else. I think your photographer showed bad taste." I let her know I disagreed.

When news of the incident reached Chris Cronyn, he said to me humorously, "I hear a pornographer has been at work in women's dresses."

Thank God for the humor. Humor kept us going and kept us sane. Mark Burchard, during the last weeks of production, began putting a vase of red roses on my desk, another on Richard's. They were delivered fresh to the studio every morning, for whose department and for what purpose I never found out. Perhaps they were used as props and set dressing on the Vera's Club set. The note on my first bouquet read, "For Tom—for always having a smile and a sense of humor." Well, it *was* a howl. In two senses: a howl like in a horror movie and a howl like in a hoot. We went through the movie in a state of laughing disbelief. Louis de Esposito, like Bronchtein an assistant director, said to me once, "Have you ever seen anything like this?" I said no, and neither had Francis or anyone else. And it was not likely that any of us would see its like again.

Theo Westenberger's time with us was not sequential but scattered through the last several weeks of production. On her last day, I was supposed to have the Cotton Club set all to myself and a crew assigned to work with us. Unfortunately, her last day coincided with the last day of filming inside Astoria Studios when it seemed that three days of work was being crammed into one. Agendas grated against agendas. It was total nightmare. Francis and the first unit were on the third floor in Studio F shooting Vera's Club, and the four principals that Theo had hoped to shoot were involved in filming there. The dreaded second unit was nowhere to be seen, but Gio was like a cattle rustler. He could be on you before you knew it, riding off with one of your lassoed stars. But at the moment I had no stars to lasso.

Theo Westenberger's auburn hair was piled up on top of her head and her pert face was alert and lovely atop a body made bulky and lumpy by layers of clothing, the outer garments fitted with oversized pockets from which photographic equipment bulged. She told me she wanted to shoot at a table against one of the murals. I would have liked that too. The murals were beautiful as artwork and would be wonderful for background and composition. Adger had done some great color shots of them, unfortunately none with major actors that also really featured the murals. But today's shooting was mostly to show off Milena Canonero's work: we wanted to emphasize costumes, not wall murals, no matter how beautiful the latter. I suggested the bandstand, against a silver curtain. Theo liked the idea but hated the bandstand carpeting. A carpenter with us said he could cover it with material that corresponded to the curtain, if we liked. We liked. He did, after I had the musical instruments removed so that we had a bare stage elevated some three or four feet above the dance floor. Theo, shooting from the main floor, would need a tall, sturdy ladder. We found that too.

We had everything but the stars.

It was mayhem on Stage F, we heard. There was great pressure to finish the scene. Nerves were frayed. The whole thing was about to blow. Periodically I had the production assistant assigned to me check with the assistant directors there as to when Gere and Lane would be available. Finally the production assistant said to me, "If I ask Henry Bronchtein one more time he's going to have a stroke." She said that Bobby Girolami had already spoken to Bronchtein about yelling at her.

Although we finally had Gregory and Lonette, I was increasingly concerned that we might not get Richard and Diane. I sought out Barrie Osborne and explained the situation. He pulled Louis de Esposito aside. "It's important that Tom get Richard and Diane. Look at them, they're just sitting over there. Why can't they be sent down for stills? If Francis needs them, they can be back in a minute."

I waited outside the door of Stage F for the decision. Fred Roos and Joey Cusumano came out the door and saw me waiting. "Just the man I want to talk to," said Fred. "Come with us, it'll take just a few minutes."

"Not now, Fred. I'm waiting for Richard and Diane. Theo's set up on the main stage."

"You're not going to get them right away. It'll just take a moment."

Reluctantly I went.

It had been decided, Fred and Joey told me, that a wrap party open to selected press would be given on the Cotton Club set on the Saturday following our all-Friday-night shoot at Grand Central Station, exactly one week away. Cusumano had the idea that since we'd had a closed set during production, this would be a nice goodwill gesture. Also wouldn't it be nice if the black Cotton Club performers all did their acts. Would I ask them about it?

I was numb. I couldn't respond.

I told them they would have my response in a memo that I would write at home the next day,

Saturday, and deliver to appropriate desks to be found on Monday morning.

I thought it was one of the worst ideas I had ever heard.

I returned to the stills set. Richard, Diane, Gregory, and Lonette were all on the bandstand being photographed, the very shot I had been hoping for and one that I feared would begin in my absence. I braced myself for repercussions.

Gere in black tuxedo, Lane in black evening dress with black sequined skullcap over her blond wig, Hines in an exquisitely tailored and textured white suit, McKee in a shimmering beige evening dress: the contrast of costuming coupled with the contrast of skin coloring was exciting and arresting.

The production assistant tipped me off that Richard was angry because I hadn't been there when he and Diane were brought down from the third floor. He had wanted to talk to me about the session before he did it. Theo, I was told, was if anything even angrier than Richard, who was giving her a hard time and being uncooperative. He had threatened to walk.

Theo was the first one to see me. "It's all because of you! Of all times to disappear!"

When she calmed down, I explained and apologized.

Richard moved out of the blinding lights into shadow so he could see me. "Where were you?" he asked evenly.

Again I explained.

Once he understood, he forgave. As for his problem with Theo, the tail end of which I had witnessed, he said soberly and gently, "I'm sorry you weren't here. I like to be talked to. I liked to be coaxed into something. You coaxed me into doing this. Now you've got to coax me into continuing with it. I don't understand what we're doing here."

Standing stiffly in front of a silver curtain, dressed like he was dressed, he felt he was nothing but a model. The shot had nothing to do with the film. It was phony. Of course he was projecting annoyance. There was no other emotion to project.

Never before had he spoken with me so candidly.

While we were talking, his hair was being retouched, perspiration wiped, makeup patched. All the right moves, just as though he intended to return to the bandstand. None of us was convinced that he would.

"This four-shot has nothing to do with the characters we play. What's it all for, Vicar?"

He wanted motivation. For a *still*. I had never before been asked to supply such. I was not skilled in providing it. His complaint about what had been happening to him throughout production now seemed to be transferred directly to me and the area of special photography. He had been thrust into *yet another* situation without adequate preparation. "What am I supposed to be projecting? How is this to be *used?*"

I wanted to say, "Oh, come off it!" Our time was limited. He owed me this. Did I dare remind him that I had gotten Herb Ritts for him? Would he ask Herb for motivation?

"It's just a glitzy glamour shot," I said. "Like they did in the 1930s." He'd been studying my books on the work of Hollywood photographers, so surely he, of all people, knew what I was talking about. This I hadn't expected from him. I was annoyed. What was the motivation of those 1930s and 1940s movie stars—Garbo, Gable, Flynn, Crawford? Obligation, maybe? To their producers and to their public? Not to mention to their publicists.

Don't piss me off any further, Richard. Get the fuck back up there.

Oh yeah, sure.

I was starting to sweat.

I argued that since the period of *The Cotton Club* was the 1930s, the present shoot should be thought of as the kind of publicity stills studios once used in promoting films. "It's *Boom Town*," I said, remembering a classic four-shot from that old MGM movie: Gable and Colbert and Tracy and Lamarr, their arms interlinked, heads thrown back, all smiling broadly, all with one foot forward as if in purposeful stride toward the camera, a great example of the old tradition of lining up your stars four abreast.

Boom Town was not a movie I expected Richard to know. He surprised me, yet again. "In *Boom Town* they interact with each other. I interact with Diane, but I have no interaction with Gregory and Lonette. Our so-called plot doesn't involve all four actors with each other like *Boom Town* did. Which clarifies the whole problem for me. I don't want to do this, Vicar. It's misleading."

I could see the shot going down the drain. I heard the dreadful gurgle. *Life* had first refusal of the day's shoot. Since Theo was one of their photo editor's favorite photographers, we were practically a shoo-in. Theo and I, and Lloyd and Bobby, and God knows how many others of us, were hoping for a *Life* layout, maybe even a cover, using not just Theo's photos but Adger's as well. But no Richard, no nothing.

I continued arguing. Not well, I'm afraid. I wished makeup would come mop *my* perspiration. But however weak my argument, it must have struck some chord to which Richard responded. Maybe he felt sorry for me or remembered his obligation not just to me but to his three co-stars, all of whom so very much wanted this four-shot. He shook his head, gave me half a grin and half a grimace as if to say he was doing this against his better judgment, greater love hath no man, and I don't know what-all, and returned to the bandstand. Hosanna in the highest. Theo looked at me gratefully. The production assistant hugged me. The shot continued in spite of Richard's continuing to be stiff and unyielding. At one point, to lighten the mood and to insure our keeping Richard there a little longer, Gregory switched places with Diane so that he was with Richard and Diane with Lonette. Richard was amused in spite of himself. He couldn't very well reject Gregory Hines, could he?

The shots were choice, but then so were the ones with the four of them heterosexually paired. On some level I respected Richard for both his complaint and his compliance. But when he saw the pictures after they had been returned by the lab, he said, "I'm not going to approve any of these."

I wondered if this was his way of assuring that Ritts's material would be given preference. I asked him, "This is a tentative no, is it not? It's possible when the time comes that we can take this to Ed Limato for arbitration?"

In time he did approve the pictures, or maybe Limato did. We got our great *Life* layout. The shot paring Gregory with Richard and Lonette with Diane was prominently featured.

It wasn't until I read Michael Daly's *New York* story that I realized that I wasn't absolutely the first person to think of *Boom Town* in connection with the movie: ". . . Evans gave a party for the foreign film distributors who were attending the American Film Market. He screened *Boom Town*, and he tried to compare this film starring Clark Gable and Spencer Tracy with his own project featuring Richard Gere and Gregory Hines. The guests cheered."

I had wanted the *Boom Town* shot particularly as a courtesy to Lonette McKee. One day I had taken advantage of a photo opportunity for Gere, Hines, and Lane. Gregory said, "Lonette should be in this," and she would have been had she been available. I had seen the three actors elegantly dressed walking about the Cotton Club set between takes, talking not with each other but to various members of the cast and crew. I rounded them up, and grabbed Adger, and although the lighting (as with Lucas and Spielberg) wasn't the greatest, asked them to pose.

"What's this for, Vicar?" Richard asked.

"*Time*," I told him.

He quipped something negative, but seeing that Gregory and Diane were amenable to the shot, he consented to pose. After several shots, I asked them to hold while I got into the composition along with Bob Girolami.

"Who is *this* for, Reverend Tom?"

"Me."

"I figured," said Richard.

I positioned myself between Richard and Diane, only my head visible. But then Richard began moving his head mischievously to block me. I moved elsewhere, same routine. A giggling conspiracy to crowd me out. Finally I was positioned on the fringes of the group and holding Diane's outstretched and sympathetic hand to confirm my connection with the group, all of us laughing. I found the four resulting shots personally rewarding, but nothing that could be sent to *Time*: the lighting had been too flat, as we suspected it might be.

Right after that pose, Richard had been called for his next shot. Mark Burchard was putting the finishing touch on his costume, his hand at the bottom of Richard's vest, giving it a good straightening yank downward just as a Polaroid shot was taken for use by the wardrobe department. When the Polaroid was developed, it looked like Mark was groping Richard. Richard's expression was unbelievable, a kind of goofy rapture with his mouth open in pre-drool. The "grope" wouldn't have been nearly as funny without the expression. Mark couldn't resist showing it to Richard. Mistake, of course. "I want that picture," Richard said. He reached for it, and Mark ran from him. Richard didn't refer to it again for two weeks, the last night of production. "I want that picture, Mark."

"I haven't got it," Mark said.

"If you ever show that picture to anyone, you'll never work in this town again."

Mark said, "If I sell that picture to the right people, I might never *have* to work again."

After Theo got the *Boom Town* four-shot, she planned to take shots of four showgirls, each in a representative costume. Karen Wilkins came out first wearing a "Stormy Weather" dress. "How do you like this?" she asked me. Somehow I thought Milena was still in the dressing room with the other girls, and I answered truthfully. I didn't like it at all, the set or the costumes for that number. They were gray satin, loose about the stomach. The women who wore them, slim and sleek as they were, appeared to be hiding (and none too successfully) volleyballs.

And then Milena, standing right beside me, said with a small laugh, "Well, you can't please everyone."

I tried to apologize. I softened my criticism. We compromised: the dress, yes, the hat that went with it, no, and Karen would model from a reclining position so that the slit up one side would be emphasized and the volleyball-effect stomach not visible. (During production the "Stormy Weather" dress became the "Ill Wind" dress when the latter song was substituted.)

Gay Thomas (yes, *that* Gay Thomas) wore a "Dinah" dress, although that number, the only one to feature a male vocal chorus, had been cut from the film. The dress seemed to evoke the floating-petal softness of moonlight; and if that element had composed its threads, the garment couldn't have cost much more. An assistant of Milena's told me, "Initially they cost $2,000 apiece but by the time Milena got through fussing with them they cost $8,000 apiece." That sounded like hyperbole to me, but another wardrobe person commented, "Not by much, if at all."

Ann Palmer looked regal as a "Copper Colored Gal," and Rima Vetter wore a "Mooch" costume that gave me a clearer understanding of what Cab Calloway was talking about when he sang "Minnie the Moocher." The costumes were composed of disparate bits of clustered black feathers at the hips, wrists, and ankles, these decorating a garment of sequined sections that could pass for lingerie. The shoes, custom-made in Italy, were luxuriant, rich green leather. The headdress consisted predominately of a plume of feathers which arched from a sequined band at the forehead.

Mark Burchard had told me a funny story about the headdress. Milena had located an original headdress which she took to her in-house milliner, Bruce Harrow, to duplicate. She would need ten of them, she said. "I want them made *exactly* like this one." She placed the hat on his workbench and left. The next day she passed the workbench, saw the hat where she had left it, and thought it was a duplicate. And she didn't like it. She scolded, "Bruce, I said *exactly* like the one I left with you! What have you done? This is ugly, ugly."

Bruce hardly had the heart to tell her she was looking at the original. But he did.

"What did she do?" I asked Mark.

"She just walked away. What would you have done?"

"Did she laugh?" I hoped that she had.

"Would *you* have laughed?"

"I think I would have."

"Later you might have. I think you'd do just what she did. You'd turn and walk away."

You thought you had heard the end of the second unit, maybe? Not quite. Gio and his crew had set up shop to one side of the Theo's bandstand set. They hoped to shoot a small section of the club that included the passageway to the men's room. No sound. They'd be very quiet. No need to worry, he had told us. Coppola was summoned to look at the setup before it was shot. He okayed it and then stopped a moment to watch the girls being shot by Theo. He kibitzed a bit with those not in front of the camera. Theo and I tried to get him to pose with the girls. So did the girls. He said, "You know what they'll say if I did. 'All Coppola does on set is fool around with the girls.' And now you want me to furnish them with *proof*?" He gave his regrets to all, waved, and walked away.

When we got through with the four showgirls, I began bringing any actors I could find who were available and in costume to the bandstand: Lisa Jane Persky, Allen Garfield, Larry Fishburne. I tried to get James Remar, but I was told to stay away: he was needed on Stage F and under serious pressure.

A dinner break was called at eight o'clock. Our days by then were *very* long. I found Remar and Gere just outside my office on a banquette eating sushi, both of them in sweat-sopped and unbuttoned dress shirts. When Remar got through eating, I asked him to come down to the main stage where Theo was waiting for him.

He blew up.

"I've slept beside you for three months," he shouted (he meant in the room right alongside mine), "and this is the first time you've asked me to pose for pictures! No! I'm not going to do it, I haven't got the time and I'm in no mood!"

It was all coming out: his frustration at having to look like and act like a bloated malignancy throughout the production and my being unable to get him even the slightest Liz Smith mention that I'd hope for and assured him he would get.

He pushed through the glass door to return to Stage F, darting up a narrow stairway outside our foyer that led to the third floor. I followed him right up the stairway, both of us continuing to go at each other. I don't know why I did it. Sucker for punishment, I guess, and I was tired and my nerves were frayed too. Maybe it was in part my embarrassment at having Richard witness the scene and my futile efforts to mitigate it somewhat, which of course was ridiculous. Jimmy was in no mood. His feelings were hurt. I should have let it go at that. I was holding a mad tiger by the leash, one I should have turned loose the first time he snarled.

What he had said was true: I had not asked him to pose for special photography. For one thing, I'd thought Adger's coverage of him was not only adequate but excellent in quality. For another, as often as I'd intended to take him to Adger's gallery for a special sitting, circumstances just as often prevented it, not the least of those circumstances his own need for rest and sleep when he wasn't wanted on set. If he wasn't resting, he was preparing a scene or working with his makeup people or sequestered with one of his buddies like Tony Dingman. And since I had such ready access to him, I thought there was plenty of time for him. (One more rule, and not just for the budding publicist: there is never plenty of time.)

Jimmy left me in anger, his voice still raised. Richard had kept his seat in the foyer, watching what he could, listening to what he could not see.

About an hour later Jimmy was released from Studio F. He came to my office, still in his tuxedo and looking like Dutch Schultz but addressing me as himself.

"Tom, I didn't mean to yell at you," he said, his demeanor one of grief. It suffused his voice and his body language. "Never would I yell at *you* . . ."

His voice trailed off. His apology was touching. He found it hard to say what he meant and said more than he meant to say. When he came in I was on the phone with Jonathan making plans for a late dinner. He heard it all and was touched. I put the receiver down and stood.

He took me in his arms, holding me close to him, crying openly. I told him it was all right. And it was.

Since Richard had witnessed the blowup, I thought he should be made aware of its aftermath. I told him about Jimmy's apology. Richard said, "He's a very sensitive guy. Can you imagine what it's been like for him all these months having to get under the skin of such a monster, and with his great looks to be made up to look like such a monster? He's probably had it rougher than any of us."

I asked Richard if he'd had any casting input with either James Remar or Bob Hoskins. He had worked with both of them before, Remar on stage in *Bent* and Hoskins more recently in *Beyond the Limit*. He shook his head. "It just worked out that way, although I'm glad it did."

Later I told Jimmy what Richard had said. "Thanks for telling me. I'd wondered about that myself."

* * *

The area of special photography was always a headache that frequently escalated into a migraine. Herb Ritts was scheduled to work for only three days. I realized that a big production number, "Daybreak Express" staged to a 1934 Duke Ellington composition, had been rescheduled to shoot on his first day, Friday, November 18, a day when Richard Gere would not be working, a problem because Ritts was there primarily for and at the instigation of Richard. Richard was penciled in to work all of the following week except Thanksgiving Day. Since Ritts did not come cheap and it would be a shame to waste him, I got on the phone with his agent in Los Angeles and was able to reschedule him for the first three days of that next week.

When Ritts got to New York on November 17, he called me to say he would be available to work on Friday if I needed him. No, I said, Richard would not be working. In that case, Ritts said, he would take another assignment for Friday.

Of course, when I arrived for work on Friday, I discovered that the schedule had been completely changed. Gere would be working that day and not at all the following week! We were locked into Ritts for exactly the three days Richard would be off, and we would have to pay him for those days no matter what.

Richard Gere to the rescue! He consented to come in for special photography for each of Herb Ritts's contracted three days. Since James Remar was off, Ritts was able to shoot Richard in Remar's room, a great location with fireplace and mantle and natural lighting. Ritts posed Richard against a mirror over the fireplace that was splashed with sunlight. Richard was dressed in his casual Dixie Dwyer costume wearing a hat and holding his cornet. The resulting pictures were superb. Ritts had one blown up and presented to me, autographed. He also got great shots on the studio roof.

On Tuesday, Gregory Hines said that he and Lonette McKee would like to talk with me. We met in Lonette's dressing room. They wanted to know why they hadn't been put on special photo call to be photographed by Ritts like Richard and Diane had. I told them that Ritts was there to strike a balance. Theo had got excellent pictures of Gregory and Lonette—"our black stars," as I phrased it—but virtually nothing on Richard and Diane, "our white stars." Ritts was there to remedy that. But of course, I said, Ritts would be doing shots of Gregory and Lonette as well, probably on Wednesday when it appeared that their schedules were more likely to permit it. I told them that Milena and I were already selecting evening gowns and furs for Lonette to wear, and we would want Gregory in his white evening suit.

Gregory exchanged glances with Lonette and Thelma Carpenter, who played his mother in the film. "This movie is just like life," he said, "like Lila Rose in the movie. No matter what kind of blood is in you, if some of it is black, you're all black." He laughed ironically, underscoring for Lonette, "Our black stars."

Even though I was speaking in categories embedded in our script, I felt semantically chastened. Gregory hadn't meant to make me uncomfortable. He had, however, heard about a letter Lloyd Leipsig had written to me. Word about it had gotten around. Something to the effect that we weren't doing a new edition of *Blackbirds of 1928*. His gripe was that we were emphasizing the musical aspects of the movie to the detriment of the element he really wanted to sell, the shooty-shooty-gang-bang gangster stuff. The trouble was the shooty-shooty stuff hadn't been filmed yet. Most of the scenes involving white actors (the gangsters) had them sitting around tables looking at a floorshow. Naturally a stills photographer was going to concentrate on the floorshow, the visuals, no matter how much they evoked in some minds a "black-and-tan fantasy," as Leipsig had phrased it. His contention was that black-and-tan fantasy was not going to sell the movie. Not by itself. Yet it seemed to him that it was all we were giving him. "I'm truly sick and tired of being jerked off in the area of special photography. I'm getting the feeling that the ten days of Theo Westenberger will result in great coverage for *Ebony* magazine and huge expenditure for Orion. I'm counting on you to do your utmost to make this a false assumption."

Meanwhile Adger had continued with his gallery as best he could. I had to leave him pretty much on his own. I was tied up seeing that Theo and Herb got their shots. When I reviewed his gallery portraits, I did wonder why Adger was photographing so many peripheral people, dancers and showgirls with no featured moments in the film. Beautiful people, beautiful lighting. Great stuff, but who was it for? I even wondered whether Adger might be marketing the stills directly to them. Orion, who had initially financed the gallery, finally pulled out. All Lloyd Leipsig was seeing was too many gorgeous but unknown black faces. Chris Cronyn questioned me about the continuing huge cash outlays the gallery project required. It was a hassle to keep it going, but ultimately it was worth all the lies and evasions it took. Adger's work got better and better, his lighting improving enormously. I showed Francis some of Adger's and my favorite shots. He said, "The stills on this movie are all wonderful, but who's going to see them? All you're going to see in connection with this movie are pictures of Robert Evans."

Francis asked for as many stills as I could let him have to pass along to Gio and the second unit. I gave him not only a good deal of Adger's work but some of Theo's as well. Herb's work wasn't available yet. When Francis finally saw Herb Ritts's work for the first time at the beginning of the long night's shoot in Grand Central, he told Stephen Goldblatt, "Maybe *he* should have shot the movie instead of you." We took it as a joke. Ritts (who I was able to bring back for the one extra night's work) laughed appreciatively, Goldblatt less so, directing at me a cocked eyebrow.

Wednesday the day before Thanksgiving was for me a horror show compounded of pressure, temper, frustration, and exhaustion. It was Herb Ritts's last contracted day. (Since Theo had been granted ten days, I expected Herb to be given five at least and had talked with his agent and with Gere in terms of that. Leipsig said four, and then cut it back to three. Then later I was able to persuade him to allow Herb to return for the all-night filming at Grand Central Station after I received Coppola's okay.) Also that same day a photographer and two reporters from *Time* were allowed to visit the set. Big mistake. I later detailed in it a memo to Bobby Zarem:

Kim Steele, photographing for Time *Magazine, had an appointment to shoot the set during our lunch hour from 2 to 3 p.m. I gave up my lunch hour waiting for him. He showed up at 3 p.m. when the crew was reporting back from lunch. I was so angry that I at first refused to allow him to shoot. He said he'd be fired. He apologized profusely, saying he'd underestimated traffic, etc. At any rate, I relented, but I knew I had to keep him as far away from Francis as possible. Tension on the set was extremely high. I told him to hurry, to get a few shots of the Cotton Club set before we resumed filming on it. Sylbert joined us and posed with a couple of female extras who were fully costumed and just hanging around.*

Kim left about 4:15, and shortly afterward the two Time *writers arrived. I introduced them to Richard, Diane, Fred Roos. They started to intrude upon Francis at one point, but the asst. director and I converged on them and I maneuvered them away unto the 2nd unit stage where reactions of the "celebrities" were being staged.*

I had told both Francis and Gregory that the Time *guys were coming—for Gregory.* To *speak with Gregory. I had it worked out. Had Francis seen them in Gregory's company, I'm sure I could have gestured to him at an appropriate moment and he would have come over and spoken with them. However, they didn't want to spend any time with Gregory. Nor talk with him. Which was an embarrassment for me and which killed any chance of their getting to talk with Coppola. Francis likes Gregory, and due to what Gregory had told me about "You wouldn't know there were any black actors on this picture . . ." Francis agreed for the* Time *people to come. I thought they understood their obligation. It was with this particular understanding that Fred Roos and I decided, despite the tension of the day, that we would risk having the* Time *people come, even though I should have spent my time with Herb Ritts and even though I'd agreed to accommodate* Time *with respect to a photographer for the proposed piece on Sylbert.*

I gave the Time *guys a tour of the building and then got rid of them, saying we would have them back another time; which of course we won't. I told them I would send a picture of Gregory, Richard, and Diane. I strongly suggest that they be required to use a quote from Gregory, if they use a photo. I know they refuse to be dictated to, but that's how it is; otherwise, forget it.*

While all this was going on, Herb Ritts was set up in the Vera's Club set on the 3rd floor, shooting Richard and Diane, after which he was to shoot Gregory and Lonette in their best costumes. You won't believe what I had to go through to accomplish half of this. I caused Lonette's special makeup man to have a nervous breakdown. He became hysterical screaming at me in the hallway of the makeup/hair unit in front of untold actors. He screamed that I was utilizing every makeup person on the film for stills, some for Richard and Diane, others for Gregory and Lonette. "Who's to do all these other actors!" he wanted to know. "Me?" My blood pressure must have shot through the roof. I gave him scream for scream. Then we ended up hugging one another, him practically in tears. I would rather have choked him.

Gregory and Lonette were scheduled for Herb at 6:30. At 6 p.m., Gregory and Lonette were dressed and ready. Thinking that we had a half hour before Herb would be ready for them, I marched them to Adger's gallery. We were intercepted before we got there. Francis himself called for them. I only hoped he would be through with them by the time Herb was ready for them.

Lonette's makeup man was on another tear. This time I wasn't going to hug him, no matter what. Lonette had been taken back to him for a makeup adjustment for the scene Coppola wanted her for. The guy said, "Well, that's it. I'm not doing her again for stills. I am not going to allow her to pose for stills." Lonette, usually the soul of sweetness, lost it. "This is something I'm not going to lose out on," she snapped, "and you can either do me or leave."

Well, lose she did; and Gregory too. They were furious, hurt, disappointed. I could have cried for each of them.

Since they were unavailable, tied up with Francis, Herb continued shooting Richard and Diane. And that was another problem, as I can tell you as I was there; and just thinking about it I feel that I was everywhere at once. A day I never want to relive. Bill Kennedy and his wife and son were on the set. When they found out what we were doing on the 3rd floor, they joined us there. The kid had a flash camera. He wanted a picture of Richard and Diane and was going to take it while Herb's strobe was working. Herb wouldn't let him. The flash would kill the strobe. I tried to let the kid get his picture whenever Herb paused. But he never paused long enough. He was shooting hot and shooting fast. Kennedy got kind of pissed off. Before I knew it they had flounced off. I ran after them. "Billy, don't run off. It'll just be a minute. Please." They returned. It was only a minute. The kid did get his shots of Richard and Diane with his daddy.

Herb finished about 7 p.m. Maybe five to ten minutes before. I hurried to the main stage to tell Gregory and Lonette, still working, that Herb was wrapping. I told them that we hoped to get him back for the Grand Central shoot and maybe he could photograph them then. "But I won't be in this evening dress!" protested Lonette. "I want him to shoot me in this" Gregory asked Francis if they could be excused. He told him why. Francis excused them. We rushed back upstairs to Stage F. The set-up had already been struck, and Herb Ritts, his assistant told me, had already left the studio for an appointment in Manhattan.

Gregory and Lonette's disappointment was so palpable it hurt me to be in its presence. Jennifer, a black wardrobe woman, felt it too. She also felt my anguish and sensed my predicament. She suggested a possible palliative. "They're all dressed, they're beautiful, they're hurt—why don't we take them down to Adger?"I could have kissed her. I should have thought of it myself. We located Adger. No easy feat, especially at this time of night in all this confusion. They sat for Adger a good half hour or so. But sill it was a downer for all of us, 7:30 in the evening, the night before Thanksgiving; when they had been hoping for a session with Herb.

In summation:

It is necessary that as much as possible be done for the black actors in the movie . . .

* * *

Weeks back, shortly after our starting work at the studio, Barrie Osborne had sent for me to come to his office. With him were the Ralph Coopers, Junior and Senior. Junior I had seen around the set, a friend of one of the male dancers or singers. He was nothing if not engaging. It was his stock in trade, I decided. I had difficulty in learning what else he did. The senior Cooper was trim, solid-looking, dressed correctly if a little rakishly. Cooper Sr. talked about how we must allow the black press to cover the film. I tried to explain (yet again) Evans's policy about publicity.

"I can convince Bob," said Cooper.

Sure. Be my guest.

I listened politely as he outlined not so much a plan as his hope: that the *Amsterdam News* and other black publications be allowed to do a story on the construction of our Cotton Club exterior set on Seventh Avenue (actually Adam Clayton Powell Boulevard this far north) between 131st and 132nd Streets. "*Everything* was in that block," he said enthusiastically, "on those *two* blocks—Connie's Inn, Lafayette Theater, the Tree of Hope . . ."

The Tree of Hope was a tree on a strip of green that divided the street. I had read about it in my research. I listened while Cooper gave it to me again. "Actors would stop and say a prayer beneath the Tree of Hope. They thought the tree brought them luck."

"At least it brought them *hope*," Jr. threw in lightly, flashing a smile. His smiles were always invitations, warmly delivered. You accepted with alacrity. Glad for a little levity, I flashed one back.

"It was a tradition," the elder Cooper said. "A lot of Harlem tradition is rooted in that block and will be rooted in this movie about the Cotton Club. At least we're assuming it will be. There is interest in this picture in the black community. There is a feeling about it. The black press demands to respond to that feeling and interest."

He suggested that community support for and cooperation with the production might be withheld should publicity barriers not be lifted, at least for the black press.

I could see that Barrie Osborne was giving serious weight to this.

Cooper alluded to the fact that should the black press not be given access, it might be wondered in print why a white man should be the "publicity director" in a film that dealt so intrinsically with a part of Harlem culture of the late 1920s.

Nothing about the whiteness of the film's producer or director.

I didn't know what political cards or position Cooper held. He was listed on *The Cotton Club* crew sheet as "community coordinator." I had seen him around, and I'd heard Maurice Hines, Sr. and Stretch Johnson speak of him disparagingly; but I had chalked that up to peer rivalry. I had assumed that Cooper, like them, was on the payroll as an untitled consultant in matters pertaining to Harlem of the period. We had two locations people working with the Harlem community. Except for political purposes, why would we need a "community coordinator"?

(After the movie wrapped, I asked Grace Blake about Cooper Sr. "Well, that's another story," she said, prefacing it with a laugh. "There is more there than meets the eye. Or less. Decidedly less. His title was, how do you put it, 'honorary.'" In honor of what she didn't know and hesitated to guess. "He wasn't in the Koch administration, but he was mixed up in government somehow. Like one of those agencies you have to deal with in order to get a movie made. It was probably thought that he had influence, and with what we were paying him and calling him, he probably did have. He really never *did* anything in connection with the movie that I could tell you, but he made it appear that he did. Memos, that kind of thing. From his attitude and that of his son, you'd have thought they were producing the picture.")

At the time Osborne and I were meeting with him, I was more than willing to grant that the elder Cooper knew what he was talking about: that the black press wanted access to our sets and locations. But so did the white press. We were a media event in the uncomfortable position of rejecting the media, which made us even more of a media event.

I resented Cooper's intrusion into my territory. On a film you discover squatters everywhere. Everybody wants to be a publicist. Some make anonymous telephone calls to gossip columnists; others write unauthorized letters. Cooper wrote letters, with copies to me and to Barrie Osborne. Like the one to the assistant news editor of NBC: ". . . When the Cotton Club Motion Picture is closer to completion, I will be pleased to help you work out the segment you desire."

Santa's little helper.

Publicity can be a form of gratuity, a kickback, a payoff. A favor given for a favor granted. A location manager—perhaps even a community coordinator, if I knew what a community coordinator did—preparing a community for the arrival in its neighborhood of a multi-million-dollar production and helping pave the way for it, often goes around with one hand in his pocket, the other on his upturned figurative hat. Giving favors, getting them, getting the job done.

Apparently Cooper had managed to convince Barrie Osborne that there could conceivably be roadblocks from a truculent community should attention not be paid to them and paid in the press.

I don't believe in "permissive" publicity on just any film, and *The Cotton Club* was far from being just any film. By permissive, I mean publicity that is officially sought and sanctioned for publication *at the time of the film's production* or shortly thereafter. It's another thing to prepare material and to authorize publicity—magazine stories, layouts—whose distribution and publication will be synchronized with the release of the movie, months, or sometimes as in the case of *Mikey and Nicky*, even years away. It is hard to strike a balance. There is often producer as well as crew pressure to see news items about the film right now, an ego trip that usually goes down the drain.

In the case of *The Cotton Club*, I agreed with Zarem and Orion Pictures that it was a waste not only of present time but also of future time for the film to take up print space while in the process of being made. The print space could be used far better at the time of the film's release when it would benefit from a carefully mapped-out and controlled publicity campaign in which the black press would figure largely. Why subtract from that future space with dribs and drabs of *now* material that would long be forgotten by the time the public got a chance to see the movie? Material whose too-early use would tend to make the movie seem like yesterday's news.

But then there's the politics of it, which does argue for local and neighborhood press stories during production that in theory might help allay community fears about the content or nature of the film. Such publicity might make possible certain types of community cooperation: residents, say, appearing in crowd scenes, opening rooms in their homes for the comfort of key personnel, putting up with some degree of added inconvenience in their daily lives.

But the original order had been confirmed from on high: closed set, no press.

Cooper did have a point. Reams of material leaked to the press continued to give a negative slant to the entire production. This negative slant had not happened with the black press yet. Cooper didn't want it to, I am certain, although that was not indicated as part of his concern at the time. Nor did Barrie and I want the black press to turn against us. If I had been allowed from the outset to deal forthrightly with the press, especially the columnists, the mentions of the film might have had a more affirmative balance. As it was, Liz Smith tried to balance every negative with a positive. But it was the negatives that hurt, with so many of the negatives for Coppola, so many positives for Gere.

Still trying to sell us, Cooper said, "Your construction crew in Harlem is mixed, black and white. For the good of both the community and the movie, photographers should be allowed to take pictures up there of that mixed crew, black and white working side by side."

Barrie looked at me. "I think he's right."

Not entirely hypocritically, I said, "I do too. It's a wonderful idea."

It was a moderately good idea but time-consuming, not worth one-tenth of the time and energy that would have to be expended on its behalf. "If we can get Evans to agree to it, I'll help in any way I can."

I added, as though really getting into it, "Perhaps I can even get Gregory and Maurice up there on a day when they're not working, to give the story that much more news value."

We left it that I would talk with the Zarem office and that Cooper would call Evans about it. By the time I left Barrie's office that day, I had put the matter on a very back burner.

Robert Evans, in the collection of essays *The Motion Picture Book* edited by Jason Squire, said this about premature publicity in connection with *The Great Gatsby*, produced while he was head of production at Paramount: "Months before the film opened, the country was Gatsbytized; the effect snowballed with Gatsby hats, shoes, suits, and so on. By the time the picture came out, most people thought they had already seen it. Excitement about the film peaked well before it opened, rather than just before its release . . ." By contrast, he cited *Star Wars*, which had no pre-opening publicity. "When it opened, the lines were around the block."

Just as he had described with *Gatsby*, I was afraid that any great want-to-see buildup about *The Cotton Club* would segue by time of the movie's release into a jaded "Haven't we seen this already?" But I still believe that had I been given a little more freedom, I would have been able to manage a more appropriate balance and tone.

* * *

When I first heard about the grand finale that Francis was planning to shoot at Grand Central Station, I thought it was a joke, a parody on the extravagance of thought and cost that had permeated the production. Gaetano ("Tom") Lisi told me about it. Tom was now a location manager. He had been promoted to Cronyn's job when Cronyn stepped into David Golden's. I'd known him for over ten years, ever since the Paul Newman-directed *The Effect of Gamma Rays on Man-in-the Moon Marigolds* when he was a hippie-dressed gofer and protégé of Newman's and Joanne Woodward's. He would marry Katharine Ross of *Butch Cassidy* and *The Graduate* fame. I could hardly believe it at the time, hardly believe it even now. Tom's was a generous and embracing personality that operated effortlessly on all cylinders, and he had a goofy warm Chico Marx kind of smile. We were having breakfast together in the commissary. I laughed, plainly disbelieving him.

"I'm serious," he said. "I thought you'd heard about it. Not only is Dixie getting on the train, but we see Dutch's coffin being put on as well, and the kicker is that Gwen Verdon will be dancing with some porters, maybe on top of a train!"

It sounded too unbelievable, but unbelievably wonderful.

Cronyn and Sylbert both confirmed it. It was all true.

Except for the bit about Gwen Verdon dancing on top of the train. She didn't get to dance with porters, but she did get to shimmy a bit with a young black girl at a track gate.

Lisi had trouble finding period railroad cars on short notice. He came up with three, fewer than Coppola wanted, but Coppola made do.

The shoot was scheduled for Friday, December 16. The crew call was for eight in the evening but I got to Grand Central by six. I needed the extra time to investigate the possibility of using one of the period train cars for special photography. I also wanted to check out the lower concourse where the company would be filming and see where Herb Ritts might set up his equipment in relation to it.

The men who represented the consortium of owners of the railroad cars had no objection to our taking still photographs aboard them, although they found the request a bit confusing since they had been told the train interiors would not be photographed. Not by the filmmakers, I explained, but by us, for publicity purposes. They were more than agreeable when they learned that Richard Gere would be among those being photographed. That would pose a problem for me in the wee hours of the morning when one of the men insisted that his picture be taken with Richard.

The three cars would represent the 20th Century Limited, with the end car having an open rear-facing canopied platform with brass railings and vestibule steps. Gere and Lane would be photographed boarding it at the end of the movie and have their final fade-out clinch there. Although the end car contained an observation lounge, a dining room, and staterooms, it was not as good for taking stills as the middle car, a standard Pullman with seats that made up into beds. Dixie and Vera undoubtedly would have had staterooms, but it was the Pullman that we wanted. Ritts was delighted with it. We began staking claim to it immediately. Richard was costumed and ready, but Diane's transition would take another hour or more. We decided to go ahead and get shots of Richard alone. Herb's two assistants set up the shot while Richard hung out in a stateroom with Ritts and a guest of Richard's, *Rolling Stone* editor Jann Wenner. I tried to spend time with both groups. Finally, the lighting ready, I went for Richard and Herb. They'd flown the coop. Nowhere to be seen. I found out they'd gone to dinner at a midtown restaurant in Richard's limousine. Richard had been told that his scenes in the movie wouldn't be filmed until early in the morning, so off they go. Nice if someone had told me, or hey, even told Herb's assistants who had been working their asses off getting ready for him. Needless to say, I was pissed.

One o'clock in the morning. No Richard, no Herb. I wouldn't see either of them until after two-thirty. The company broke for a meal at two o'clock. I sat at a table with Gwen Verdon and music staff Bob Wilbur (musical recreations), and Sy Johnson (associate music supervisor/arranger). When Richard and Herb finally returned, Richard went to his camper and Herb pulled up a chair beside me. I was in no mood.

I told him he had been discourteous not only to me but to his own assistants. I reminded him that I had put myself out on a limb to get him here tonight and that he was on salary and expected to work like the rest of us, during the same hours the rest of us did. It was improper for him to disappear for two hours with the star of the film no matter what their personal relationship was.

Gwen Verdon, opposite me, sat quietly and attentively. I hate making scenes, even quiet ones like this was, but it had to be made. Even with Herb Ritts, whom I liked and respected. Even though it would get back to Richard. In reprimanding Herb, I was reprimanding Richard. Hey, I was a vicar: who better had the right to moralize?

Herb's purpose in being here, I reminded him, and the understanding of Orion Pictures who had allowed me to have him here, was to shoot Gregory Hines and Lonette McKee, whom he had been unable to shoot during his other days with us, as well as more of Richard and Diane, as well as Gwen Verdon and a few others. It was almost three o'clock in the morning and not a single frame of Herb Ritts's film had been shot.

He apologized and set to work, accomplishing everything I had hoped he would. Richard and Diane were photographed inside the Pullman card and in the station itself, and Ritts got great shots of Gregory, Lonette, Gwen, and others.

The dancers had been told that the Pullman car would be their holding area. Nobody had told me that when I made arrangements for Herb to use it. The dancers were moved to the third car. They complained that it was uncomfortable and "smelled of urine." They made the complaint official by taking it up with the Actors Equity representative on location. He took it up with Osborne and Cronyn. They in turn jumped on me. Under whose direction, they wanted to know, had I "usurped" the Pullman car for *my* use? Only beginning with our two location managers earlier in the evening, I told them, and continuing with requested permissions with declared intent and receiving cooperation on down the line. The dancers were told to stay where they were. We kept the Pullman.

A dancer muttered sweetly to me as we passed later in the early hours of the morning, "Train robber!"

The area of the Grand Central concourse where we were shooting was roped off, but guess who I spotted pressed against the rope. The "flasher" from the *New York Post*, the guy who had been hustled off crying false arrest on Richard's first working day before the camera. He wasn't alone. I identified other paparazzi. I alerted production assistants, and we were especially careful that none of them had access to the area where Herb was set up to shoot.

Adger had his own problems.

He went to the vans for more film. The cops guarding the entrance wouldn't let him back in. Did he explain in a reasonable tone of voice who he was and what he was doing? Knowing Adger, I doubt it. Anyway, he exploded. The cops were going to arrest him for being abusive. He was going to sue them for false arrest. I was able to intervene and verify who he was and guarantee his safe passage back into the terminal with no charges pressed. I asked why he hadn't shown or worn his identification badge. I'm not sure I got an answer. He was in a blue and furious funk. Later he was playfully apologetic and laughed about it, chagrined, I'm sure, at how he had lost his temper and gone quite wildly off the deep end.

But there were lost, damaged, sulking tempers everywhere you looked that night and deep ends just a step away. In any direction.

I had never been aware of Gere drinking anything stronger than Perrier or a cola. The night at Grand Central was an exception.

Diane led me to his camper. She took a drink from a bottle of tequila that Richard kept in an icebox. Something to see them through the long night's shoot, Diane told me. I gathered they had both been nipping. I was offered, but I didn't accept. I was afraid tequila would put me to sleep. I think it did put Richard to sleep. He crawled into one of the Pullman car berths that had been made up for sleeping and pulled the curtain shut. Diane crawled into a nearby berth. The costume people had a rough time drying out and shaping and ironing her costume all evening.

I enjoyed watching Diane with Richard. He was good to her, perhaps not quite as good as he might have been; but then he was Dixie Dwyer, and he was in character. I thought back to the quasi-Apache dance Richard had performed with Diane a few days earlier for the cameras, that bit of ritualized S&M put to music in which dancers slap each other around and which is identified with Paris joints in the 1920s, a dance floor number when Dixie and Vera got really nasty with one another. During the scene, Gere got too rough with Diane. When Francis had called "Cut," Diane had run off the set. It was reported that she was hysterical. Gere had to be talked to and told to tone down the rough stuff, otherwise Diane wasn't returning to complete the scene. Richard looked befuddled though chastened. He was only playing the scene the way he thought they wanted it played and was not aware of having been unduly rough with Diane. When the scene was reshot, it looked to me like he played it at exactly the same pitch, with not one iota less energy than he had put into it before. Diane was plainly angry, as herself and as Vera Cicero, and she gave as good as she got. She was ready for the violence and angry enough to respond appropriately and ably to it.

That last long night at Grand Central, Richard and Diane posed for Herb Ritts and posed again and yet again, exhausted from their lack of sleep and dubious fortification with tequila and all this boring still-taking. They did not get to do their big movie scene until well after daybreak. They were still doing it at ten-thirty in the morning when Herb and I finally left for home. On the platform beside the mock 20th Century Limited, Dixie discovers Vera sitting on a geometrical mountain of luggage. She has changed her mind: she will go to California with him after all. Except for cutting back to the stage of the Cotton Club where dancers are performing a "boarding the train" number followed by the end credits with the haunting music underneath, it was the end of the movie.

* * *

The company's big shoot that Friday night at Grand Central Station lasted until one o'clock in the afternoon on Saturday. Those long hours no doubt accounted for the large number of actors and crew who did not attend that evening's wrap party. Richard didn't come. Diane didn't make it. Lonette didn't come, but she had the excuse of a bad cold. She had been taking antihistamines all the evening before to keep her runny nose from showing on screen. Coppola arrived late, after midnight, just after I had left. Robert De Niro came, as did Mickey Rourke. Robert Evans came with retinue including various Las Vegas investors and several photographers. He posed for a few pictures and left before chancing an encounter with Coppola.

I am invariably in a work mode at every wrap party I attend. I'm overstating a bit: a couple of them have been blasts. I wouldn't call this one a blast, although I might say I was blasted.

I stopped by a table where William Kennedy was sitting with Richard Sylbert to exchange what I thought would be pleasantries. Not to be. Kennedy took me to task for a recent *Wall Street Journal* piece by William Woolf which still adhered to the Evans-inspired party line that it was Mario Puzo, not Kennedy, who was co-author of the screenplay. The Woolf piece had been prepared—with Sylbert's cooperation, by the way—before I was even hired. I was annoyed that Sylbert didn't speak up on my behalf. I had been through all this with Kennedy before. He knew Evan's reasons for maintaining the charade, and he also knew that he would get his credit in due time.

So far as I know, it was the only time I've ever been chewed out by a Pulitzer Prize winner.

If the party was the resounding success that some called it, maybe I had played a small part with my memo to Joey Cusumano and Fred Roos with copies to "all concerned" about the proposal that black *Cotton Club* actors and singers and dancers perform on the Cotton Club set at the wrap party for guests and invited press. It brought them around to my view that it would be a mistake to invite press, not just a mistake but an invitation to disaster, and that no actor should be asked to perform: this was to be a party and not a benefit.

TV's *Entertainment Tonight* had been suggested as an invitee. I asked all to consider, if they would, Richard Gere, say, after working from ten to twelve hours the previous night, being subjected to eavesdroppers, microphones thrust in his face, lights in his eyes.

I had tested on Gregory Hines the proposal that actors and dancers and singers be "invited" to entertain the crowd.

"I go to a party as a guest," he said. "If I'm expected to perform, I get paid, I have fees for that sort of thing. I want to get swacked at a wrap party. I don't want to have to keep looking at my watch and thinking, 'I'm on in ten minutes.'"

The actors came as guests. Those who danced did it on their own volition and of their own good will, exuberantly and joyfully, Maurice and Gregory Hines among them.

When I was getting ready to leave and was in the process of securing my office, Mickey Rourke and retinue of twelve showed up at my door asking to use the telephone. No doubt the retinue as well as Mickey. Sorry, Mickey. I had ordered a car for myself and my guests, and they were awaiting me out there on the cold twenty-six-degree street. My guests were freezing. I had to lock up and get out. I suggested where they might find a phone. Profuse apologies and all that.

As it was, my guests had to fight off groups trying to commandeer our car.

Yes, cold out there, but not as cold as it would be the next week in Harlem.

The wrap party was over but work on the picture wasn't, and even when principal photography ended a week later on Friday, December 23, 1983, my job didn't. Even with three weeks off from January 14 through February 5 when I went to Texas, New Mexico, and California to visit family, I would have had twenty-two weeks on *The Cotton Club*. Because of the time worked on that film, I made more money than on any other on which I've ever worked. Usually you're lucky to have eight weeks and out. Often you're glad it's only eight weeks and out.

The week after the wrap party, I was busy getting the souvenir books ready, getting a stack of 8 x 10 pictures to location for Richard Gere to autograph, updating production notes and biographical material, and making determination about the disbursement of transparencies, contact sheets, and negatives, the sheer mass of which shocked the Orion publicity department when finally I was allowed to relinquish them.

With Gere and Remar on location and not planning to return to the studio, it was decided that our joint suite should be closed down and locked up. Getting in and getting the heat turned off took half the morning. Then Gere called me to meet him on location. As long as you're going, take the Eddie Bauer foul weather coat to Joe Cusumano, somebody instructed me. When I found him, he had practically turned blue.

It was at this Harlem location that Nicolas Cage proved he had a temper to match his uncle's. He found release in wrecking his camper, an act of violence in which he was assisted by the actors who played his fellow hoods, James Russo and Bruce MacVittie. Russo had just completed a successful run as a rapist in the off-Broadway hit play *Extremities* opposite first Susan Sarandon, then Farah Fawcett. I asked Russo once why he took such an insignificant role in *The Cotton Club*. He said it was the only way he could get out of the play. "My contract said if I had a movie assignment I could get out, and this was it. I couldn't go on playing that role. Everybody was always getting hurt, including me."

Russo told me about the wrecking of the camper.

The day had been extremely cold, prohibiting their getting out much to let off steam. They were costumed in the early morning. By late afternoon they still hadn't worked. Cage touched something, a sconce, I believe, and it fell. Then he opened the camper door, and it partially collapsed. Something snapped in Cage. He began ripping everything apart. Russo and MacVittie joined in the mayhem. The camper driver heard the commotion, but he was in the cab and couldn't see inside the camper. He thought that the actors had left the camper and that Harlem toughs had gotten in and were wrecking it. It was a natural assumption: we were shooting in a deprived and potentially hostile neighborhood. He was reluctant to investigate.

"Something snapped in all of us," said Russo, "and I joined in."

George Cantero, who was also playing one of Vinnie's hoods and was in the camper at the time, refused to participate in the vandalism. Cage threatened to beat him up. "Go ahead," Cantero had said, "I might like it." The idea of that caused Cage to back off.

Go ahead, I might like it.

The sentence in a way delineated the character of a movie that owed as much to initial and continuing improvisation on theme, character, and period as it did to scripted plot.

It summed up the creative masochism of the experience of all of us involved with the project.

Going over it all again, jotting down these recollections, I feel like a magnifying glass, skimming days, slowing down here, stopping there for a clearer look at some detail.

A metaphor called to mind by a memory of Francis Coppola one day on the Bamville Club set. He sees me with a magnifying glass and asks to borrow it. He pulls from his wallet a small piece of paper about the size of a credit card. It appears to be the page of a screenplay in miniature.

"Is that a new script page?" I quip.

"Actually, it is," he replies.

He explained why the page was reduced to this size. Because of the confusion surrounding us, I didn't really catch the explanation, not enough so that I feel qualified to repeat it.

There was so much I didn't catch because of the confusion surrounding me and because of the level of intensity at which I was doing my own job. But even so, I did have my antenna up and pointed in every direction.

The coalescence of pain and humor behind the make-believe was epitomized for me by another incident on the Bamville Club set during the filming of the bomb sequence. In the script, one of Dutch Schultz's associates is called "The Sullen Man." His sole function in the film is to have his arm blown off in the explosion. The actor playing the sullen man was standing on the set wearing the costume he would appear in after the explosion. His prosthetic arm was on, the bloodied, gaping wound in it showing through the ripped cloth sleeve of his coat. A crew member stopped to admire the craftsmanship of the mangled arm, then looked about the young man's body to see where the real arm was tied up out of sight.

"Where's your arm?" he asked.

"Somewhere in Vietnam," said the actor.

When the company moved out of the studio to the Harlem location for the final scenes, I mostly stayed at the studio, rarely getting to location. It seemed as though I were on a ship where most of the interesting people had gotten off. The festival cruise was over. I had the big stateroom, not to mention the dance floor, all to myself. I got a lot of work done, but somehow the excitement was out of it.

And then I was even moved out of the stateroom.

The Diana Ross Suite would be dismantled. Workmen had started tearing it apart even before I was resituated.

The ghost of Gloria Swanson began her long mourning.

The suite was destined to become the offices of a company called Tomorrow Entertainment. All the old wallpaper and dressing-table mirrors were ripped out, along with Richard's "good" new door. I was moved to an office known as the Sidney Lumet Suite. Lumet had made a lot of movies at Astoria Studios, and this had been his office for some of them. During our studio shoot, our assistant directors had hung their hats there. It was located a half floor above the Little Theater. Now I was even more isolated. The door to it had a peculiar locking mechanism. Inadvertently I locked myself in. My telephone wasn't yet connected. I couldn't get out. I couldn't call out. Would anybody ever find me, I wondered, or would my ghost join that of Gloria Swanson wandering the studio at night.

It was Gregory Hines who found me when he came looking for me. He was unable to open the door from the outside just as I was unable to open it from the inside. He went for Astoria security people who finally freed me. They reminded me of their service to me on my last day of work.

I passed by the Cotton Club set daily, watching it torn down little by little until only a corner of it remained, a piece of a mural.

I felt the trip was finally coming to an end.

The Cotton Club opened in New York in early December, 1984. Some liked it more than others. I liked it. It wasn't the box office hit its creative team had hoped for. Its competition, *Beverly Hills Cop*, didn't exactly wipe it off the map. It just made a smaller dot of it.

The trip was over. Really over.

Tom Canford/Tom Miller
October 24, 1922 - December 6, 2007

FAREWELL TO A MOVIE PUBLICIST
(The Editor Says Good-Bye)

Me again.

Why Tom Canford? That name was cobbled together from part of his real name (Tom) and one fake name (Canford). Canford sounds like it ought to be somebody's name, but it's not. Once upon a time back in the dim dark past when Tom was working in name clearances for television shows like Dr. Kildare, "Canford" turned up on a list of "safe" names. If you had a raping murdering drug-addicted lying traitor in your story, you didn't really want to name him John Q. Smith for fear that one of the real ones out there might take offense and sue. "Canford" sounded like a "real" name but nobody was named Canford. Hence he couldn't sue. If a dastardly villain could be named Canford, then why not an author?

Yeah, but why did he want a pseudonym in the first place? The problem was his real name: Tom Miller. Thousands of them out there. Check it on Google sometime and just see how many hits you get. Heck, narrow it down to the Internet Movie Database and you'll find some 47 in the movie business alone (of which our Tom is number III).

He played around with it a bit: Thomas Canford. Tomas Canford. Tom Canford Miller. Then he decided to opt for simple.

Even his "real" name had its variations over time. When I first met him in 1966, he was already Tom Miller, using middle initial J (for James) for more formal occasions. A nice, neat, "adult" name. During the Second World War, the United States Coast Guard knew him as Tommy Miller, and that name stuck with him through his post-war college years in Los Angeles and well into the 1950s. His family called him Tommy (still do) and so did his friends from the time. Actually, if you dig way back to the certificate of his birth in Carrier Mills, Illinois, on October 24, 1922, you'll discover another interesting variant: Tomi James Miller. Nobody knows where that "Tomi" came from. Maybe the registrar of births simply made a mistake, or maybe a drop of ink got smeared.

The name Miller is itself suspect. It is known that even farther back in time, Tom's father, James Clyde Miller, was sired by someone other than his mother's husband. But like his father, Tom was raised a Miller, lived his life a Miller, and died a Miller. A Miller through and through. Except when he wrote.

And write is what he did. Words were life's blood to him from his earliest memories until the day before he entered the hospital for his last illness. He was in his office working away at the computer on his new novel, *The Wiretapper's Daughter*, right up until two o'clock when he had to begin taking the "prep" for the next morning's surgery. I have this fantasy that it was not the pulmonary embolism that took Tom away three weeks later on December 6, 2007, but rather his being kept away from his writing for so long a time.

* * *

When Tom was about seven years old, his father and mother moved with their son and the two younger twin girls Jane Rose and Betty Jo from southern Illinois to Las Cruces, New Mexico, to join their first-born child, Norma, who had already moved there and was teaching school. The family move was prompted by the discovery of a scar on Tom's lungs, and the high desert country of southern New Mexico was believed to be better for him than the coal mining community of Carrier Mills. Tom was raised in a houseful of strong women (including his mother), and I believe that contributed greatly to his lifelong interest in, fascination with, and comfort with members of that sex. There would have been one more sister, Evelyn, born between Norma and Tom, but she had died of complications from the 1918 flu.

Tom adored his mother, and I believe the central tragedy of his life was her death from pneumonia following a hysterectomy when Tom was thirteen. Norma, who was about thirty at the time, became the surrogate mother for her much younger siblings, a role she filled until her death in September 2000. After the death of Tom's mother, his father married an old friend and fellow teacher of Norma's, to Tom's great distress. Certainly Clyde Miller needed all the help he could get with his three youngsters. Gradually Leanah Miller won Tom's affections, and he grew to love her.

As a young boy, Tom fell in love with the American popular song. For years, to write songs for the movies or the Broadway stage was his great ambition. And he did write. After his death I had to deal with a trunk packed full of his lyrics and lead sheets

I believe his early childish songs showed great promise. Tom always had a wonderful facility with images and words and rhyme. Making a telephone call one day, he got an answering machine with a humorous message about calling back. On the spot, Tom composed and sang a rhymed reply that referred amusingly to the message he had just heard and left an intelligible message to boot. Anything could trigger a quatrain. Or (shudder) a limerick. This could be a mixed blessing to anyone around Tom, I must confess. I have a sense that Tom's great facility with song was the enemy of great accomplishment: he could come up with a good lyric so easily that he often settled for that and did not make the extra effort at the time to perfect the song. Of course he never threw a lyric away: decades later he might haul one out and work on it again, but by then the world of music would have moved on.

Somehow, Tom didn't care. While fame and fortune would have been nice, it was the writing itself that sustained him. In addition to song lyrics, he wrote short stories, radio stories, comedy skits, plays, and musicals. His musical *The Darwin Theory* was produced successfully at Los Angeles City College (where Tom was an advanced student in playwriting) in June 1949. Book, lyrics, and music by Tommy Miller. (The musical director and arranger was one Jerrald Goldsmith: he went on to fame, fortune, and awards as movie composer Jerry Goldsmith.) Dealing with the human fallout from the battle between science and religion at the Scopes trial in Tennessee, it preceded the hit play *Inherit the Wind*; it is said that the authors of that play attended a performance. Meanwhile Tommy was working on his musical version of Voltaire's *Candide*, but Leonard Bernstein got there first. At the suggestion of screenwriter Ben Maddow and composer Lukas Foss, Tommy submitted a selection of lyrics including the riotous "I Was Buggered by a Tall Bulgarian" to Bernstein, who declined the offer on the grounds that he had already selected a lyricist.

Tom worked in order to write. At various times in Los Angeles he worked as an elevator operator, a clerk in a shipping room, and a postal clerk. When he moved to New York in the 1950s, he fairly quickly started getting jobs in the movie business (most folks move to Los Angeles to do that: Tom always did things his own way). At various times he held staff positions, primarily in publicity, at MGM, Embassy Pictures, and American International Pictures. The movie work was interesting and varied and not so challenging as to interfere with his writing and his active and adventurous life of the flesh.

A co-worker at MGM, one Walter Brown McCord, was from my part of Alabama. Walter Brown and I had become friends after we both moved to New York. In the fall of 1966, Walter Brown's psychiatrist dared him to have a party and invite all his friends, whom he had always kept separate from each other. He did, the party was a great success, and Tom and I met for the first time and took an immediate liking to each other. Walter, you've got my eternal gratitude. Had it not been for you and your psychiatrist and your party, my life would have been so very different and not nearly so interesting. Tom too shared in that gratitude. I like to imagine you and Tom sitting together at a bar on the other side of the Pearly Gates telling tales tall and otherwise to each other.

In the fall of 1968, Stanley Kubrick's *2001, A Space Odyssey* was released, and it immediately joined Michelangelo Antonioni's *L'Avventura* as Tom's two favorite movies of all time. Initial reaction in the New York press to Kubrick's great movie was more negative than not, and Tom took particular umbrage (something he tended to do quite easily) at Renata Adler's review in the *New York Times*. Tom struck back with, of course, words, in a letter to the *Times*:

TO THE EDITOR:

In what was meant as a put-down, Renata Adler dismisses the "murkier" and more metaphysical aspects of Kubrick's "2001, A Space Odyssey" as being "simply there, like a Rorschach."

True, but what a Rorschach; and what a revelation. A searing inkblot of modern thinking man's apprehension as to the ultimate place of technology in the celestial scheme of things. Death and resurrection sanctioned by what? A machine? God, the perfect machine, overseeing decay, death and a new Immaculate Conception.

Who is triumphant in the here or in the hereafter, man or machine? Study the Rorschach. The answer comes from the individual viewer. Interpretations abound, and will proliferate. Is HAL, the computer, in a foreboding and unsettling manifestation of an Age of Anxiety neurosis, becoming humanized, memorizing, learning the emotions of jealousy, fear, hate? Or has he become subverted by a Higher Computer, an agent and representative of a culture in which the machine has emerged as the dominant and evolving form of life? God (perfect machine or standard variety) knows.

The film is a ghost story of the spheres, a veritable haunting of heaven's doorstep, eerie, spellbinding, beautiful; and in form an orchestral composition of sight, sound and the senses.

Like a Rorschach, it is an insight, an experience. As an experience and as art, it is a masterpiece. TOM MILLER New York City.

Mike Kaplan, an old friend of Tom's in the movie publicity business, was working on the United States release of *2001*. He read the letter over the phone to Kubrick, who reportedly was pleased. A few years later, Kaplan was hiring unit publicists to work on MGM movies during production. He remembered Tom's letter as well as Tom's abilities as a staff publicist and called Tom to inquire about his availability for unit jobs. Tom made himself available, and except for a few special assignments like dealing with stars and press during the New York premiere of *Ryan's Daughter*, escorting an actor dressed up in a monster suit to the 1976 Democratic Convention headquarters to publicize *Godzilla vs. Megalon*, and occasionally filling in for a staff publicist on leave, he never held any other job.

He loved the work, and the episodic nature of the assignments gave him plenty of time off for his own creative activities. He was good at the work. He quickly earned a reputation for working well with black creative artists and performers and with actors and directors with "difficult" reputations.

In 1989 family circumstances encouraged me to retire from my job at Columbia University and move back to the house where I grew up in Alabama, and I was able to talk Tom into moving as well. He was offered more movie jobs, but the move itself interfered with one and a knee procedure with another. That was all right with Tom, for he was more than contented with his life in rural Alabama. We had set up a great office for him, and he spent his days at his electronic typewriter and later his computer. Although we both missed the cultural advantages of New York, we were able to fill the gap with our books, CDs, DirecTV, videotapes, laser discs, and DVDs. Tom expressed interest in a dog; and not two weeks after we had settled in, Tom found an abandoned white bundle of fur down in the pasture with the four goats that came with the place. We named her Huckleberry, and she was a great friend for her too-short ten year life with us. A month after her death, we stumbled upon Orozco Cahaba (Roscoe for short), a six-pound black and tan Rottweiler mix who wormed his way just as deeply into our affections and grew into a sturdy eighty-pounder. He managed to outlast Tom by two and a half years.

Tom wrote and wrote and rewrote, by now working mostly but not exclusively on novels. I was cook, gardener, chauffeur, and in-house editor (did a little writing on my own, but that's another story). During the last few years he finally became satisfied enough with three of his novels so that he was willing to have them published. All were deeply influenced by his life, but only the first, *Boy at Sea*, life in the Coast Guard in WWII, had any autobiographical content. The second, *The Curse of Vilma Valentine*, his funny and astute account of shenanigans involving Hollywood in the forties and sixties, Nazis, murder, stolen art treasure, and the vicissitudes of fame, draws heavily on his knowledge of movie history and movie publicity. The final one, *Ghost Guitars*, is infused with his knowledge of the music industry, songwriting, the 1960s war protest movement, and again, Hollywood. Author's copies of *Ghost Guitars* arrived in the fall of 2007, just as he was starting to exhibit symptoms of his final illness.

Tom had written accounts of some of his movie experiences over the years. He polished the memoirs a bit in the 1990s and put them on a back burner except for a few more recent emendations and updates. It was his intention to add at least one more major section for possible publication in a year or so. Unfortunately that was not to be. As I was going through his papers after his death, I set aside the relevant manuscripts and finally got around to reading them again. I found that they were as interesting and amusing as I had remembered, and I thought that his worm's-eye view of the movie-making process offered insight and perspective worthy of sharing.

So here they are, for your enjoyment, very much as Tom left them. My editorial hand drifted lightly over the words; and changes tended to involve commas and semicolons, spelling, and the occasional repositioning of a word or phrase or sentence, mostly just the neatening up that Tom had not gotten around to doing.

Tom liked people. He liked weird people. He liked difficult people. He had a great knack for getting along with people. Fellow publicists would warn him about actors from whom he might expect a hard time, a list that includes but is not limited to Robert Mitchum, Rita Hayworth, Ryan O'Neal, Peter Falk, John Travolta, Louis Gossett, Jr., and Richard Gere. Yet with all of these he had wonderfully positive experiences, and his memories of all of them were warm and friendly. None of them were pussycats, but Tom just had a knack. His words about the people mentioned herein certainly reveal his great affection for them.

Once at a party in Tuscaloosa, Alabama, someone asked Tom who, of all the actors he had worked with, was his favorite. It was a hard question, and Tom gave it some thought. He was able to narrow his list down to two: Robert Mitchum and Paul Newman. And then came the question: who did you like least? He had the answer to that one immediately, but I will not share it with you other than to say he was not written about in this memoir. And over time Tom even mellowed about him.

Tom accumulated quite a bit of movie-related material in his lifetime: thousands of still photographs, books of contact sheets, press kits, preliminary press kits, screenplays (not just those he was issued while working on films but also ones from files that were being weeded over the years at AIP, MGM, and Embassy Pictures), working drafts, notes, screening programs. He had wanted this material to go to a library, and in the late summer of 2007 he had written to one library in New York making the offer. He did not get a reply. After Tom's death, I mulled the matter over with John Dartigue, an old friend from Tom's publicity days. John put me in touch with the Margaret Herrick Library of the Academy of Motion Picture Arts and Sciences, and in the spring of 2008 I shipped nine large boxes of material to the library. Thanks for the idea, John. Tom would have been delighted.

Let me share one little anecdote about Tom:

Tom never went anywhere without a notebook in which he would write down everything he could, even if just a brief note to use later as a reminder. He continued the practice in Alabama with a notebook he kept in the pocket by the passenger seat in our car. When we ate at a restaurant in Tuscaloosa, he would always ask the name of our waiter and write it down when we got back to the car so that he could greet the waiter by name the next time we dined there.

Some time after Tom's death, I dined alone at Maharaja, our favorite Indian restaurant. A young waiter asked me, "Where's your friend?"

I replied, "He passed away last month."

The waiter was visibly moved. "I'm so sorry. He's the only customer who always called me by my name."

I think that story suggests at least one reason why Tom got along so well with the people he met in his movie publicity career. He liked people, and he cared about them. To all of his colleagues mentioned in this memoir, Tom would want me to tell you that he liked you enormously and loved the opportunity to work with you.

I wanted Tom to have the last word in this book, and that made me think of his song "Boardwalk."

Tom considered the movie *Boardwalk* to be one-half an excellent movie about growing old and the rest an indifferent (at best) tale of a budding rock singer with a crappy ending. He believed that the film should grow in importance over time because of the intersection of talents Lee Strasberg, Ruth Gordon, Janet Leigh, and Lillian Roth (returning to the screen after many year's absence), all of whom gave excellent performances.

Tom wrote the lyrics for a possible title song (music by our late friend William Dyer) which Lillian Roth recorded on tape for Tom. He offered it to the director, but the song was rejected because only rock music would be featured. Noted songwriter Sammy Cahn also expressed interest (through Tom) in supplying a title song. Also rejected. The style of Bill Dyer's music is that of a *valse triste* and it is quite lovely, as is Miss Roth's recording. The point of view of the song is that of the Ruth Gordon character in the movie, who becomes ill and dies, leaving her husband, Lee Strasberg, bereft.

BOARDWALK

Music by William Dyer
Lyrics by Tom Miller

We've eaten the hot dogs,
We've taken the rides,
Done the fun-house mirrors
Front and sides.
Am I burned,
Am I tanned?
Want to walk in the sand,
Or like this, hand in hand
On the boardwalk?

The salt water taffy
Has loosened a tooth.
Do you think the gypsy
Tells the truth?
Pass her by,
Let her be.
My good fortune she'd see—
You here standing with me
On the boardwalk.

We've come a long way.
What didn't we do!
It's been a lark,
An amusement park
Any day with you.

But a chill in the wind now.
I ought to go home.
Is this Brighton Beach
Or is it Nome?
Oh, this day's
Been a friend,
But I now recommend
You walk me to the end
Of the boardwalk.

Made in the USA
Middletown, DE
09 April 2021